STO

from the

SEA

Peter Young

GREENHILL BOOKS

This edition of *Storm from the Sea* first published
2002 by Greenhill Books, Lionel Leventhal Limited, Park House,
1 Russell Gardens, London NW11 9NN
www.greenhillbooks.com
and
Stackpole Books, 5067 Ritter Road, Mechanicsburg, PA 17055, USA

British Library Cataloguing in Publication Data
Young, Peter, 1915–1988
Storm from the sea.—(Greenhill military paperback)
1. Great Britain. Army. Commando, No. 3—History
2. World War, 1939–1945—Personal narratives, British
I. Title
940.5'4'81'41

ISBN 1-85367-511-3

Library of Congress Cataloguing-in-Publication Data available

Publishing History
Storm from the Sea was first published
in 1958 (William Kimber & Co. Ltd), and reprinted in hardback, with
additional material, in 1989 by Greenhill Books. It is reproduced here
in paperback, incorporating the introduction by John Adair from the
1989 edition, and with minor revisions, a new index, publishers note,
and newly reproduced photographs.

Printed and bound in Great Britain by
Creative Print and Design (Wales), Ebbw Vale

PUBLISHER'S NOTE

IDENTIFICATION OF COMMANDO UNITS
From 1940 Army Commando units selected
volunteers from many regiments and corps. They
were disbanded after "VE Day". Almost all
mentioned in this book had a single digit number.
Royal Marine Commando units mentioned herein
had a double digit number and usually the initials
"RM". They preceded today's Royal Marine
Commando Brigades which maintain the proud
Commando tradition in Britain's permanent
Armed Forces.

If they be well ordered and kept in by the rules of good discipline, they fear not the face or the force of the stoutest foe, and have one singular virtue beyond any other nation, for they are always willing to go on; and though at first they be stoutly resisted, yet will they as resolutely undertake the action the second time, though it is to meet death itself in the face.

Donald Lupton on the English soldier, from his *Warlike Treatise of the Pike,* 1642.

ACKNOWLEDGEMENT

Officers and soldiers of the Commandos, too numerous to name, have helped me in the writing of this book. I am deeply grateful to them all.

At the risk of seeming unfair to the rest I must mention one by name, Henry Brown, the Secretary of the Commando Association.

PETER YOUNG

Brigadier Peter Young, DSO, MC and two Bars, fighting soldier and military historian, first achieved distinction as an intrepid leader of the Commandos in the Second World War.

In 1939 he was commissioned in the Bedfordshire & Hertfordshire Regiment and was wounded during the evacuation from Dunkirk in the following year. As soon as he was fit again he volunteered for the newly-formed Commandos. With No. 3 Commando he took part in the raids on Lofoten and Vaagso, where he won his first MC. After a period on the staff at Combined Operations HQ, he became second-in-command of 3 Commando and took part in the Dieppe Raid for which he was awarded the DSO. In 1943, in Sicily, he was awarded a Bar to his MC and then, when commanding 3 Commando in raids on Italy, received a second Bar. In 1944 he was back in Normandy, serving with distinction in the D-Day landings before being posted to the Arakan, Burma. When the war ended he was commanding the 1st Commando Brigade with the temporary rank of Brigadier and aged only 30. These adventures he vividly recounts in *Storm from the Sea*, a classic memoir of a young man going to war.

The golden period of Peter Young's subsequent years of military service was undoubtedly his three years in command of 9th Infantry Regiment in the Arab Legion. He told that story in his first book, *Bedouin Command* (1956).

When Peter eventually retired from the Army with the rank of Brigadier in 1959, he became Reader in Military History at the Royal Military Academy, Sandhurst. He brought to the study and teaching of military history his stimulating and original mind. Like Churchill, whom he much admired, Peter tended to treat the young about him as his equals and contemporaries. With his encouragement and practical help, the young lecturers in the Department of Military History produced a remarkable number of good books in their chosen fields, some of them now regarded as classics.

Like Churchill again, Peter could entertain as well as inform when he spoke – always without notes – to a large audience. He was at his best when commenting upon presentations by officer cadets, some of them based on raids described in this book, notably Vaagso and Dieppe. Therefore he had a great effect on the generation of future officers who passed through Sandhurst in the 1960s: he was an inspiring teacher and a lovable man.

The Royalist Army in the English Civil War was the first and deepest love in his life as a scholar. His interest in the Cavaliers went back to pre-war days reading history at Trinity College in Oxford. After leaving the Army, Peter wrote much more widely on that "war without an enemy", as one contemporary called it.

Twenty years ago, the publication of one of his most characteristic books, *Edgehill: The Campaign and the Battle* (1967), led Peter to arrange a re-enactment of Edgehill that led in turn to the formation of The Sealed Knot. This society, dedicated to promoting interest in the Civil War by recreating the battles and sieges of the 17th century, soon numbered thousands of members, united by its deep respect and abiding affection for its founder and Captain-General. Peter died in September, 1988, at the age of 73, a Cavalier to the end.

As *Storm from the Sea* reveals, Peter was in his element in the Commandos during the Second World War. With characteristic simplicity, he used to say that leadership should be done from in front. Self-confidence and the ability to inspire confidence in others lay at the core of Peter's natural leadership. Apart from battlefield courage to an unusual degree, he had the rare ability to think quickly – as if from first principles – in military situations. That intelligence and commonsense, together with his bravery, robustness, sense of humour and personality, live again in these stirring pages.

John Adair, 1989

CONTENTS

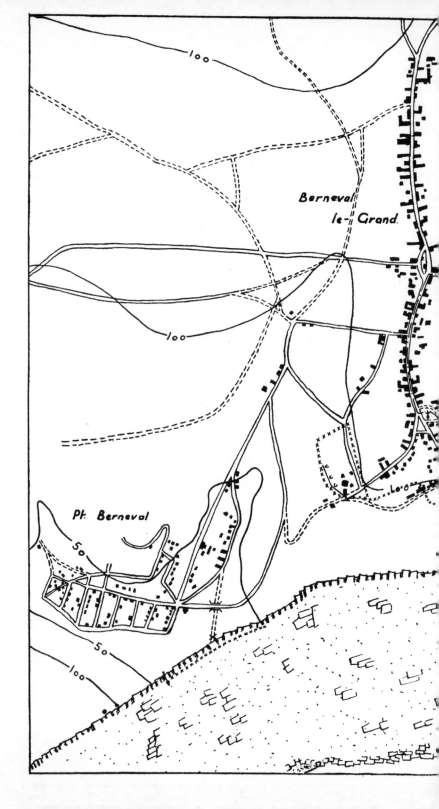

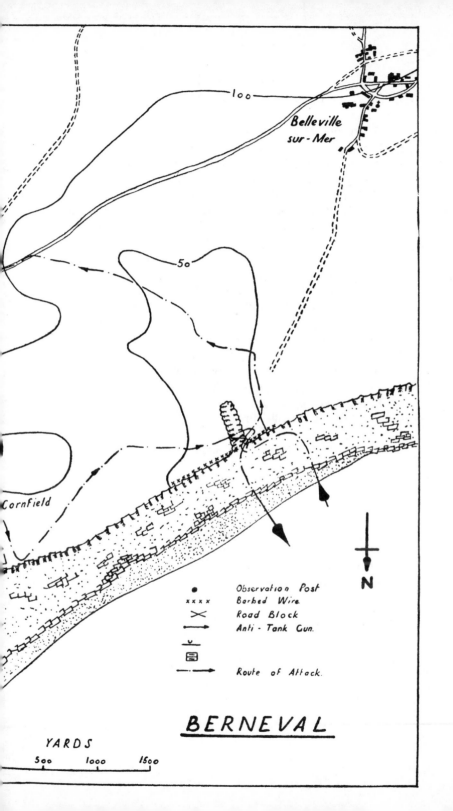

Belleville sur-Mer

100

50

Cornfield

●   Observation Post
x x x x   Barbed Wire
✕   Road Block
→   Anti - Tank Gun.

→   Route of Attack.

N

BERNEVAL

YARDS

500   1000   1500

ILLUSTRATIONS
Appearing between pages 64 and 65

1. Destruction of a waterfront warehouse at Vaagso.
2. The main street at Vaagso. In the centre is a demolition group.
3. British troops at Vaagso, returning to their ships.
4. A blazing storehouse at Vaagso.
5. Men of 3 Commando on their way to Dieppe in an LCP(L).
6. Lt. Col. Peter Young (right) at La Plein, with Brigadier John Durnford-Slater (centre) and Captain C. A. Head (left).
7. Peter Young.
8. Some officers of 3 Commando, just before Normandy, at the Limehouse street-fighting training area.
9. The eve of "D Day". 4.30pm at Warsash on the Solent.
10. After dawn on "D Day". Six landing craft heading towards the Normandy beaches.
11. After "D Day". Aerial view of la Brèche and the beaches.
12. Peter Young briefing snipers at Amfreville, 1944.
13. Aerial view of Amfreville, Normandy.
14. "Typical of my followers"—Peter Young.
15. Robert Christopher.
16. Memorial at Petiville, France.

PLANS

PART I

NORTH-WEST EUROPE

CHAPTER I

IN WHICH I JOIN NO. 3 COMMANDO

WHEN war was declared I was a second lieutenant and commanded 7 Platoon of A Company in the 2nd Battalion of
the Bedfordshire and Hertfordshire Regiment.

I had joined them at Gravesend in the previous February, shortly
after coming down from Oxford, where, despite four years' residence,
I had obtained a rather indifferent degree. My knowledge of the
Royalist Army in the Great Civil War was, I considered, unrivalled,
but in 1938 the examiners had not seen fit to set any question on that
entertaining subject. I had vague plans of becoming a schoolmaster,
and had even received an invitation to join the staff of a military
academy in the United States. But this hung fire, and in view of my
qualifications—or rather lack of them—I now decided to abandon the
teaching profession. The next step was not so clear: still, the Second
World War cast its shadow before and by the summer of 1938 it was
obvious that it could not be long deferred. Perhaps, I thought, it would
be as well to have some practical knowledge of soldiering before it
began.

And so almost a year later I found myself sitting with three or four
other subalterns in one of the old Officers' Quarters in Milton Barracks,
Gravesend. We listened to tunes from *The Pirates of Penzance* and
waited for Neville Chamberlain to come on the air and launch us
against Hitler. When he spoke it was rather in sorrow than in anger
—no heart-stirring call to action. Somehow, this did not seem the
way to declare war; how differently these things had been done in
the past, in 1914 or in the old Boer War days. There was an

atmosphere of anticlimax. Yet his words seemed strangely in keeping with the mood of the hour. Reluctant reservists swelled our thin ranks; lieutenants of highly unsatisfactory seniority appeared from the Supplementary Reserve; generals inspected us; and eventually one dull morning, at some ungodly hour, weighed down by an enormous pack, I stumped off to Gravesend station with 7 Platoon. The drums rattled away at the head of the battalion, but the scene lacked drama.

However, if a mood of disenchantment was abroad it was not universal. My Company Commander, who had fought on the Somme and seemed to me at once venerable and formidable (I suppose he was at least as old as I am now), was Major G. A. Anstee, M.C. "Now we can get back to normal," was his comment on hearing that war had broken out. Then fixing me with a steely gaze he followed this up by saying:

"In a year's time you will be a company commander."

I thought it far more likely that I should be dead. However, I had by this time fallen, half unconsciously, into a habit of believing everything Geoffrey told me, particularly when he appeared to be joking. I therefore had no difficulty in believing that by September 1940 I should be a captain, which, I thought, would be very fine. At the same time it occurred to me that, if that should come to pass, in 1941 I might become a major. The thing had endless possibilities. War had its points. In peacetime I could expect to be still a captain in 1945.

. . . . .

The battalion arrived in France on 1st October, spent a cold winter around Lille, had its baptism of fire in the Saar and then fought the brief, chaotic campaign of Dunkirk. It was a time of confusion, rumour, even humiliation; but the 10th Infantry Brigade came through with credit, and the battalion, over 570 strong when it re-formed at Yeovil, came back still an efficient fighting force. One lesson had become clear: good though they were, we were overrating the Germans. This, at least, I had learned. If you took them by surprise, they would run away; if you opened fire on them, they would take cover; if you shot them, they bled. In a word, they were human. They disliked being bombed and shelled just as much as we did—only in those days they did not get quite so much of it. Their turn was to come.

The campaign of Dunkirk was certainly less bad than I for one had expected, and a great deal less awful than the Great British Public has since been led to believe.

.   .   .   .   .

The battalion was at Yeovil when a letter arrived outlining the terms for "special service". It chanced that the Colonel and the Adjutant were both away on a few days' leave, and Major Ashby, the Second-in-Command, and I were in their chairs. The letter detailed various requirements: Commanding Officers were to ensure that only the best were sent; they must be young, absolutely fit, able to drive motor vehicles, and unable to be seasick. It was a leap in the dark, for absolutely nothing was said as to what they were to do, and in any case most regular soldiers make a point of never volunteering for anything. I would leave the decision to fate. A draft of about 135 men, including five officers, was about to join the battalion to replace our Dunkirk casualties. At this time I was looking forward with impatience to the fulfilment of Geoffrey Anstee's prophecy and weighing up my chances of getting a company. I decided, therefore, that if any of the five officers turned out to be senior to me I would put in for this "special service". Sure enough, there was among them a lieutenant of some forty-eight summers, and so the die was cast. I wrote a letter in which I strongly recommended myself, and Ted Ashby signed it without demur.

Several weeks went by; the battalion moved to Bognor Regis and I forgot all about my application. We settled down to guarding the beaches: stand-to at dawn and dusk—pretty dull. One day I was summoned into the presence of "Pip" Birch, the Commanding Officer, who gave me a rocket because a letter had arrived asking that I should be sent up for an interview.

"What's all this about?"

I defended myself by pointing out that there had been no opportunity to ask his approval since he had been on leave. To make matters worse, Bob Senior, the Adjutant, refused to provide transport to take me to Romsey where this appointment was to take place. He relented after a while and said I could take a motor-bike.

"But I've never ridden one in my life!"

"The first time I rode a motor-bike was on a march across the Yorkshire moors at Catterick," he replied, "—at night."

Further protest was useless. Seeking out Private Fetter, one of the dispatch-riders, I rode for ten minutes round and round the tennis court of the house where Battalion Headquarters was installed. By the end of that time I knew at least how to start the thing and thought I'd better set out before I discovered something disheartening.

The straight bits were all right and I was able to tell when I was going too fast because the wind made me weep. When I came to a corner I just slowed down as much as possible and wobbled round it. All went well until I came to a level-crossing—with the gates shut. I switched off and let the machine shudder to a halt; the gates immediately opened. After some hearty kicks on the starting crank the engine roared into life; the gates shut again. This went on for some time. Altogether too long, in fact. I pushed the thing across to a garage on the other side. Taxis were advertised, and I would gladly have hired a Rolls-Royce. No vehicle of any sort was available. By the time I reached Emsworth I had managed to wreck the kick-starter, but fortunately was able to get it repaired. Soon afterwards I had a stroke of luck—I got in the wake of a motor coach which was batting along at a good pace, and followed it for miles.

By the time I reached Romsey I was in a desperate mood and ready to volunteer for anything, particularly if it did not involve motor-bicycles. I was an hour late. The interviewing officer, happily, was two hours late.

Eventually I was ushered into the presence of a captain who bore, I thought, a superficial resemblance to Mr. Pickwick and certainly looked benevolent. This, I said to myself, will be some staff officer from the War Office. He asked me in a quiet mild voice whether I was "all for this sort of thing". His precise meaning was obscure, but the answer was suggested by a story of my mother's. It seems that Captain Scott was selecting men to take to the South Pole, and one of the keenest candidates, hesitating for an instant when asked how he felt about the expedition, had been turned down. Thus prepared, I stared at my questioner with the look I imagined people use in the wide-open spaces and said "Yes". He asked next if I knew anything about small boats: much experience of canoeing on the River Isis justified me in assuring him that my knowledge was extensive. I was in.

About two weeks after I left the 2nd Battalion the elderly Lieutenant, who had been the unwitting instrument of fate, departed to hospital, as I am told, and never returned. . . .

Various other officers had also been selected. Captain de Crespigny, R.A.S.C., Joe Smale of the Lancashire Fusiliers and myself were told to interview the volunteers from the 4th Division and to raise our own troop from them. It now appeared that the interviewing officer was to be the Commanding Officer of our new unit. Such was my first meeting with John Durnford-Slater, who, for more than three years, was to be my C.O. and was to become one of my firmest friends and allies.

De Crespigny, Smale and I spent the last days of June 1940 in touring the 4th Division and selecting men for H Troop. We had a free hand, for this was before commanding officers grew cunning. Later they learned to keep back their volunteers or to clear their prisons, but at this time we only met one company commander who would not play.

One of the first battalions we visited was the 2nd Lancashire Fusiliers, where, thanks to Joe Smale's local knowledge, we picked some likely men. The Adjutant was good enough to point out that one of them was awaiting court martial, but we liked the look of him and airily dismissed so trivial an objection.

We visited Geoffrey Anstee, who had taken over the 5th Northamptons halfway through the Dunkirk campaign. Here we found, among others, George Herbert, who had already won the M.M. for his gallantry at Oudenarde. He proved to be a fighting man in a class by himself.

From the 2nd Battalion of the 16th Foot we took Hopkins, the brothers Drain, and two characters who had been D Company's runners, "Curly" Gimbert and "Duff" Cooper, most of whom were well known to me already.

We did not take our full complement of N.C.O.s, preferring to promote our own men when they had proved themselves, a stroke of genius for which we were to be deeply thankful later on. The great majority of our men were reservists, who had served seven years with the colours, mostly in India. Their average age was about twenty-six, and they were well-trained, keen, professional soldiers in the prime of life. They knew their weapons, had seen some fighting and wanted more. Nobody will be surprised to hear that they were the best troop in the Commando—indeed in any of the Commandos. . . .

Guernsey, 14th/15th July 1940

John Durnford-Slater gave us early proof of his wisdom by selecting H Troop to do the Commando's first raid.

The troop arrived at Plymouth, where the Commando was concentrating, on 7th July.

Training began at once. On the 8th we practised pulling a cutter under the instruction of naval petty officers, and in the evening there was a conference at Commando H.Q. about Operation "X", as it was called. Next day we rehearsed our rôles on the football ground of Raglan Barracks. One night we did a landing at Saltash from a lighter; later we had some shooting on Tregantle Ranges and went thoroughly into the question of equipment, but we had not much time for preparation and when the men said they could swim we believed them.

The raid was twice postponed for twenty-four hours, but on 14th July the troop and a small detachment from Commando H.Q. left for Dartmouth in two Western National buses. I travelled with de Crespigny and his servant, McGovern, in the former's car. It was beautiful weather and there was a holiday atmosphere about the whole proceedings. As we drove along the narrow, high-banked Devon lanes we got stuck behind a car in which two men in flannels were driving to a cricket match. They dawdled along and de Crespigny could not pass. After some time and much hooting I suggested firing my pistol into the bank. The result was highly satisfactory, for they shot off with commendable speed—not without backward glances.

We arrived at the Royal Naval College at about midday and were given the run of the Gymnasium. The Physical Training Instructor's office served as a conference room and here we were shown the map of our objective. It was explained that we had been rehearsing for a landing on the north of the island of Guernsey, but the plan had just been changed and we were now to land in Petit Port Bay on the south-east.

The enemy, who had landed by air on 1st July, were 469 strong under a Doktor Maass. One of our agents had landed from a submarine a few days previously and had got the ration strength from the contractor! The Germans were holding the coast with a chain of machine-gun posts, many situated in old Martello Towers, dating from the Napoleonic Wars. Their main body was concentrated in St. Peter Port and there they had collected all available motor transport. It was thought that they could reinforce any part of the island in about twenty minutes. The men were young soldiers, and rather to our surprise we were told that they were not badly behaved—in 1940 it was difficult to imagine that any German was not a monster.

Besides H Troop the British force was to include No. 11 Independent Company under Major Ronnie Tod of the Argyll and Sutherland Highlanders. They were to land and attack the airport while we made a diversionary attack against a machine-gun post at Telegraph Bay and the barracks on the Jerbourg peninsula. The task was to inflict casualties, take prisoners and destroy aircraft. The force was to be conveyed in two destroyers, H.M.S. *Scimitar* and *Saladin*, 1918 vintage. For landing-craft we were to use seven R.A.F. crash-boats, two of which were allotted to the troop.

The Directorate of Raiding Operations had only been formed twelve days previously, but the arrangements for this raid were very good. The intelligence included such interesting information as that moonset on 15th July was at 0153 hours. It was arranged that Ansons should fly over the island to cover the noise of the landing-craft running in and it was emphasized that re-embarkation must be completed by 0230 hours.

The Petit Port beach was reported to be sandy, gradually sloping to the top, where it was shingle and small boulders—a good enough beach if there was no swell. Two paths led up the cliff, the best being on the right, where steps 250 feet high led to the Doyle Column.

The 14th of July was a Sunday. The cadets, who had been having their prize-giving and were leaving next day, were intrigued by our tommy-guns and insisted on loading the magazines.

After tea in the College Dining Room we boarded H.M.S. *Scimitar*. Only five of the crash-boats had turned up. We proceeded to sea, increased speed to 18 knots, and shaped a course for Guernsey. About midnight the crash-boats, which had been keeping station about one hundred yards away, came alongside and the soldiers transferred to them as silently as possible. The crash-boats made a terrible noise and the sound of the Anson's flying low over Jerbourg peninsula to drown our noise was most welcome. These craft were very high out of the water; moreover, we were very crowded. The idea of coming under aimed small-arms fire in such a craft was unattractive, but no machine-gun opened up.

We landed at about 1 a.m. The craft could not get right into the shore, for the tide was high and the cove rocky. We had to lower ourselves into the water; it came well up to my chest, and almost at once a wave put me right under. As I struggled ashore water poured from every part of my equipment: we wore battle-dress, steel helmets, canvas shoes and army gaiters. In an old-style officer's haversack I had three Mills grenades, a drum magazine for the tommy-gun and a clasp-knife. In my breast pockets were more magazines of the clip type. My armament included a .38 pistol, and I had also some five feet of cord with which I intended to secure my numerous prisoners; maps, saws, compasses and other impedimenta were sewn into various secret parts of my costume. For some obscure reason I was carrying an additional fifty rounds of .303 rifle ammunition—we took our soldiering seriously in 1940! Thus burdened, we began the weary climb up the steps to the Doyle Column.

We plodded up the steps with a dreadful squelching noise, half expecting to be ambushed any minute—and that in a place where it was impossible to deploy. Our worst fears seemed to be realised when, as we neared the top, there came a sudden burst of fire. Everyone froze. The shooting was only just ahead, but nobody cried out—evidently nobody had been hit.

"It's probably only some windy b—— shooting at shadows," I whispered to de Crespigny.

"Come on," he said, and in a few seconds we were over the edge of the cliff. "What was that shooting?" he hissed.

"It's all right. I only tripped and let off my tommy-gun," said Joe Smale, who was crouching in the darkness nearby.

There was no hostile reaction, so we pushed on.

We skirted the Doyle Column and, to the barking of many dogs, pushed on down the road towards the barracks. Finding a telegraph pole with rungs, Lance-Corporal Rann climbed it and cut the wires. Meanwhile de Crespigny was questioning an old man whose cottage was near the road in the hope of finding exactly where the Germans were. The man knew nothing, which made de Crespigny very angry indeed. The whole incident caused a useless and noisy delay.

Suddenly we heard the footsteps of an approaching patrol. Taking cover in the hedge, we let it come close and then challenged.

"Desmond," came back the password.

It was the Colonel, who had been the first up the cliff; he announced that both barracks and machine-gun posts were unoccupied; he must have gone at a great pace. He now gave us orders to withdraw.

I was walking just in front of John Durnford-Slater as we went down the cliff. In one hand he had a torch, in the other he held his pistol. As he went he gave the signal for the boats to come in—five red flashes with his torch. These were followed by a loud explosion just behind me.

"What was that, sir?" I asked.

"Er, it's nothing. I slipped and my bloody gun went off. Ha-ha-ha!"

It seemed to me that for an unopposed landing this was proving unduly hazardous.

A German machine-gun over in Saints Bay now opened up with tracer, presumably firing at the Independent Company; a searchlight played for a few seconds, and then switched off. When I got down to the beach I disposed my men behind rocks to watch the steps. We now found that it was impossible for the boats to get in at all, owing to the rocks and a slight swell.

The sailors did not want to throw us a line for fear of being dragged aground—not very flattering. Durnford-Slater ordered de Crespigny to put off in a dinghy; on its second or third trip it upset. Smale led his party into the sea and, although a very strong swimmer, was almost drowned by the weight of his grenades!

After a time the Colonel stripped to the waist and swam off. Johnny Giles came up and said that our orders were definitely to dump our kit and swim for it, so I ordered my party into the water. Looking around, I found that three men were left—non-swimmers, as it now turned out. I gave them three hundred francs and my tommy-gun and told them that in two nights' time a submarine would be at Le Creux Mahie to pick them up. They were very philosophical about it. I said I hoped we would be able to send the dinghy for them.

"Well," said Corporal Dumper, "to tell the truth, I'm not sweating on it." It turned out that his guess was right, for the dinghy was no longer in action.

With the help of a Mae West I reached one of the crash-boats without much difficulty and spent most of the return journey in the *Scimitar's* engine-room, drying off!

On checking up we found that McGoldrick was also missing. My own party returned to England without loss.

.   .   .   .   .

This raid was rather a fiasco, but still it was an experience. The planning and improvisation was of a high order and gave us all confidence. We in H Troop certainly paid lip-service to the idea of lightness and mobility, but on this occasion we went loaded like donkeys. That was a lesson learned. It was at this time that we began to suspect that steel helmets were not much use for this sort of work. And we also held swimming tests. . . .

Almost a year later I received a letter, dated 27th April 1941, from Private Frederick Drain, who told me that the other missing men were also prisoners with him . . . *and I must say that we will certainly be glad to get back to the old country. I hope that my brother is still with you and also carrying on some good work.* It was perhaps just as well that he could not foresee the four years as a prisoner of war that still lay ahead.

.   .   .   .   .

Searching back through the long history of these islands it would, I suppose, be hard to find a period of greater danger than the summer of 1940. Overhead raged the Battle of Britain; as the weeks wore on invasion loomed ever nearer. Yet looking back I remember few happier periods. It was a glorious summer, lovely weather; Plymouth was a good station, and the people, long used to service folk, were kind and hospitable. As the troop settled down we realised that we had chosen well. These men were ready to have a go at anything; coming as they did from a dozen different units, they brought with them their own regimental traditions, which fused to make a troop spirit. The most arduous training exercises were a game to them. I had been used to the formal atmosphere of a regular battalion, and to colonels in their late forties. It was a novelty to find ourselves at the end of a desperate assault drinking beer in the local pub with a colonel in his early thirties, who could dash through thick and thin with the best.

John Durnford-Slater was a gunner and was not then well ac-quainted with the details of infantry work. He had, however, certain basic ideas which guided him while he was hammering the unit into shape. The first was that 3 Commando should be the Greatest Unit of All Time, and the second that it should operate before any other. He had served for six years in India and had loved it, particularly racing and pig-sticking. But from 1935 to 1939 he had been serving at home with raw recruits and regiments below strength; that had lacked charm. When he raised the Commando to go raiding he felt he was getting back to something not unlike pig-sticking; for he had distinguished himself in the Kadir Cup Competition. In fact he trained the Commando very much as if it were a horse: he didn't believe in keeping it always at the peak of training. He would work up to a climax and then let it relax a bit.

Of middle height, he was sturdily built, with a massive head, well-nigh bald, set on his square shoulders. His eyes were of a bluish-grey, bright and twinkling. A smile usually played about his lips, but this was deceptive; it was still there when he was angry. John was tough. He still played Rugger—he was fast too—and I can see him now dashing straight down the wing, knees coming up like battering-rams, as easy to stop as a runaway horse. His ideas were old-fashioned; in any raid he must always be the first man ashore and the last away. When he had no preconceived notions he was the easiest man on earth to reason with, but once his mind was made up all argument was vain; one might as well save one's breath, for then he was about as pliant as concrete.

Not all our time was spent training. My sister came down to stay at Plymouth, and de Crespigny drove us in his car to Polperro, where we bathed during most of a glorious day. Pam was then about twenty-one, and not altogether ill-favoured. A few days after her arrival John Durnford-Slater said to me:

"Peter, your sister knows more of the officers in this unit than I do myself."

On 14th September Admiral of the Fleet Sir Roger Keyes watched us training near Plymouth and was particularly impressed by the keenness and fitness of all ranks. He promised that 3 Commando would be the first to be employed in active operations. It seemed that we were already beginning to make "friends in high places"— a favourite expression of our Colonel's.

At the same time we were informed that *as a temporary measure Commandos and Independent Companies should be added to the troops already employed in the primary duty of defence of this country.*

This meant that we would come under the operational command of G.O.C. Home Forces, an arrangement which was not greeted with the enthusiasm its authors would have wished. It meant that for the time being 3 Commando was acting under the orders of the Commander of South-Western Area for the defence of Plymouth and spent many hours rehearsing this rôle in the Tamerton Foliot area—though I do not recall that we ever went so far as to dig ourselves trenches.

On the same day, 14th September, I took over H Troop and was promoted captain. Thus Geoffrey Anstee's prophecy turned out to be accurate to within a fortnight—which is a great deal better than most minor prophets can do.

One of my two subalterns was Dick Wills. I well remember his joining us at Plymouth. As a newly-promoted Captain I rather hoped that he would prove to be an innocent young subaltern like Raleigh in *Journey's End*—someone I could impose upon. I was somewhat put out when I found that he was a graduate of Cambridge University and several years older than me. But all was well. At this time we used to send parties to sea with the Plymouth minesweepers for sea experience, a taste of Active Service which involved sailing to within sight of the shores of France—which was not unduly dangerous—and drinking drams and chasers with hardbitten sea-captains—which was very hazardous indeed.

The very first time that Dick was due to go on one of these expeditions he overslept and missed the boat. His detachment went without him and, as usual, returned without seeing a sign of the foe. The incident was reported to me and I busied myself devising all sorts of splendid rockets, beginning, "Never in all my service . . ." and based entirely on similar speeches received from Major Anstee in 1939.

However, I missed my chance, for when Dick eventually awoke and reappeared he looked so much like Dreyfus about to leave for Devil's Island that I could only laugh; the rocket remained undischarged and we became good friends.

Commando soldiers lived in billets instead of barracks, and received 6s. 8d. subsistence allowance. This arrangement worked very well, and the men liked it. For training or for an operation everyone came under starter's orders; nobody had to be left in barracks to do the inevitable chores of the spud-bashing variety. The administrative tail therefore consisted of a body of some five hundred landladies, who, whether in Plymouth, Largs, Seaford, Weymouth, Worthing or wherever else our journeyings took us, proved a fine body of women with a tremendous *esprit de corps*! Some of the soldiers developed the system to such a fine art that they would get the people in their billets to clean their equipment, or would send them round to Troop Headquarters to read Orders!

The Commando left Plymouth in October and moved to Inveraray, where a large force of Commandos was concentrating for a projected operation—the invasion of Pantellaria. Here we were quartered in a half-finished camp: the huts were complete, but the plumbing was not.

At Inveraray I first got to know Charley Head who had recently joined us and later, as Adjutant, was to become one of the great characters in 3 Commando. He was already an old ally of the Colonel's, for when John Durnford-Slater had been seconded to a Cornish Territorial Anti-Aircraft Regiment he had found Charley in charge of the Helston detachment. He had gone to sea as a boy and one of his best stories was of his shipwreck in the Black Sea. He had then joined his father as a veterinary surgeon and had learned the valuable knack of dealing with Cornish cows, who were dumb, and Cornish farmers, who were not. At sea, as a vet and as a Territorial, Charley had picked up a fund of experiences which had made him a wonderful judge of character. Caustic, yet not unkind, he was seldom wrong.

On our first morning in Inveraray we were introduced to the Assault Landing Craft. Sir Roger Keyes had succeeded in producing two of them. Armoured, and with a low silhouette, they could do about six knots—a big improvement on the crash-boats in which we had raided Guernsey. The Colonel soon had each troop in turn rushing in and out of these craft like madmen. Before long thirty men, fully armed, could clear one and double up the beach to cover in about fifteen seconds. Night and day we trained—there was nothing else to do! The long treks over the craggy hills soon broke anyone who was not fit. It was a good way of weeding out the unit.

After a time it became evident that the operation was not going to come off and we were moved to the seaside town of Largs in Ayrshire. Here the soldiers were very comfortably housed and very hospitably received. There were plenty of good hotels, and with the aid of the local police billets were not hard to find. The country at the back of Largs is rough moorland, ideal for field firing exercises, and altogether the town was an excellent base. I doubt if it had seen so many soldiers since the seventeenth century—which may account for the warmth of our welcome.

In December the project came to life again and we moved over to the Isle of Arran. For many days we lay in Lamlash Bay waiting for the *Glenroy* to take us to the Mediterranean. No. 8 Commando, under Lt.-Colonel R. E. Laycock,[1] was with us, and indeed for a time 3 and 8 were joined together and known by the slightly sinister title of the 3rd S.S. Battalion. Bob Laycock, a dark, stocky, tough-looking man in his early thirties, was very much the professional soldier; staff-trained and a specialist anti-gas officer. Even in those days of peace he had never tolerated among his friends any who did not come up to his own hard standards. He believed that the war would be long and boring and for that reason had deliberately gathered his friends about him in 8 Commando. Most of his officers were Guardsmen, and there were at least three members of the peerage. Evelyn Waugh and Randolph Churchill were among his junior officers. The officers of 3 Commando seemed practically like Roundheads—horrid thought —by comparison with this glittering band. And yet of all their officers none impressed me more than their Administrative Officer. A big Captain, with close-cropped hair and flashing eye, who used to go striding about the *Glenroy* darting fierce glances in every direction and evidently ill-content with what he saw. It was a long time before I plucked up my courage to make the acquaintance of this formidable yet admirable person. This was Captain J. E. Martin, alias "Slinger", who had served in the 1914–18 war as a trooper in the 9th Lancers and was therefore thought "too old" to go to the Middle East in 1941. To our very great advantage, he was transferred to 3 Commando, so in time I came to know him well.

Posted to the 16th Lancers after the First World War, he rose to be Regimental Sergeant-Major and eventually Quartermaster. In the process he had greatly distinguished himself by winning numerous Army championships in both shooting and riding—no mean achievement, particularly when one considers the standard of those competitions, open to the whole Army. His example as a professional soldier of the Old School was of great value in the unit, and as an Administrative Officer there were few to touch him.

[1] Now H. E. Major-General Sir Robert Laycock, K.C.M.G., Governor of Malta.

Eventually we were told that Pantellaria was definitely off. Nos. 7, 8 and 11 Commandos, now known as Layforce, sailed for the Middle East, taking with them about one hundred of our men, including the whole of A Troop.

The concentration of Commandos broke up, but not before Sir Roger Keyes had addressed us, enjoining us to "keep our spearhead bright". But this was easier said than done. It seemed that we were *never* going to see a German. The fire-eaters—who were legion —vowed they would go back to their units. John Durnford-Slater collected his disgruntled followers in one of the mess-decks and gave them the speech of his life; he went round each troop in turn, picking on some characteristic of its men and drawing roars of delight from his audience. "H Troop are the old soldiers, just like the men I used to have in India before the war. I'm very fond of H Troop," he said. Content to have our throats cut at a later date, we all went off on leave.

Early in 1941 the Commando was reorganised when the original war establishment was changed from ten to six troops, an organisation in every way better than the original establishment. Three officers and sixty-two men fitted well into two assault landing-craft, while it was much easier for Commando Headquarters to control a unit of six troops; the standard rose higher and became more even. H Troop became 6 Troop. We were the strongest troop at this time and ran little risk of being joined with another—a great advantage, as a merger would have given us too many N.C.O.s. Although each troop retained its individuality, the old "Wild West" days were over. No longer did one see officers sporting deerstalker caps, or soldiers with kukris hanging from their belts. With this reorganisation 3 Commando came of age. The Colonel took the opportunity to get rid of a number of misfits and almost at once his prayers were answered; at long last we were sent on an operation.

CHAPTER II

LOFOTEN

O N 4th March 1941 we raided the Lofoten Islands—the first amphibious operation in which 3 Commando as a whole took part.

The objects were to destroy fish-oil factories whose produce the Germans used to make glycerine for explosives, to sink enemy shipping, and to enlist recruits for the Norwegian Navy and arrest Quislings.

The objectives of 3 Commando were the ports of Stamsund and Henningsvaer; the other Commando (4) being allotted Svolvaer and Brettesnes.

Each Commando was about two hundred and fifty strong. Brigadier Charles Haydon commanded the force which was embarked in *Princess Beatrix* and *Queen Emma,* Dutch cross-channel steamers converted to carry assault landing-craft.

For my part I had never heard of the Lofoten Islands before this raid, and I doubt if any of the troop had. Eagerly we devoured the latest intelligence reports, which were very complete. German military posts of about twenty men each had been reported in the Islands, but there were none at Stamsund or Svolvaer. The nearest garrisons were Narvik, a hundred miles to the north-east, and Bodo, sixty miles to the south. In January U-Boats had been seen in Narvik. Armed trawlers escorted the coastal convoys, but there were no warships in the area. Even in the air the enemy were not particularly formidable since at this season the airfields as far south as Trondheim, three hundred miles away, would be unfit for any aircraft not fitted with skis. A mail steamer, usually with German troops aboard, was said to visit the Islands daily. Most of the navigation lights on the coast had been obscured or were only lit occasionally and with altered characteristics.

The troops embarked at Gourock during the afternoon of Friday, 21st February, and sailed for Scapa Flow the same evening. Scapa was reached at about 2.30 p.m. on the 22nd, and *Queen Emma* and *Princess Beatrix* were anchored between H.M.S. *Nelson* and *King George V*. We had about a week in which to put the final touches to our arrangements. Plans and operation orders were to be written and circulated; the soldiers were briefed. The crews of the landing-craft were able to train with the various troops, while the sappers and Norwegians had a chance to get to know the Commando soldiers.

My troop (6) was in one of the leading craft acting as a scout, so that the whole Commando would not come under fire at once, and the Colonel himself elected to ride with us.

The covering force, under the Commander-in-Chief, Home Fleet, himself, included H.M.S. *Nelson, King George V, Nigeria, Dido* and five destroyers, while the submarine *Sunfish* was to see that the raiding force made a successful landfall.

.   .   .   .   .

On 1st March we received the signal: "Carry out Operation Clay-more." The force left Scapa Flow at midnight and sailed to Skaalefjord in the Faroes, arriving at 7 p.m. that day. The destroyers refuelled in the Faroes, and after a stay of five hours the force sailed once more. During the night of 3rd March we entered the Westfjord, and by four o'clock in the morning of the 4th many navigational lights in the neighbourhood of the Lofotens could be seen.

So far, everything had gone precisely according to plan.

.   .   .   .   .

John Durnford-Slater, as was his custom, had issued a cut-and-dried plan which went into great detail. No. 5 Troop, under Sandy Ronald, was to deal with Henningsvaer, while the remainder of the Com-mando was to land at Stamsund.

My troop, still some forty strong, was to secure the landing-place and approaches; control communications; protect the landing-craft after disembarkation; and, lastly, to cover the withdrawal of the force from Stamsund.

Other troops were to arrest Quislings and Germans, enlist Norwegians and distribute gifts to the inhabitants and to carry out the demolitions. Two troops were in reserve. A bugler was to sound the Cookhouse Call half an hour before the time for re-embarkation. All troops were then to report back to the landing-place by 12.30, and those not present at that hour would be left behind.

I divided my troop into three sections. Bill Bradley, my senior subaltern, was to secure a stone house near the landing-place and the post office; Dick Wills was to take over the telephone exchange and telegraph station, and the third section I kept under my own command as a reserve.

The morning of 4th March was very clear and calm. It was broad daylight long before the landing-craft neared Stamsund, and one could see the snow-clad mountains rising straight out of the sea. There were few signs of life, though one could just make out buildings on shore. Our landing-craft, with forty-one officers and men aboard besides the crew, was considerably overcrowded; an occasional wave came over the side, splashing icy water on to the passengers, though our weapons were protected by oilskins.

Legion was leading us in; suddenly she opened fire, and at once everyone was on the alert to see what danger this portended. The least we expected was a German-armed trawler, but in fact the destroyer had fired to turn back Norwegian fishing-boats which were putting to sea. They hove-to and soon we were running past them at close range, the fishermen greeting us with enthusiasm. Each vessel ran up the Norwegian flag, which had been flying at half mast since the invasion, to the masthead.

"*Hvor ar Tuska?*" we cried as we passed and were told, to our disappointment, that no Germans were present.

My interpreter, a Norwegian corporal, seemed quite certain that there really were no German troops in Stamsund: nevertheless we approached the quay fully prepared for an ambush. It was a complete anticlimax when crowds of Norwegians of both sexes descended upon us, tied up the landing-craft, reached down for our weapons and hoisted us ashore. We had been assured that the landing-place was a "gently shelving beach", but in fact the quay was so high that had the landing been opposed we would have been a sitting target.

The stone house, Bradley's objective, was nowhere to be seen, but Wills quickly found the telephone exchange and telegraph station. This was in our hands by seven minutes past seven, before any report of the landing had been sent out. The mail at the post office was seized. A lighthouse where there was supposed to be a wireless station was found to be on another island.

Since there was no opposition we established posts on the outskirts of the town and the work of destruction began. The troop took some part in this, rolling oil drums into the sea and putting a few bullets into each. We had also to assist in driving Norwegians from the factories during the demolitions. These people were carrying off everything of value and running considerable risks in doing so. Dick Wills, bored after his capture of the telephone exchange, organised a Quisling hunt, which produced a suspect from an hotel next door.

I had a long conversation with Mr. Johannsen, owner of some of the principal oil factories. He said that the wireless station for which we were searching did not exist! He was in the habit of listening to the B.B.C. news in Norwegian and was not afraid to do so, saying there was no danger of being discovered. Gestapo men had paid Stamsund a visit, but no German troops had been stationed there, although a German motor torpedo boat had been in a few days earlier. Johannsen was surprised that the British had not been to the West-fjord before.

The inhabitants were extremely friendly. We had been told that they would be suffering considerably from food shortages of one sort or another and for this reason about a ton of gifts were landed at each of the main towns. In fact the people looked healthy and well clad. A number of us had been given Norwegian money in case we were cut off and had to make our way overland to Sweden. One sergeant, not in my troop, who had been issued with one hundred Kroner, gave thirty to a young woman in return for her kindness . . . he never lived this down and was called "Thirty Kroner So-and-so" from that day forth.

There was no shortage of Norwegian volunteers and in all over three hundred were taken back to Britain. A soldier in full fighting equipment came out of his house wearing a well-kept green uniform, his pack on his back and his rifle in his hand. Thus accoutred he reported for duty! At the end of the 1940 fighting he had simply demobilised himself!

All this time my Troop Headquarters was in communication by civil telephone with Commando Headquarters. About 10.45, when the demolitions were completed, word came that 6 Troop was to move to the quay and cover the re-embarkation. This presented only one problem, traffic control; the whole area of the quay was thronged with Norwegians who were enjoying their day's holiday and crowded round the departing troops, making it almost impossible to preserve any military formation.

At Commando Headquarters I found Colonel Durnford-Slater, who was in a very good humour. The Provost Sergeant, who was guarding a number of Quisling suspects, inadvertently loosed off his tommy-gun. A burst riddled the floor between the Colonel's feet.

"Yeah, well, Chitty, you want to be careful of those bloody things, they're dangerous!" said John, quite unmoved.

He shrewdly suspected that most of the alleged Quislings had been denounced by their business rivals and did not feel that any of them deserved a free passage to the United Kingdom. Shortly before departing he had them drawn up in a single rank before him and delivered a speech to this effect:

"Yeah, well, I don't want to hear any more of this bloody Quisling business. It's no bloody good, I'm telling you. If I hear there's been any more of it, I'll be back again and next time I'll take the whole bloody lot of you. Now clear off!"

This was delivered at great speed in John's characteristically mild yet energetic manner, his feet apart, his left toes sticking up in the air, his left thumb stuck in his waistband, a steely look in his eye. The Norwegians departed—considerably puzzled. I have often wondered what they made of *Quisling-business* which he pronounced as one word.

At 11.05 the last of us re-embarked without misadventure, and by 12.58 H.M.S. *Legion* and *Princess Beatrix* were ready to sail and the expedition was ordered to proceed homewards. At 3.15, while the coast of Norway was still in sight, an enemy reconnaissance plane caused an alarm; its report was intercepted by the Admiralty, deciphered and swiftly wirelessed back to *Somali*. The Germans do not appear to have taken any action, and we reached Scapa on the morning of 6th March.

It was estimated that, in all, 800,000 gallons of oil and petrol were burnt during this raid. Eleven ships, whose total tonnage was over 20,000 tons, were sunk. One trawler was taken back to England. Eighteen factories were destroyed; 314 Norwegians returned to Scotland, besides 216 German subjects, and some sixty Quislings. In addition, the British manager of Allen and Hanbury's was rescued from Brettesnes. All this was achieved without a single battle casualty, though one officer—not of our Commando—succeeded in shooting himself with his own pistol, which he had stuck in his trouser pocket.

·   ·   ·   ·   ·

This raid, coming as it did after a long period of frustration, was a great encouragement for the future. It was, indeed, unsatisfactory that there had been no fighting, but most of the soldiers were content that our objects were achieved. A raid with no fighting was better than no raid at all.

·   ·   ·   ·   ·

In 1955 Charley Head and his wife took a holiday in Norway, sailing from Bergen round the North Cape as far as the Russian border. They spent an hour ashore on Stamsund Island with Mr. Johannsen, who told them that the Germans had arrived next day and burnt a few houses, but they had shot no one. Later Johannsen drove the Head family round the beautiful island of Svolvaer, where 4 Commando had landed. Near the church they saw a war memorial bearing the names of eight of the Norwegian volunteers whom we had taken to England in the *Princess Beatrix*. Seven had lost their lives serving with the Royal Navy and one with the Norwegian Troop of 10 Commando.

CHAPTER III

VAAGSO

IN December 1941 No. 3 Commando had its first taste, so long and eagerly awaited, of serious fighting. The Lofoten Islands raid had been something of an anticlimax, for there had been no real opposition. When we went to Vaagso we knew for certain that we would find German troops there; we knew too that they were from the 181st Division, which had seen service in Norway in 1940.

The strategic object of this raid was to harass the Germans, and by so doing to induce the enemy to employ more troops on coast defence duties in Norway—troops who from their point of view would have been far better employed in Africa or Russia. The tactical aims were to destroy the garrison, blow up the local fish-oil factories, sink shipping, seize Quislings and bring home volunteers for the Free Norwegian Forces. In addition it was thought that the long-suffering British public might not take it amiss if it were given a victory, however small, by way of a Christmas present.

Sör Vaagso is a small port on Vaagso Island and by the most direct approach, through Vaagsfjord, lies four miles from the open sea. Its garrison consisted of about one hundred and fifty infantry and one hundred men of the Labour Corps. A four-gun battery on the little island of Maaloy covered Maaloy Sound and defended Ulvesund, an anchorage used by the Germans for the assembly of coastal convoys. Another battery on Rugsundo Island, by covering Vaagsfjord, was sited to give further protection from the south. Although the smaller German ships, those under 3,000 tons, used to pass inside Vaagso Island when northward bound, the navigational hazards were such as to rule out the approach of the British force from the north. There was, in addition, a mobile battery of 105 mm. guns at Halsor on the north coast of the island.

The Germans had no warships in the neighbourhood though the convoys were escorted by armed trawlers. At the nearest airfields, Herdla, Stavanger and Trondheim, there were believed to be a total of twenty bombers and seventeen fighters.

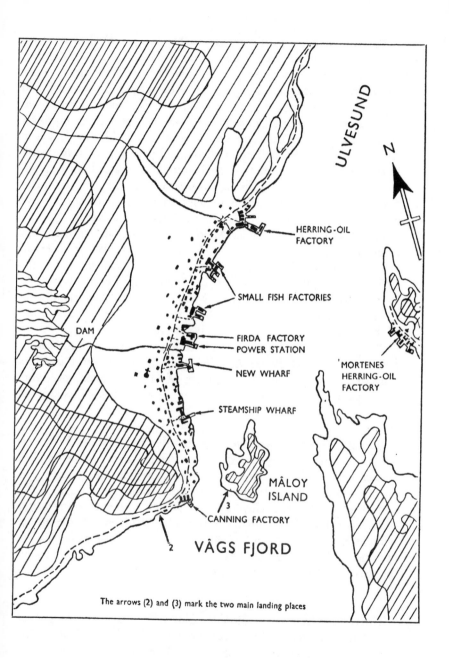

ULVESUND

N

HERRING-OIL
FACTORY

SMALL FISH FACTORIES

DAM

FIRDA FACTORY
POWER STATION

MORTENES
HERRING-OIL
FACTORY

NEW WHARF

STEAMSHIP WHARF

MÅLOY
ISLAND

3

CANNING FACTORY

2

VÅGS FJORD

The arrows (2) and (3) mark the two main landing places

The Commando was still at Largs when we got wind of this new raid. John Durnford-Slater vanished on a mysterious trip to London. Doubtless with a view to security, John went there fairly often, so this was no proof that a raid was brewing. After a space he returned and summoned the troop commanders to Broomfield House. I remember him drawing a rough diagram of the job in a large fat buff notebook which he kept on his desk and which was used for all his jottings as to exercises, conferences, postings and so on. There was no security risk in this practice, as his handwriting is more like Arabic than English.

For this operation our Commando was reinforced by two troops of 2 Commando, and the whole military force was divided into five groups of varying strength. Durnford-Slater placed Sandy Ronald's troop (5) and mine (6) under Major Jack Churchill, his Second-in Command, for the assault on the Maaloy Battery. We in 6 Troop were somewhat offended at not being chosen once more for the Colonel's own group, but he put us off with fair words, saying that he expected the stiffest resistance would be on Maaloy Island, and indeed it was obvious that until the battery was captured the future of the whole force would be distinctly uncertain.

On 13th December the Commando embarked at Gourock in H.M.S. *Prince Charles* and *Prince Leopold*, Belgian cross-channel steamers converted to carry assault landing-craft. And so we sailed once more for Scapa, where the force assembled and the final exercises took place.

. . . . .

On 24th December we sailed for the Shetland Islands. Four destroyers formed a screen ahead of the Belgian ships, while H.M.S. *Kenya*, with the force commanders aboard, brought up the rear. The operation was commanded jointly by Rear-Admiral Burrough, R.N., and Brigadier Charles Haydon, D.S.O., an excellent arrangement, since it left John Durnford-Slater free to fight his own battle ashore without having to concern himself with the details of inter-service co-operation. The submarine H.M.S. *Tuna* was to ensure that we found the narrow entrance to Vaagsfjord.

. . . . .

The passage from Scapa Flow to Sollum Voe was pretty rough, for a westerly gale (force 7 or 8) was coming in from the Atlantic. The storm did considerable damage and delayed us for a day in the

34

Shetlands. The usual rumours were rife—the whole show had been cancelled, the raid had been postponed because the Pope wouldn't think it cricket if we fought on Christmas Day and so forth. As usual there were fire-eaters who proclaimed that if the raid did not come off they would go back to their units. But during the day the wind dropped.

In the evening Jack Churchill played his bagpipes on the after part of the ship. When some wit threw a copper on the deck and shouted "Next Street!" Jack pocketed it without turning a hair. Our new Second-in-Command cut a dashing figure. The crowns on his shoulders were very large and it was said that they were really those of a sergeant-major; and he had, moreover, round silver buttons on his battledress, exchanged with a French officer in 1940. His equipment was a Sam Browne belt, with one of Wilkinson's fighting knives in the sword frog. All this, not to mention his bow and arrows and his bagpipes, provoked a sergeant to remark on this occasion:

"If Robin 'Ood were alive today he'd be f—— blushin'."

As darkness fell, about 4 p.m., we put to sea again in bad weather, but throughout an uneventful passage it was improving all the time.

The officers visited the mess-decks and gave the men their final briefing. I particularly remember impressing on my troop the need to take prisoners, thinking that with Dunkirk in the back of their minds some of the men would be little inclined to do so. I need not have worried.

Some of us had a long talk with a few of the sergeants. We discussed the chances of the various groups, and most of the party, officers and N.C.O.s, insisted that the battery was the toughest proposition. I gave them my opinion, which was that the fight in Sör Vaagso, which the Colonel's group was to clear, would be the deadliest part of the operation. From the model and the air photographs it was evidently just one street, bordered by houses and factories; on one side was the icy fjord, on the other a bare snow-clad hillside. In the fight up this long street troops would get split up into small parties, some halted by snipers, some pushing on; control would be lost and confusion would reign. So it seemed to me. This view was considered quite reasonable, though since nobody present was in the group concerned—or so we thought—the discussion was purely academic. Sergeant Culling of 2 Troop, who impressed me by his calm, almost fatalistic attitude to the whole affair, delivered his opinion, brief and to the point. "I am afraid of damn all," was more or less what he said, quite quietly and without any trace of boasting. He was as good as his word.

．　　．　　．　　．　　．

In the early hours I got up, put on my equipment and, while it was still dark, went on deck. It was very cold; we had all been issued with a leather jerkin or a thick sweater.

I found my way down to the mess-decks for a final check-up to see that nothing had been forgotten. This was really just something to do. I hardly expected to find anything missing, and there was not much I could do about it if there was. After breakfast, somehow nobody felt very hungry, the troop assembled on the boat-deck. It was still dark but rapidly getting lighter. I could see the mountains of Norway rising sheer out of the sea, fantastically beautiful; here and there lights twinkled from the few scattered houses on shore.

Tuna was sighted, and her presence removed all possible doubt as to the position of the force, which was only one minute late at the rendezvous, a fine feat of seamanship on the part of H.M.S. *Kenya,* our Headquarters-ship, though I was far from appreciating the point at the time. Like most soldiers, I had a touching faith in the navigational abilities of the Royal Navy—fortified by an intimate acquaintance with the career of Captain Hornblower—and did not for one moment imagine that they could not find their way anywhere, by day or night, with perfect ease.

Since the Hordenoes and Bergsholmene Lights were burning normally, though at reduced brilliancy, it seemed that surprise was complete —so far.

As the force entered Vaagsfjord *Kenya* moved over to the southern shore, while *Chiddingfold* led *Prince Charles* and *Prince Leopold* to the bay south of Hollevik. *Onslow* closed on *Kenya's* starboard quarter, and *Offa* came up astern. *Oribi* remained near the entrance to the fjord to cover the force from the west.

Dead on time the Hampdens came over, causing a diversion while the landing-craft were lowered and drawing the fire of four or five light anti-aircraft guns. Far away up the fjord I could see the streams of tracer climbing into the sky. The Hampdens were on their way to bomb the Rugsundo Battery. It was at about this time that one of the destroyers, *Chiddingfold* if I am not mistaken, loosed off a burst from a Bofors gun into the morning sky, probably by mistake. "That's given the position away," grumbled some pessimist behind me in the craft.

At 8.42 the landing-craft began to move up the fjord. For more than half the run-in we were hidden from the Maaloy Battery, but as we neared the point at Halnoesvik I could not help wondering what sort of a reception awaited us round the corner. The idea of steaming straight into the mouths of four guns firing point-blank lacked charm: I wished that it had been decided to approach Ulvesund from the north. The big guns on Rugsundo did not worry us, it was the battery on Maaloy that mattered. No. 2 Troop were lucky; before we reached the point their craft turned away to port and ran in to Halnoesvik, where the air photographs showed some kind of gun.

As our craft moved on George Herbert spoke to his men, asking those who had not been in action before whether they felt all right. One of them was Roger Hilton, an artist. His only comment was:

"What beautiful scenery. Wish I could paint it."

Six minutes had passed since the craft left the ships, when at 8.48 *Kenya*, still moving slowly ahead, fired star-shell to burst over Maaloy Island and illuminate the point of aim. Half a minute later she began to bombard.

The flotilla rounded the point, and now we were in full view of Maaloy, indulging in a sort of amphibious Charge of the Light Brigade. By now the salvoes of 6-inch shells from H.M.S. *Kenya* were crashing down on the battery, but still no reply came from the Germans. As we drew nearer I could see the huts bursting into flames and being hurled into the air, until gradually the whole battery became crowned with a cloud of dust and smoke. Now *Onslow* drew ahead and when clear of *Kenya* joined in the bombardment; soon *Offa* followed. Every shell seemed to strike home, and still the battery made no reply.

I told the men what was happening, and every now and then one would stand up to get a glimpse of what was going on, only to be told sharply to get down. Spirits rose almost visibly; Jack Churchill took up his bagpipes and began to play *The March of the Cameron Men*, standing the while, fully exposed, in the front of the craft and gazing calmly ahead. The men liked that.

Meanwhile, at 8.56 the Rugsundo Battery, despite the bombing it had received, had opened fire on *Kenya*, though its fire, not unnaturally, was slow and erratic. From our craft we did not even notice it.

We were getting slowly closer now; the run-in seemed interminable. At last, at 8.57, the Colonel in his craft, a little way to port, began to put up a series of ten red Very lights, the signal for the ships to cease fire. The bombardment had lasted over nine minutes. *Kenya* now changed from Howitzer to Full Charges and began to deal equally faithfully with Rugsundo, silencing that battery in two and a half minutes.

At least two machine-guns had now opened up from the hillside and a factory near the beach where the Colonel's group was to land. As the craft chugged slowly in the Brens replied with good effect; from Dick Wills's craft a Bren-gunner knocked out a party of four Germans who were running to their alarm post.

Seven more Hampdens now came in very low and dropped 60-lb. smoke bombs to cover both the main landing-places. On Maaloy an anti-aircraft gun behind the battery began to fire furiously.

·   ·   ·   ·   ·

Not a shot greeted us as we sprang ashore, dryshod, onto a rocky ledge. Lieutenant Hall, our boat officer, had put us ashore in dead ground, exactly as planned, at the foot of a low cliff. As we touched down Jack Churchill was busy stowing away his bagpipes and so I was able to brush past him and land first. At the top of the cliff I paused for a moment to give the men time to climb up, deploy into extended order and fix bayonets. During the few seconds that this required, Major Churchill, sword in hand, dashed past with warlike and impatient cries and vanished into the smoke. I did not see him again until the end of the action, and nor did his servant, Guardsman Stretton, who, not being a member of my troop, had been put in the stern of our craft.

On our right 5 Troop had got ashore without mishap, but the smoke was too thick for us to see them once we had landed. My troop, three officers and fifty-two men, advanced, well spread out, peering ahead for signs of opposition; one could see perhaps twenty yards. Almost at once we came to a single apron of barbed wire, weak and sagging. This obstacle, in which a shell from *Kenya* had torn a breach at one point, did not delay us for an instant, and we passed it without a shot fired. Nobody ever goes to the trouble of making a barbed-wire entanglement without siting machine-gun posts to cover it, but there was still no shooting—and no minefield. Where were the enemy? It was very odd. We pushed on through the smoke, still going uphill, and then suddenly found ourselves looking at one of the gun positions, about thirty yards ahead. Dashing forward, we found it empty and climbed in over a low wall—still not a German in sight. It seemed unreal.

We manned the inland side of the gun site and put up a white Very light to show that we had got our first objective. At once this was answered from right and left by more lights, so the sections on each flank were still level with us. Thus far not a shot and not a casualty. This was the last thing in the world that we had expected. I felt that the Germans should have put in an appearance by this time.

No. 3 gun was surrounded by a low wall, perhaps two and a half feet high and fairly thick; behind this cover we paused for a moment to weigh up the situation. Ahead we could make out the outline of wooden huts looming through the smoke. Suddenly things began to happen. A little way to the right a grenade exploded, and almost simultaneously a German soldier appeared twenty yards away charging towards us—perhaps the leader of a counter-attack. I was glad I had got the men under cover ready to receive it. Kneeling inside the gun position, my rifle resting on the wall, I was able to shoot him. He screamed, spun round and fell. Sergeant Vincent and one of the Norwegian guides fired too. "If I'm killed today at least I take one of them with me," I said, a barbarous sentiment with which Vincent was in full agreement.

The grenade which we had heard just before this incident had caused our first casualty, Walsh, the Irish Guardsman. Connolly, now one of my sergeants, saw two Germans in a small wooden hut about thirty yards away and ordered one of his men to throw a bomb at them. Walsh, who was a little deaf, had dashed forward at that moment and had been hit in the neck. The two Germans promptly surrendered and he escorted them back to the beach. He thought so little of his wound that when he was sent off to H.M.S. *Kenya* he did not report for treatment until next day, since there were already many casualties whose condition he considered more serious than his own. It so happened that the wound had narrowly missed his jugular vein!

Through the smoke I could see No. 2 gun position to our left, and I sent a group to take it, which was done without opposition. A

German, wounded by the shelling, was found in the position. Dick Wills and his party meanwhile had captured No. 1 gun. In one at least of the gun sites empty shell cases were found, but though this gun must have fired at the flotilla during the run-in, amidst the rain of shells from *Kenya* nobody in the landing-craft had noticed it.

A few seconds passed, and as nothing more happened it was clear that no counter-attack was coming after all. If the enemy would not come to us, we must look for him.

"Push on."

We advanced down the slope into the huts, bombing them and searching them. They were empty, but at this moment George Herbert and his section appeared escorting about fifteen German prisoners. Their commander, a stoutish middle-aged officer, an Iron Cross on his chest, walked behind them. As there had been no more firing this was a considerable surprise. George Herbert explained what had happened. His men had been on my right, and he also had seen and taken aim at the German I had shot, but his rifle had misfired. In action nobody's brain worked quicker than Herbert's and in a flash he deduced that there was a shelter beneath the very hill where his men were posted. Ordering his soldiers to cover him, he ran down the slope and found that his guess was right. Inside sat Hauptmann Butziger and his men, fully armed. Herbert had a grenade in his hand, but before he could toss it in he heard Halls and Hughes, who had got to the other entrance, shouting: "It's all right, George! We've got the bastards!"

I sent Herbert and his section to escort the prisoners back to the beach. I went on among the huts, and walking round the corner of one I found myself face to face with a German—there was another beyond him—and sprang back into cover. Only Lance-Corporal Harper, the boxer, was with me, the rest of my Headquarters party having paused presumably to inspect the prisoners.

"There's two of them there," I said to Harper. "We'll go round the corner together."

Shouting *"Hände Hoch!"* we did so, he armed with a tommy-gun and I with rifle and bayonet.

The nearest German snatched at my bayonet, and instead of sticking it into him—which did not occur to me—I drew it back, fully expecting him to surrender. Instead, he turned and ran and as he did so I pulled the trigger, firing from the hip. I was slightly surprised to see him stagger and lean heavily against the wall of the hut. In the instant that it took me to reload, Harper, behind me, let fly with his tommy-gun and gave him a burst. As the second German, an N.C.O., took aim at me with his pistol from the doorway of the building, Harper swung his gun on him and gave him the rest of the magazine. At that instant one of my party, Clark, reappeared and took a shot at him with his rifle. Both Germans fell dead. I doubt if the whole incident took more than ten seconds.

We searched the building, but found nobody else. It contained the battery office and an arms magazine and was on fire, due to the shelling—though not seriously.

Pushing on, we found some more of the troop, Lieutenant Brandwood and the demolition party, who had discovered two more of the enemy, sailors this time, crouching in a kind of cellar under the foundations of a large hut. They were so shattered by the shelling that they could not be persuaded to emerge. Gimbert, a man of bull-like physique, crawled in, grabbed them and pushed them into the open. They were unarmed and one of them, we found, had been wounded. They wore steel helmets, navy-blue jackets and white denim trousers—hardly a suitable uniform for a frosty morning, but smarter than the grey-clad soldiers. Still, they looked very miserable, and I almost felt sorry for them.

It was clear that all opposition was now at an end, so I told Brandwood to get on with the demolitions. I looked at my watch. We had been ashore eight minutes.

Returning to Butziger's battery office, we found it fiercely ablaze. I remembered that there was a large cupboard which had appeared to be full of files, books and assorted military paper. Climbing through the window, I was able to find my way through the smoke and fling bundles of documents out of the window, where the soldiers stowed them in sandbags. After a few journeys, one of the men told me that I was on fire and so I jumped out of the window, only to find that this was not true. I was able to get a few more handfuls of files before the place finally went up in smoke.

This search completed, I was about to set off and visit my sections, when Hogan, sent by Dick Wills, turned up at Headquarters with two more German prisoners, one wounded, and a Norwegian woman, who might be described as a camp follower.

Excitement was not quite at an end, for a small German ship—probably the *Föhn*—tried to escape up Ulvesund. Mapplebeck, on guard over No. 2 gun, used his initiative and, swinging it round, opened fire. While he loaded and fired the gun, Hannan acted as layer. The range was perhaps 800, and although they claimed two hits, they were mortified to see that the ship did not sink. Both were by origin infantrymen and had failed to set the fuses properly. At this juncture the Durham sergeant, Vincent, a real gunner, whom I had sent to remove the breech-blocks from the guns, came on the scene. He now took charge of the shoot and I remember his telling me in his quiet Tyneside voice:

"I laid the goon and I set the fuse when oop cooms Mad Jack and tells oos to cease fire."

While this was going on some of Wills's and Sergeant Connolly's men were shooting at this ship with Brens and an anti-tank rifle, but it finally fell a prey to the destroyer *Onslow*.

At 9.20 Major Churchill signalled that Maaloy was in our hands, and five minutes later he was instructed to send troops to destroy the factory at Mortenes. He sent Sandy Ronald and the whole of 5 Troop to carry out this task, which they did unopposed.

By 9.41 the smoke was clearing and H.M.S. *Oribi*, with Group 5 aboard, followed by H.M.S. *Onslow*, steamed past Maaloy Island into Ulvesund, under a fairly heavy fire.

Once clear of the smoke, the destroyers saw the German ships *Regmar Edzard Fritzen* and *Normar*, and the armed trawler *Föhn* beaching themselves in the small bay just north of Brandhaevnes Point. Shots were fired across their bows, and Oerlikons swept their decks, but they had gained enough time to carry out their plan.

Looking across to the town, we could see troops advancing slowly along the waterfront, and since we could hear little shooting we assumed that all was going well.

My demolition party were now laying their charges while the remainder of the troop occupied various vantage points around the island. Some of the phosphorous smoke bombs were still burning, and the Major gave orders for them to be smothered. No. 5 Troop, moving slowly in the snow, filed past on their way to the boats. A German with a broken leg, a senior N.C.O. who had fought in Crete, was carried down on a stretcher. He was quiet and stoical.

With my runners I returned to the place where the first German had fallen and found him lying at the foot of a small gallows, from which hung the alarm bell. Who had sent him? If Butziger, why were the rest of the men still in the bunker? It turned out that they thought an air raid was in progress and nothing more. Still, the Captain ought to have had advance information of our coming, for at 8.15 the naval signaller, Van Soest, had received a telephone message from a coastguard station at the mouth of the fjord to say that warships were approaching. He did not warn anybody, but rowed across to the town to fetch his mate, who for some reason had been sleeping there. They were returning together and were ten metres from the island when the bombardment began. Their information never reached their commander.

The coastguards tried to ring through to Butziger direct. The telephone rang in his quarters, but his batman, who was busy cleaning his boots, did not answer it! He put first things first. The other men were receiving a lecture on how to behave in the presence of an officer when the Hampdens flew over. Butziger came out of the officers' mess to see what was happening; fire was opened on the aircraft, the air-raid alarm sounded and most of the men followed their captain into the bunker, presumably before our flotilla rounded the point.

On our right 5 Troop had also captured their objectives at the first rush. Altogether Churchill's group had captured one officer and twenty-four men of the artillery, two naval signallers, one groom, one pay clerk and two women, one a Norwegian and one Italian. The remainder of the garrison, including the two ack-ack gunners who stuck to their post, were killed—mostly by *Kenya's* shelling.

The four guns of the battery, one of which had been damaged by shellfire, turned out to be Belgian field-guns, 75s, one being dated 1923. The 2-cm. ack-ack gun was the only piece of German make, for the men's rifles were Norwegian. Since the previous August Butziger had had a large number of mines. They were blown up in his stores.

I searched the rest of the island, to make sure that no more Germans remained in hiding; three more dead men were all we found and a Christmas tree in one of the barracks.

Two Messerschmitt 109s came over, but did not attack us. I looked at my watch again. It was now 10.12.

I went once more to the beach. Jack Churchill was there with the Medical Officer. A corporal who had been slightly wounded was sitting wrapped up in a white blanket, his back to a rock, but otherwise it was not a very warlike scene and I was quite surprised when Churchill told me that the Colonel's group had met severe opposition and that half my troop were to go at once to Sör Vaagso and join the group, which needed reinforcements. He gave me permission to go myself.

I rounded up the nearest men, Herbert's and Connolly's, about eighteen in all, and in a few minutes I had handed over the troop to Brandwood and boarded one of the assault landing-craft. As we did so two of the official photographers dashed down to the beach and joined us. One of them, Jack Ramsden, wrote afterwards: *I scrambled into a barge and heard an officer say: "Well, boys, I don't know what we're going into, but it looks pretty sticky. Remember what your job is and your drill and we'll pull through."* The officer can only have been me, and it is true that I had little enough idea of what was going on. Jack Churchill had told me nothing of the situation in the town, for he knew nothing. The boat officer asked me whether I wanted to go to the Colonel's original landing-place, but this seemed a waste of time. We could see soldiers in khaki a good way north of that, and I asked him to run in and join them. This choice of landing-place turned out to be a fortunate one; as I stepped ashore I was met by Charley Head, the Signals Officer, who, rather to my surprise, shook me warmly by the hand.

.   .   .   .   .

At 10.20 Colonel Durnford-Slater sent a signal to Brigadier Haydon saying that the situation in the northern end of the town was not clear and reporting that the wireless sets of the two forward troops, 3 and 4, had been destroyed. This signal was quickly followed by another saying: *Fairly strong opposition being encountered in centre and north end of Vaagso* and requesting that the whole of Group 4, the floating reserve, should be sent to the original landing-place. Brigadier Haydon sent Hooper's troop ashore.

At seven minutes past ten *Oribi* had landed Group 5 to cut the road between North and South Vaagso. Two Messerschmitt 109s came in and attacked with cannon fire, adding to the confusion but failing to make any hits.

Durnford-Slater went forward to reconnoitre. It was now 10.30, and 3 and 4 Troops were in fact in the midst of very bitter street fighting. Nevertheless they had pushed steadily on, rushing from house to house and wall to wall in desperate close-quarter fighting. As always happens in street fighting, there were heavy casualties among the leaders.

44

By this time the Colonel was leading the advance in person. Coming out of a factory after laying demolition charges, "Slinger" Martin ran into him, "blackened and begrimed, but always with that devil-may-care smile on his face". Ammunition, especially Mills bombs, was wanted at once. Around Headquarters were a number of Norwegians who wanted to return with us to England. Martin went over to them, and asked if they would give him a hand. They volunteered to a man and went off up the main street replenishing each troop in turn.

It was at about this time that my party of 6 Troop appeared on the scene.

As soon as I landed, Charley Head told me the sad news that Algy Forrester and Johnny Giles, the commanders of the two assault troops, had been killed, and Bill Lloyd hit. Looking around, I could see little sign of movement on the part of our own troops, most of whom were taking cover round the corners of houses. Arthur Komrower, whose leg had been crushed by a landing-craft, came hobbling along walking with the aid of a stick and wearing a balaclava instead of his steel helmet. A few of his men were with him.

They must have been pretty worried, for one of them shouted: "Good old 6 Troop!" when he saw my men disembark.

In the normal way they hadn't a good word to say for us!

"Take cover over there," I said, pointing to the corner of the cemetery and I went with Charley Head to get orders from the Colonel who was not far off.

"Yeah, well, Peter, I'm glad to see you."

He took me forward with him to reconnoitre.

The Colonel told me how Algy Forrester and the Norwegian Captain Martin Linge had fallen in an attempt to storm the German Headquarters, and how when all the officers of his troop were out of action a corporal, one "Knocker" White, had led them on in splendid style. Our losses in officers had indeed been grievous, for Mike Hall too had been shot—a bullet had shattered his left elbow. Of the first two troops into the town only one officer survived unscathed—small wonder that the attack had lost its momentum.

The Colonel had taken vigorous steps to get the advance going again. He had asked for the floating reserve, which had been sent ashore by Brigadier Haydon; he had sent in Bill Bradley with such of 1 Troop as were not engaged in demolitions and other tasks; he had summoned the party which I had brought over from Maaloy; and he had also called up 2 Troop, which had come up by road from Halnoesvik.

While the Colonel had been speaking I had been looking around trying to make out the situation, and looking for a line of advance which would offer my men at least some cover in this winter landscape. The main road was obviously covered by enemy riflemen, and the Colonel said it was no good trying to push along it. To the left the steep snow-clad hillside at the back of the town looked forbidding. Not fifty yards away to the right was the icy fjord.

The Colonel stopped talking and beamed at me. I expected him to give me some particular objective, some line of advance. There was a pause. I suggested that I should try and work forward along the water-front. He was obviously pleased with this idea, which had in fact occurred to me because it seemed that there would be cover among the warehouses. He told me that Denis O'Flaherty of 2 Troop would be under me. Charley Head was ordered to return to Headquarters, and I persuaded Arthur Komrower, who was in a bad way, to go with him.

O'Flaherty now appeared and warned me to be careful crossing the open ground leading to the factory as it was covered by snipers from the hillside which overlooked it. The body of a sergeant lay in the snow, sufficient proof of the truth of what he said.

I ran back to the troop and found that in my absence Slinger Martin had come up and replenished their ammunition. I warned them that they would probably come under fire on the way to the warehouses, which lay across the square where the Colonel had been briefing me. We rushed across in single file, running as fast as we could in the soft snow. We had not gone far through the first of the dark high buildings when we ran into O'Flaherty's party. In the first warehouse was a German lying dead, an unexploded stick grenade in one outstretched hand. From a doorway Denis O'Flaherty pointed out what he knew of the enemy positions.

O'Flaherty pointed out a yellow house in which he suspected there were Germans. In street fighting it is extremely difficult to locate the enemy, and so as soon as we got into a warehouse with a reasonable view I posted Lance-Corporal Halls with a Bren in an upper window from which he could cover our advance.

There was a small building about twenty yards away to our left front and this I made my next bound. We had to dash out through the door

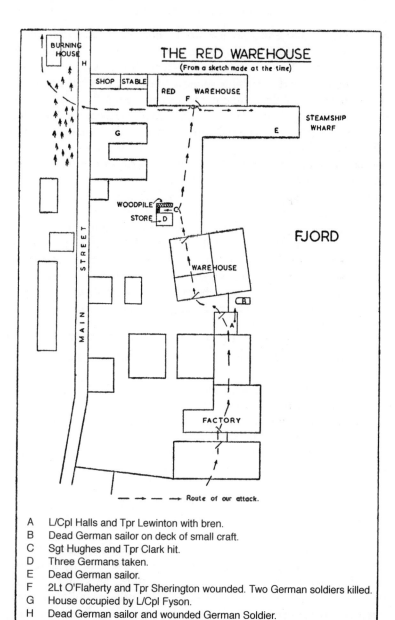

THE RED WAREHOUSE
(From a sketch made at the time)

— → — Route of our attack.

A L/Cpl Halls and Tpr Lewinton with bren.
B Dead German sailor on deck of small craft.
C Sgt Hughes and Tpr Clark hit.
D Three Germans taken.
E Dead German sailor.
F 2Lt O'Flaherty and Tpr Sherington wounded. Two German soldiers killed.
G House occupied by L/Cpl Fyson.
H Dead German sailor and wounded German Soldier.

one at a time. There was no entrance on our side, and as I ran round the corner I saw Germans in the doorway. They vanished with the speed of light and, shouting *"Hände Hoch!"*, I edged up to the door.

Sherington, a dark well-built young soldier, on fire with excitement, pushed past me and, crouching in the doorway, emptied his Thompson into the building. This did the trick. Three Germans, one a sailor, and a Norwegian came out and surrendered.[1] Things were going well —but not for long.

There was an L-shaped wood pile on the north side of the hut, and most of our party, nearly thirty strong, were now crowding into this narrow space. From somewhere not far off shots rang out; by the corner of the building a sergeant of 2 Troop and Clark had been hit. Clark, pierced through the left arm, was still standing up. Excitedly he pointed out that it was from behind that he had received his wound; the sergeant, hit in the lungs, lay on his back with only a minute or two to live. Our Bren in the warehouse behind had not spoken. I felt sure the bullets must have come from our front—no doubt the impact had spun Clark round. The first thing to be done was to get rid of the prisoners.

"Moore! Take Clark and these prisoners back to the beach."

"I'm all right, sir!" from Clark, who was white as a sheet.

"Do as you're told!"

They ran into the last warehouse and disappeared. I was told later that Clark had fainted on the way back.

The Colonel now joined us, quite alone as far as I remember.

"We must get on!" he said.

I looked in the building, an ammunition store, to see if I could find a position from which Dick Hughes, our sniper, could cover our advance. There were no windows, not so much as a loophole; hopeless.

Ahead, and about sixty yards away, stood a long red building, clearly another warehouse.

"We'll get in there and reorganise. Come on!"

It was pretty plain that the only chance of getting away with this next move was to make it fast. Despite the snow and my haversack full of bombs I was making pretty good time. Suddenly a smart-looking German in a long overcoat, steel helmet and equipment stepped into the doorway little more than ten yards away, and flung

[1] One of the soldiers, who was in fatigue dress, was said to be Alexander Holscher, an opera singer.

a stick grenade at me. It fell some ten feet to my right. I fired from the hip as I ran, swerving to the left; a second grenade followed the first, bursting almost in the same place. By this time I had reached the wall of the building and there was only a large wooden crate between me and the doorway. Within seconds George Herbert and Sergeant Connolly had joined me, and the rest were coming up at the double. Whilst we were still fumbling for our Mills grenades a stick bomb flew out of the door and fell about eight feet away. My legs will be full of bits, I thought. It did not go off. Perhaps the German forgot to pull the pin out.

We shouted "*Hände Hoch!*" several times. No result. We began throwing Mills bombs through the door. We gave them more than the ration, perhaps twelve altogether—it was a big building. Then, confident that they must have been knocked out, I walked in. There was a little hallway with a wooden staircase leading up to the right and a doorway straight ahead. The door, if there was one, was open and the room beyond was as black as night. I was silhouetted in the doorway. Two shots flashed out from a point across the room to my right. I fired and sprang back into the open. The Germans had retreated to an inner room. A direct assault seemed unpromising and I told the others that we must try to outflank the enemy. Easier said than done.

The Red Warehouse stretched practically from the fjord to the main street. O'Flaherty and I posted men to guard every window and door on our side of the building while we reconnoitred to try and find some other way in.

"We must get on."

The Colonel had reappeared again.

To rush the place was to ask for more casualties. What was the answer? I looked once more at the massive red walls. By God! They were wood! Fire!

"We must set the place on fire."

Dick Hughes went to fetch a bucket of petrol from a nearby garage; some of the others dragged three draught horses out of the stables.

At this moment, while I was organising the business of setting fire to the warehouse, Denis O'Flaherty, exasperated by the prolonged resistance, once more assaulted the front door. Sherington, who was full of dash, sprang in behind him. This was no part of my plan, but I felt I had to go too. I had reached the bottom of the stairs when there were two shots and both of them fell. I fired towards the flashes

49

and withdrew a second time, again unscathed. They were both lying in the middle of the room covered by an invisible enemy lurking in the darkness of an inner doorway not five yards away. Sherington gasped out that he had been shot from the next room. How the hell were we to rescue them?

It seemed to us that the best thing to do would be to go up the stairs and try to shoot the enemy through the ceiling, though this was obviously going to be difficult. At that moment, however, O'Flaherty and Sherington staggered out of the warehouse. Sherington had been hit in the leg; O'Flaherty's face was covered with blood. Hannan caught O'Flaherty as he fell, and Lance-Corporal Darts got hold of Sherington. I sent them back to the rear. Hughes came up with a bucket of petrol which George Herbert flung into the room. A moment later the warehouse was ablaze.

Hilton went back for more Mills bombs and I posted a corporal with some men of 2 Troop to tend the fire and keep an eye on the entrance while the rest of us moved on up the town towards the Firda Factory, our ultimate goal.

Gathering the rest of my party, now much diminished, I prepared to advance. I still had my two sergeants and we were perhaps a dozen in all.

.   .   .   .   .

Elsewhere the same kind of fighting was going on; small groups charging from one house to another in short rushes. Slinger Martin was busy issuing ammunition to men of 1 Troop when three bursts of rifle fire came from the hillside to the left. At that moment the Colonel came along, his batman at his heels. They got under cover and spotted where the fire was coming from.

"Martin, get those bastards out from there and then blow the huts up or set them on fire."

Covered by a Bren gun, Slinger and two of his men dashed twenty yards up the slope to the cover of some huts. Slinger was armed with bombs, the other two with Thompson guns. Crawling round the end of a hut, Trooper Mainwaring opened up into the entrance of the next building, about ten yards away.

"There's two in there!" he said, over his shoulder.

Martin got out two grenades, a Mills bomb and a fire bomb. He threw the first into the hut, ducked and waited for the explosion; then he threw the fire bomb, which hit the wall and burst outside, sending up a cloud of smoke and flame. It was close enough to set fire to the resinous wood. Under cover of the smoke they dashed into another empty hut. No. 1 Troop opened up with their Bren and caught two Germans, who chose this moment to emerge from the blazing hut. In the Commandos everyone came under starter's orders. Mainwaring was a storeman. . . .

•   •   •   •   •

Now we were among the houses; the warehouses were behind us. Looking up the road, I could see a wounded German soldier lying on his back—he kept looking up, but he seemed quite helpless. Nearby was a sailor, quite dead. I gathered my men by the corner and we dashed across in a bunch. So far so good. Skirting round the Hagen Hotel, which was on fire, I could feel the fierce heat of the flames, although the place had been burnt almost to the ground. Then we advanced along the hillside, crossed a wire fence and ran down the snowy slope to the back of a house standing on the left of the main road. There was no cover, but nobody had taken a shot at us. There were a number of Norwegians near the next house, but they were afraid to approach us, so I could get no information from them.

Well spread out, we pushed on up the main road. Still nobody fired at us, although we could hear bursts of firing to our left. After a time we came across some Norwegians looking out of their cellar through a window at street level.

"There are Germans in a house farther up the road," they said, not that this told us much.

Still, I decided to get off the main street and led my party to the right, down to the water's edge. Here we found our progress blocked by buildings.

At this moment the Colonel reappeared. There was a motor-car nearby and I suspected that one of the houses might be the billet of the German commander. I flung open the door and, glad to find there was no reception committee, searched the place thoroughly. In a room upstairs we found a haggard-looking German, apparently on the point of death, for he lay under his bedclothes trembling. I thought he was feigning sickness so that we would leave him. I asked the Colonel, who had come up and was standing behind me in the doorway, whether I ought to take a closer look at him, but John was kind-hearted as well as tough and said, "Let him be." I think he was right.

This must have been Major Schroeder, the German garrison commander, whom some of the prisoners said afterwards had been left dying.

The windows of the next house were barricaded and Mapplebeck and I took a few shots at one of them, but there was no response. We went out and continued the advance. I now discovered, to my disgust, that I had only one section, Herbert's. It afterwards transpired that one of the troop commanders had taken it upon himself to send Sergeant Connolly's men back to the beach carrying some of the dead and wounded. Meanwhile the Colonel had collected some of 2 Troop and his own runners, a party about equal in size to my own, and with these two sections we advanced by bounds. Herbert and I went forward until we came to a small stream which formed a natural trench; here I fanned out my men in fire positions, while the Colonel, pistol in hand, took his party through. Flanked by his runners, he walked at his usual swift pace straight up the main street. Sergeant Mills, rifle in hand, was level with him on the left of the road. Suddenly we could sense from their movements that something was wrong. George Herbert was pointing like a hound, yet we could see nothing to fire at. Suddenly there was an explosion, the Colonel hurtled through the air and vanished, a shot followed and two figures came limping painfully back along the side of the building where we had last seen John. We rose from our trench and rushed forward about forty yards to the scene of the calamity. The Colonel's orderlies had both been badly wounded by a stick grenade. He himself by a fantastic dive had reached the cover of a doorway, escaping with nothing worse than grazed knuckles. In the snow a German sailor lay dead. Directly after the explosion he had walked out of a side street with his hands up. Then, seeing the look in Mills' eyes, he had cried:

"*Nein, nein!*"

"*Ja, ja,*" said Mills and shot him.

"Yeah, well, Mills, you shouldn't ha' done that," was all John said.

To our left we could hear occasional bursts from a Bren—probably Chatton and a party from 2 Troop working along the back of the houses—but in the main street there were few of our men to be seen.

We went on until we got near the edge of the town and the Firda Factory, and then the Colonel put us into a good solid house on the right of the road and told us to act as a "stop" in case the Germans counter-attacked down the road before the demolitions could be completed. Some way off we could see the Youth Hostel to our left front where there seemed to be fighting going on. Later the Colonel held a conference in a garden behind a wooden fence. Bill Bradley was ordered to destroy the Firda Factory.

John now handed over to me and told me to fall back not later than 1.10. He returned to his Headquarters to report progress to the Flag Ship. It was about 11.45.

At 12.37 three Heinkel 111s came over and from that time air attacks continued until after dark, although no ship was hit. *Prince Charles,* however, sustained some damage from near-misses. The sight of the German bombers put new life into the men of the Rugsundo Battery, who opened fire again, and this time hit the *Kenya.* It was soon silenced again.

At the end of the town we had not been long in our new position when Mapplebeck acquired a prisoner, captured, I think, by 2 Troop, and brought him upstairs to be examined. He was a small man, deplorably scruffy, enveloped in a long greatcoat. A search revealed nothing of the least interest amongst his belongings.

"Are you a Prussian?" I asked him.

"Nein, Pommer!" he said hastily, in a perish-the-thought sort of way, which made Bill Bradley and I laugh immoderately. It seemed an odd thing to be, anyway.

By one o'clock the whole area had become as quiet as a grave. There was no sign of either side. Clearly the Commando had pulled out. I decided to start my withdrawal, and so, with our prisoner in the van, encouraged with cries of *"Vörwarts, Hermann!"* we made our way back along the street. Bill Bradley led and I brought up the rear.

Two Norwegians came back with us as well, each of them carrying a sandbag full of 36 grenades. I had sent our artist, Hilton, back to the beach to fetch a fresh supply and he had caught us up when the fighting was over. He was a recent arrival in the troop, having previously been a clerk in Regimental Headquarters. He had persuaded the Adjutant to give him a chance of more active work, but he had not done very much infantry training. In the innocence of his heart he rejoined us, with two sacks of grenades, by the simple process of walking straight up the main street. How he survived remains a mystery, for the sandbags were very heavy and he was an easy target. It is said that when he returned on board he asked George Herbert to show him how to unload his rifle.

When we reached the site of the Red Warehouse we found it a blackened ruin, but the area was still so hot that we had to pass it by crossing the road and moving along the hillside. We felt very naked. Our blood had cooled while we were in our house at the end of the town, and I remember thinking that, having survived so many hazards that morning, it would be a pity if we got shot up now. But by this time the snipers and machine-gunners on the hillside had either been silenced or had hidden themselves and we passed unmolested.

As I went I counted the enemy dead. I saw about fifteen lying in the open, but, of course, most of their casualties had been inside buildings, and again there were many places which I did not have a chance to inspect. As we passed the German Headquarters, the Ulvesund Hotel, I took an epaulette with yellow piping from one of the casualties. Here the dead lay thicker, some of them horribly burned.

We reached the main road at the point where our solitary 3-inch mortar had been in action and gathered up quite a number of bombs which the detachment had left behind when they withdrew. It was not until we reached the beach, where the Adjutant and the R.S.M. were marshalling the men into the boats, that we saw any of our own side.

As we arrived Slinger Martin came up and told me that there was still one more big demolition to be done, a factory nearby. The Colonel had given orders that it was not to go up until the rearguard had passed through and that on a whistle signal everyone would have three minutes in which to go to ground. We looked around for some cover.

A sergeant entered the building, there was a pause, then a blast on the whistle and he came running out and dropped down behind a rock where Slinger was crouching. Two seconds later the earth shuddered. Through the smoke we could see the building gently collapse in a heap, half the roof hanging over the jetty into the water.

By this time the wounded, the handful of prisoners and most of the loyal Norwegians, who included several aged men and women, and even young women with babes in arms, had embarked: so had most of the other troops.

I sent off George Herbert and his section, with Hermann, our prisoner, and had a look round to see if there were any more of my men about. They had all gone, so I embarked along with Hooper's Troop. My two Norwegians elected to come with us and, after picking up yet another volunteer between Sör Vaagso and Halnoesvik, we made for *Kenya*; Hooper and his men went aboard. Not long after,

54

we got back to *Leopold*, where I found that all 6 Troop had already arrived.

· · · · ·

While we had been away the party left on Maaloy had carried out the demolitions. Altogether they made a thorough mess of everything on the island which had survived the naval shelling.

By 2.45 all tasks had been completed, all troops had been re-embarked and the force withdrew. Altogether the Navy sank about 16,000 tons of enemy shipping.

· · · · ·

Just before the landing-craft reached the side of our ship two enemy bombers appeared overhead. The naval escort and both the infantry assault ships let fly with everything, keeping them at a good height. Even so, a stick of bombs was near enough to *Prince Charles* to put one boiler out of commission.

Otherwise the journey home was uneventful; the storm had now subsided. Our chief interest was the interrogation of prisoners. Stoutly though the enemy had fought in the town, the men of the battery were poorly clad and generally of low intelligence. Most of them had been in the infantry and knew little about guns, and some had been sent straight to Norway without much training. Few were Party members, and some were anti-Nazi, two being Czechs who had preferred the German Army to a forced labour camp. Service in Russia was already unpopular, and men on leave from that theatre were forbidden even to discuss it. There had been four suicides on Maaloy Island, presumably from sheer boredom, though most of the garrison had been home on leave. Half of the men had seen active service in Norway.

Among the papers which I took from the burning hut was one signed and dated 26th December 1941. In it Butziger informed his commander that on 29th October the anti-aircraft gun on the island had fired upon and beaten off a British aeroplane which was attempting to bomb the shipping. This was in fact the reconnaissance aircraft taking photographs for our raid, which performed its task and returned undamaged.

· · · · ·

The most important result of the raid was that the enemy proved sensitive to harassing tactics of this sort and began to increase the strength of his outlying coastal garrisons at the expense of his field army. It is said that by the end of the war there were 300,000 German soldiers tied up in Norway.

Besides the shipping destroyed, four field guns, one tank, and one anti-aircraft gun were demolished. About 150 Germans were killed and ninety-eight captured.

In addition numerous factories were blown up, and this was a blow, if not a very important one, to the German war effort.

Seventy-seven loyal Norwegians came back with us to Britain, and many of them enlisted in the Free Forces. The name of Captain Martin Linge, who had been with us at Lofoten and Vaagso, is still honoured in the Norwegian Army, for they still have a Commando Company which bears his name.

Our losses were twenty killed and fifty-seven wounded, mostly from 3 Commando, besides several aircraft.

Vaagso was that rare thing, the operation which went according to plan. That is not to say that every detail worked out with meticulous precision, but simply that the group tasks detailed in the Force Commander's plan were carried out successfully. The plan called for the closest co-operation with the Royal Navy and the Royal Air Force, and their successful intervention in the actual battle, quite apart from the passage to and from Norway, was vital to the success of the operation.

Without *Kenya's* bombardment we might never have got ashore. Without the air attacks on the neighbouring airfields we might never have got away again! It was a true combined operation, with each service making its contribution in full.

Although Brigadier Haydon had been the overall military commander, and had dealt with the Navy, John Durnford-Slater alone was responsible for the fighting ashore. He had made the plan while the Brigadier was away on another operation, and he had seen it carried through to the bitter end. It was a flexible plan, which gave him a good reserve. This he was able to throw in when the first attack on Vaagso got held up. In the second phase he was everywhere, spurring us on and leading the advance in person. In the early stages he went forward accompanied by Charley Head, himself not the most cautious of men. There was a lot of shooting going on. Charley said:

"You keep a lookout for snipers on the left, sir, and I'll take the right."

"Lookout nothing," John snapped; "I'm in a hurry."

And that was the form all day. He bore a charmed life. Armed only with a Colt automatic, usually walking in the middle of the main road, nobody who saw him there will ever forget his inspiring leadership. He had always meant 3 Commando to be the greatest unit of all time and he certainly made it show its paces at Vaagso.

. . . . .

Returning to the *Prince Charles*, Slinger Martin saw two *matelots* with fixed bayonets on guard outside a cabin.

"Who's in there?"

" 'Ave a look, mite."

Inside were four shapely blondes in various stages of undress.

"Jerries' floozies! Yer can't keep 'em down. Me an' me mite's been 'avin' 'eart attacks," the sailor winked, and Martin went into his cabin.

These ladies, it seemed, had been segregated from the other prisoners —perhaps it was thought that they might have a bad moral influence on them.

Later the gallant Captain had occasion to pass the prisoners' cabin a second time. Two rifles, bayonets fixed, were leaning against the door.

CHAPTER IV

DIEPPE

AFTER Vaagso one of the first jobs I was given was to go round various units and select volunteers to replace our casualties. By this time Home Forces had clamped down on recruiting for the Commandos and the units I was allowed to visit were all Young Soldiers' Battalions. No. 6 Troop had always consisted for the most part of old soldiers, reservists with pre-war training and previous battle experience at Dunkirk, and I was a bit dubious about taking men of eighteen and twenty. As it turned out, these young soldiers were to have nearly eighteen months' training before operating in Sicily and Italy, where they did very well. Young soldiers will follow their commanders out of the innocence of their hearts.

. . . . .

Soon after this I was asked by John Durnford-Slater whether I would like to go to Combined Operations Headquarters and serve for a time on the planning staff. This sounded interesting, and early in March 1942 I joined the staff at Richmond Terrace, Whitehall, as a major. I worked directly under Robert Henriques, who had been Brigade Major of the Special Service Brigade, and Charles Haydon, now a major-general, was the head of our branch.

Our job was to select suitable targets, submit appreciations and outline plans, and when these were approved by the Chief of Combined Operations, Lord Mountbatten, to work out the details of the raid. At this time the scope of any raid was governed by two main factors: the range of fighter cover, then not more than seventy-five miles; and the availability of landing-craft, which were still in very short supply.

During the months that I spent at C.O.H.Q. the most important raid was that on St. Nazaire. The cover plan was beautifully simple; the officers and men detailed for demolition parties from various Commandos were assembled and trained on the pretext that they were

58

doing a demolition course. At the end of the course, instead of dispersing, the students went off on the raid.

This operation, which was carried out by 2 Commando, was a desperate venture, involving as it did a six-mile run up the mouth of the Loire under the fire of many batteries.

After this operation I asked Charles Haydon if I could return to 3 Commando. By this time Sandy Ronald had left to become Second-in-Command of 6 Commando, and Jack Churchill had succeeded to the command of 2 Commando. And so I became Second-in-Command of 3 Commando, which I now rejoined at Largs.

. . . . .

Jack Churchill once told me that it was the Second-in-Command's duty to sit and wait until the Commanding Officer got bumped off. However that may be, I found that John Durnford-Slater liked to leave a great deal of the training to me, an arrangement which suited me down to the ground. Besides the normal training, to a very great extent he allowed me to select and train N.C.O.s. In this way I got to know all the officers and very nearly all the N.C.O.s and men, which was to prove invaluable to me later on.

I thoroughly enjoyed my new job. John is the most reasonable of men unless he has finally made up his mind. This, rightly or wrongly, was my opinion of him long before I became his Second-in-Command and I acted upon it throughout. It seemed to work. At any rate, in all the time that I was associated with John Durnford-Slater I do not remember having a single row with him, although we once had a near miss.

. . . . .

By this time, of the twenty-seven officers in the Commando only six had joined when it was formed: the Colonel, myself, Charley Head, Joe Smale, Bill Bradley and John Pooley. We had lost two of the best at Vaagso, several had gone to the Middle East with Layforce, a few had been promoted; others willingly or unwillingly had gone back to their own regiments.

To be honest, at least half of those who had left the unit had done so for the unit's good. John Durnford-Slater gave his followers a lot of rope and was an unusually sweet-tempered Commanding Officer, but once he had decided that someone was useless or crooked or had "had it", that man was out.

. . . . .

In the summer of 1942 we left Largs for the last time and moved to Seaford, where once more we went into "civvy billets". The town was rather too small for the whole Commando, and so 5 Troop was billeted at Alfriston. The move to Sussex made a great change in the life of the Commando because we now found ourselves in a countryside teeming with troops, whereas in Ayrshire we had been able to train, and to a great extent to shoot, almost where we pleased.

The planning for Dieppe had begun as long ago as April when I had been on the planning staff at C.O.H.Q. Dieppe was selected because it would not be one of the invasion ports whenever it was finally decided to launch the Second Front. It was within the range of fighter cover. It also had obvious disadvantages. The whole coast for some miles on either side of the town is a wall of chalk cliffs, like those between Newhaven and Brighton, and this limited the number of suitable landing beaches. The planners had to decide whether to land several miles from the town, which meant crossing small rivers on the way, or to land on the waterfront of the town in the teeth of the garrison. A landing at Dieppe itself would call for the maximum of fire support from the Navy and the Royal Air Force.

Three Commandos were allotted to the force. Nos. 3 and 4 Commandos were to silence the two coast defence batteries on either flank of the port, while No. 40, the first of the Royal Marine Commandos, was to attack shipping in the harbour and to be available as a floating reserve. The main assault was to be made by the 2nd Canadian Division.

The task of 3 Commando was to land in two groups at two beaches, near the village of Berneval, "Yellow 1", and near Belleville-sur-Mer, "Yellow 2". The Colonel was to land on Yellow 1 with the main body of the Commando, while I was to land on Yellow 2 with 3 and 4 Troops and a 3-inch mortar section. The two groups were then to move inland and together destroy Goebbels Battery of 5.9-inch guns, 450 yards inland on the outskirts of Berneval, between the village and the cliffs. The Colonel, with the general layout of the battery and its neighbourhood clearly in mind, was able to organise thorough rehearsals which were carried out on the downs behind Alfriston.

In July the raid was postponed for a month, which gave rise to the usual rumours that the whole show was off, but towards the middle of August it became obvious that it was really going to happen. First of all a detachment of U.S. Rangers arrived and later some Fusiliers-Marins—these last to act as guides.

The force embarked on the evening of 18th August and sailed from Southampton, Portsmouth, Shoreham and Newhaven about 9 p.m. No. 3 Commando sailed from Newhaven in a flotilla known as Group 5, consisting of twenty Eurekas.[1] These unarmoured landing-craft—designed, not for a seventy-mile channel crossing but only for a run of five to ten miles—each carried about eighteen fully-equipped soldiers. We were escorted by a steam gunboat, a motor launch, and a larger landing-craft carrying 4 Troop. The Colonel and Commander E. B. Wyburd, R.N., were leading the flotilla in the steam gunboat, so as to ensure that we did not lose our way. The Eurekas sailed in four waves five abreast, and I was in the starboard craft of the first wave, which was commanded by Lieutenant Buckee, R.N.V.R., and the soldiers with me were the H.Q.s of my Group and of 3 Troop.

At first everyone was chiefly interested in watching the rest of the force moving out to sea, but after a time we tried to get some sleep; it was very uncomfortable and cramped in the landing-craft and I doubt if anyone dozed for more than a few minutes. About midnight we opened some tins of self-heating soup. It was tepid.

At 3.47 a.m., when we were still about an hour's run from the coast, a star shell went up on our port bow illuminating the group.

Immediately a heavy fire was opened up on us; 3- and 4-inch guns, ack-ack guns and machine-guns poured a stream of shells and tracer into the flotilla, while further star shells lit the sky. It was by far the most unpleasant moment of my life.

Five enemy craft were converging on us. It seemed impossible that our wooden landing-craft could survive for more than a few minutes. The tracer seemed to come swooping straight at us. In a few minutes we would be dead and there was absolutely nothing we could do about it. We crawled upon the face of the ocean, and always nearer to the deadly line of enemy ships. It was certainly very frightening—far more so than any land battle I ever saw before or since. I began to ram a clip into my Garand rifle. There wasn't much else to do. In the dark I found it unfamiliar. I wished I had stuck to my old Lee Enfield. Craft and Clark were at my side. I sensed that they were as unhappy as I was—which comforted me to some extent.

I was in the stern of the craft, where I had been trying to sleep;

[1]Landing-craft Personnel (Large).

there was more room there. Now I wanted to speak to Buckee urgently. He was up forward beside the steersman. It was impossible to get to him through the soldiers crouched beneath the awning. I climbed up on to the narrow deck and ran along the side. We were still heading towards the Germans and every second brought us nearer the muzzles of their guns. I suggested to Buckee that it might be better to take some sort of avoiding action, but he replied that we were to follow the steam gunboat, which was navigating, so long as she was in action. Commander Wyburd had decided beforehand that, should he meet the enemy at sea, he would continue on his course and fight his way through, for he felt quite rightly that any alteration in course or speed would so disorganise the group that an orderly landing would become impossible. In any case, the destroyers *Slazak* (Polish) and H.M.S. *Brocklesby* were to give support to the landing-craft in the event of their being attacked by German ships. We ploughed on towards the Germans for what seemed a very long time; it has been estimated as ten minutes, but can scarcely have been as much; at the end of that time the gunboat, hit many times, reeled out of action, crossing our bows. Once more I urged Buckee to alter course and he now turned off 90 degrees to starboard.

Those of the landing-craft which escaped owed their survival to Wyburd's gallantry in keeping the gunboat on her original course, for the majority of the German gunners took his ship for their target. All his guns were put out of action, his wireless equipment was hit and about forty per cent of those on board were wounded.

On the other hand, we in the landing-craft now found ourselves far too near to the German ships and attracting a great deal of fire. The canopy of our craft was full of holes, but the men crouching down below were not hit. We made the best speed we could for several minutes and at last found ourselves out of range; behind us tracer could still be seen but no sound reached us.

The destroyers, meanwhile, were pursuing some project of their own.

As soon as we were clear we looked about to see where the rest of the group was, only to find that we were now alone. This did not disturb us very much; Buckee had little doubt that some of the other craft would be able to find their way to the beaches even without the gunboat to navigate. We turned towards the shore and started looking for Yellow 2. It was not difficult to estimate its rough position, as a light some miles away to starboard was evidently the Dieppe Lighthouse. We could now see the cliffs quite clearly and a black patch which Buckee said was the gully at Yellow 2. I thought it was Yellow 1, but Buckee insisted that he was right.

"There you are," he said, "there's your beach."

"What do we do now?" I asked, rather pointlessly.

"My orders," he replied, "are to land even if there's only one boat."

Not to be outdone, I said: "Those are my orders, too: we are to land whatever happens, even if we have to swim."

Buckee offered to land with his sailors to swell our party, but I persuaded him to remain with the craft. We arranged that if he should come under heavy fire from the cliffs he would leave us and that we would try to make our way to Dieppe and join the Canadians when the time came to withdraw. He was making directly for Yellow 2, but, fearing that there would be machine-guns in the gully, I asked him to run in about fifty yards to the right. We came in five minutes early, for it was getting light all too quickly, and touched down about 4.50 a.m.

We crossed the narrow beach, reached the foot of the cliff, turned to the left and approached the gully. The narrow cleft in the cliffs was completely choked with coils of wire with a rabbit-wire fence on the outside some ten feet high in front of it. I asked John Selwyn to tell his men to bring a Bangalore torpedo and blow a hole in the fence and was told that they had not got one in this particular boat. I said that we had better get to work with wire-cutters, but he said he had not brought any. I was vexed with Selwyn. I started to climb up the left-hand side of the gully, which looked the easier, but almost immediately lost my balance and fell back on top of Selwyn, who suggested that we were not doing much good and that it might be better to get back in the craft.

Similar thoughts were passing through my own mind at that moment, but being, I suppose, contrary by nature it needed only this to make me determined to carry on. I gave a sort of surly growl by way of reply and started climbing the other side of the cleft. When about twelve feet from the ground, my Garand rifle slipped off my shoulder and into the crook of my right arm, swinging me away from the wire. I thought to myself, "If I fall off now I shall never get up," but by some miracle I managed to keep my foothold and cling on with one hand. From this point the cliff became rather less steep and I reached the top, standing on the pegs with which the Germans had secured the wire, which served as a rope. The barbs were very close together but fairly blunt and this, though it cut my hands, was not as unpleasant as it sounds. On reaching the top, I could see the back of a notice-board which turned out to have the words "Achtung Minen" written on it.

The men seemed to take a very long time coming up the cliff, though Driver Cunningham collected their toggle ropes and made a rope to help them up the worst bit. As we reached the top Hopkins pointed out some landing-craft running in on Yellow 1, five of them. Later on a small ship ran in and beached between Yellow 1 and Yellow 2. This was the German-armed tanker *Franz*, damaged by one of our motor launches.

By about 5.10 a.m. my whole party had reached the top and I led them into a small wood nearby and organised them into three groups under Selwyn, Ruxton—a recently-joined subaltern—and myself. Some of the soldiers did not look particularly pleased at the turn of events, so I gave them a pep talk, telling them that if a party of nineteen could do any good it would be something to tell their children about. They looked a bit dubious. We had an odd assortment of arms; there was one Bren, six Thompson guns, ten rifles including my Garand, which had been given to me by the U.S. Rangers, a 3-inch mortar, which we had failed to get up the cliff, and a 2-inch mortar.

I now sent out scouts and started advancing through the cornfields towards the road which runs along parallel with the coast about a thousand yards inland. Looking out across the fields towards the battery we could make out absolutely nothing, though during our advance six Hurricanes came over and attacked it and were fired at by a light ack-ack gun. When we reached the road I took a careful look at the approach to the village through my field-glasses, expecting that there would be a German post at the entrance to the village. A French youth of about sixteen was passing on a bicycle when some of the men grabbed him. Though terrified, he was friendly and told me that he was trying to escape inland to avoid the fighting and that there were two hundred Germans in the battery. It was obvious that he would not betray our presence, and when I told him he could go on his way he swiftly leant forward, kissed me on the cheek, leapt on his bogwheel and pedalled for the hinterland! Ruxton advanced with his group while the rest of us covered him. He soon signalled that the

Destruction of a waterfront warehouse at Vaagso

The main street at Vaagso. In the centre is a demolition group.

British troops at Vaagso, returning to their ships.

A blazing storehouse at Vaagso.

Men of 3 Commando on their way to Dieppe in an LCP(L).

(Above) Lt. Col. Peter Young (right) at La Plein, with Brigadier John Durnford-Slater (centre) and Captain C.S Head (left).

Peter Young.

Some officers of 3 Commando, before Normandy, at the Limehouse street-fighting training area. From left to right – Ponsford, Westley, Williams, Lewis, Bartholomew, Pollock, Pritchard, Collins, Herbert, Wardle, Cowieson, Peter Young, Johnston, Nixon, Woyevodsky, Moore, Butler, Alderson, Pollard. (Not in photograph – Pooley, Hopson, Reynolds, Martin, Mount, Wills).

The eve of "D Day". 4.30pm at Warsash on the Solent. 3 Commando embarking for Normandy. In the foreground men of 5 Troop, 6 Troop and 4 Troop.

After dawn on "D Day". Six landing craft of the flotilla carrying the 1st Special Service Brigade, plough through heavy seas towards the Normandy beaches.

After "D Day". Aerial view of la Brèche and the 1st Special Service Brigade's "Queen Red Beach", littered with landing craft.

Peter Young briefing snipers at Amfreville, 1944.

Aerial view of Amfreville, Normandy. The road running from the centre top to bottom left was the German front line; to the left of it was No-Man's land.

"Typical of my followers" – Peter Young

Robert Christopher

Memorial at Petiville, France (one of many to Commando units) dedicated by the people of Petiville to mark their liberation by Peter Young and 3 Commando on 14 August 1944.

coast was clear and we all arrived at the edge of the village just as the battery fired its first round. We cut some telephone wires at this point and then pushed on. In an orchard to the right of the road a French peasant woman sat calmly milking a cow.

To move through the gardens at the back of the houses would have taken too long so we went up the main street. Here we met some Frenchmen wheeling a wounded woman along on a hand barrow; she had been hit during the attack by the Hurricanes soon after dawn. The guns were still firing slowly, so the sooner we reached the battery the better; I gave the order to double and we ran down the street at a pretty good pace. I questioned several inhabitants, hoping to hear that some of the men who had landed at Yellow 1 had also reached the village, but there was no news of them and no sign of firing from that direction. We saw quite a number of the inhabitants, some of whom were members of the local fire brigade in their brass helmets; one of the houses in the village was on fire. The people very wisely kept out of the way, though several of them waved to us, and all those we spoke to were distinctly friendly.

When we came abreast of the church we were suddenly fired on by a German machine-gun post at the corner of the road about sixty yards ahead of us. Ruxton opened fire on two Germans whom we saw cross the road and get into position in a hedge. They fired their rifles at him, but he stood his ground and returned their fire with his Thompson sub-machine gun. Selwyn joined him and opened up as well; then Abbott came up and got the Bren into action. Selwyn put Lance-Corporal Bennett behind the church and engaged this enemy post with our 2-inch mortar; the German machine-gun ceased fire.

I cannot think why we had no casualties at this point, for our party must have been an easy enough target. While this shooting was going on another group pushed on into the churchyard and engaged the enemy from there. The Germans' fire was mostly high and one burst dislodged a shower of tiles from a roof which descended on Abbott, the Bren-gunner.

The doubling had done the men good. They had now got their blood up and quite recovered their spirits. They were beginning to enjoy themselves. I re-formed them behind the church, with the intention of placing the Bren and some snipers in the tower, while the rest of us held the area. It seemed certain that the belfry would overlook the gun positions, and I had visions of picking off the German gunners one by one as they served their pieces. Unfortunately, when I went inside to look for the steps leading up the tower, I could find none. The church, a lovely medieval one, vanished in the pre-D-Day bombing, but I was told several years later by the town clerk that the steps began ten feet above ground level and were reached by a ladder which had been removed. Moreover, the view from the belfry was obscured by a row of tall trees, so perhaps it was as well that I was forced to alter my plan.

We now tried to advance on the battery through the orchards at the north-west end of the village, hoping to outflank any post which might be guarding the tracks entering the battery from the rear. We passed a slit trench and the under-carriage of an aeroplane which had been camouflaged and rigged up to look like a small gun, but then came under fire again from riflemen whom we could not see. They did not hit anybody and probably could not see us very well. Next a machine-gun opened up on us, firing three bursts, but there were so many hedges that we could not locate this either. There seemed to me to be no future in advancing blind through these orchards against a hidden enemy, and it suddenly occurred to me that we might be better off in the cornfields.

We assembled again at the edge of the village and I sent Selwyn's group to the flank of the guns, with orders to get within two hundred yards and snipe them. As he moved, my own group fired at the left-hand gun and continued to shoot while Ruxton led his men out to support Selwyn. My group then joined the other two. All three parties were fired at by small arms as we dashed to take up our new position, apparently by sentry groups posted along the edge of the orchards, but once again nobody was hit. The left-hand gun, which we imagined we could see clearly, and at which we had fired a certain amount, now turned out to be a dummy!

Once we were in among the crops I formed the men into two lines in extended order, with a good distance between each man and with the second line firing between the intervals in the first line. We now opened a hot fire at the smoke and flashes around the gun positions. Groups of riflemen were still firing at us from the battery position, but they were not marksmen.

All this time the guns went on shooting at a slow rate; possibly only one gun was in action, trying to find the range. Certainly there were no salvoes, and some of us estimated that the total number of rounds fired was no more than fifteen or twenty, though there must have been more. It seemed that the gun detachments were firing on their own account and that the observation post was not doing its job properly, possibly because we had cut their telephone wires, but more likely because of the enormous smoke-screen off Dieppe. The cloud of smoke there was very thick indeed and we ourselves could see none of the ships. To confuse the gunners the R.A.F. had dropped smoke on the battery and there was still a great deal hanging about. No doubt this air attack had upset them.

We had to fire from the kneeling position because of the height of the corn, taking snap shots and moving about, so as to offer the most difficult possible target to the enemy, but we were almost exactly at right angles to the enemy gun-line and any bullet that whistled over No. 4 gun would give a good fright to the crew of No. 1 as well— at least so we hoped. I am very far from claiming that we caused many casualties, and indeed it was very difficult to see anyone to get a shot at. It was harassing fire, more or less controlled. The guns were about twenty to thirty yards apart and surrounded by concrete walls.

After a time, at about eight o'clock, we had our reward. There was a sudden explosion about one hundred and fifty yards to our front, an orange flash, and a cloud of black smoke. A shell screamed past overhead and plunged into a valley about a mile behind us. The Germans had turned their left-hand gun round and were firing it at us. Fortunately we were too close to be damaged, for the guns, not being designed to fire at point-blank range, could not be depressed sufficiently to hit us. It was nevertheless an unusual experience and for a moment I wondered what was happening. Indeed one of the soldiers came up to me and said indignantly:

"Sir! We're being mortared!" An odd deduction when a 6-inch gun was firing at us! The Germans in the Varengeville Battery used mortars against 4 Commando, but at Berneval it seems they had none, which was just as well for us. Fifteen feet of standing corn is said to stop a bullet, but I doubt if it is much protection against a mortar bomb. Selwyn told me afterwards that one of our motor launches, having taken us for the enemy, was also firing at us about this time and one of the men was hit in the ear, our first casualty. Every time the gun fired we gave it a volley of small arms, aimed at the black-and-yellow fumes which appeared. They fired four rounds at us, at the same slow rate as before, and then gave it up.

Suddenly two Messerschmitts came swooping up from our rear and flew over the battery without attacking us. Neither side seemed to know who we belonged to. We had come ashore with about a hundred rounds per rifleman. Firing rapidly it would be easy to spend that much ammunition in ten minutes, so we had to be very sparing; we were continually telling the men to fire slowly so as to keep up a steady whine over the heads of the gunners. The posts in the orchard continued to fire at us without respite, but without success. We kept all our fire for the big guns.

Coast defence guns firing at a normal rate should be able to fire one or two rounds a minute, for the operation of reloading, though complicated, should not take more than about thirty seconds. We spent approximately an hour and a half in the cornfield and during that time I do not believe the battery got off more than twenty or thirty rounds, including the four aimed at us.

The shortage of ammunition was now becoming acute, and as time went by it was becoming increasingly probable that German reinforcements, including perhaps armour, would intervene. I did not care for the idea of meeting tanks in the middle of the cornfield, so I thinned out my line and sent Selwyn to form a small bridgehead round the beach, telling him that if the landing-craft was still there he was to fire three white Very lights.

So far we had paid no attention to the German observation-post which clearly deserved a visit. While the remainder of the party withdrew towards the beach, Ruxton with Abbott, Craft and Clark came with me to a point on the cliff from which we had a good view of this pillbox. Ruxton saw two Germans standing on the roof and fired a burst at them with the Bren, at a range of about four hundred yards. They disappeared and fire was returned immediately. Ruxton continued to engage the enemy post. Clark now reported seeing three white Very lights from the beach and we wriggled back into a small valley and began to make our way back to the boat. A group of riflemen were following us, at a respectful distance, and someone else was sniping from the Dieppe side of the gully. A few of the men covered our withdrawal, firing back at the German riflemen.

Captain Selwyn now withdrew his party and embarked, while the rest of us covered their withdrawal from the top of the cliff. The landing-craft had been under fire from the observation-post for some time. Riflemen had reached the cliffs about three hundred yards to the east, and the solitary sniper was still plugging away from the west. Three men waiting on the beach to cover Ruxton and myself down the cliff were cursed at by the sailors for their slowness and told to get into the boat.

Once aboard, they engaged the cliff-tops with the stripped Lewis gun belonging to the craft, scoring several hits. One German dropped his rifle down the cliff.

By this time Ruxton and myself, with Abbott our Bren-gunner, had crossed the beach and were wading out to the landing-craft. It was like those dreams you have of trying desperately to walk and making no progress. Eventually we laid hold of the lifelines and were towed out to sea. About three hundred yards out the craft hove to and we were dragged aboard. Quite a number of shots hit the craft at this point, and a sailor a yard away from me was severely wounded in the thigh. The battery fired a few shells at us but pretty wide of the mark. A bullet hit the smoke canister in the stern and we began to give out quite a respectable smoke-screen.

Shortly afterwards we fell in with the motor launch and transferred to her. We then returned to Newhaven, being unsuccessfully attacked on the voyage by a JU.88 at 10.45 a.m. and entertained nobly on whisky, cocoa, and rum so that I felt distinctly warm, if somewhat tight, on arriving at Newhaven.

There was no news of the rest of the Commando when we reached Newhaven, and in the afternoon I went up to London to report at C.O.H.Q. Having been on the planning staff there at the time of the St. Nazaire raid, I knew with what anxiety we had waited for any authentic information and how many days it had taken to reach us. I had an interview with Lord Louis Mountbatten and with General Haydon and was told to return for the conference which was to be held next day. I asked permission to reappear in my battledress which was rather the worse for wear, and Lord Louis replied: "What the hell, there is a war on."

I then went home to Oxshott and slept the night in my own bed.

. . . . .

The Germans were very excited at capturing some Americans. One of them, a very tall man—unfortunately his name is unknown to history—was being interrogated by a German officer.

"How many American soldiers are there in England?"

"There are three million. They are all my height and they have to be kept behind barbed wire to stop them swimming the Channel to get at you bastards." Fortunately this German had a sense of humour.

. . . . .

What did Dieppe prove?

To the Germans it proved that their system of coast defence was sound, and in the two years that followed they continued to develop the West Wall with the intention of repelling invasion on the beaches. Infanterie Regiment 571, which was in the area, had only the 2nd Battalion holding the town and yet succeeded in repulsing an attack by six battalions. The Germans were convinced that they were working on the right lines.

The expedition was extremely costly. Of the 4,961 Canadian soldiers engaged 3,363 became casualties—that is to say, 68 per cent. The Germans sustained about three hundred military casualties. Only thirty-seven prisoners were brought back to England, less than the number taken by our Commando at Vaagso.

Dieppe was always intended as a reconnaissance in force, and it succeeded in rubbing in certain lessons. When D-Day came in 1944 the invaders, instead of attempting to capture a port by direct assault from the sea, took their port with them and never again did they try to carry out a large-scale landing without heavy preliminary bombardment from the air and supporting fire from the sea.

At Dieppe there was no preliminary air bombardment because it was felt that this would prejudice surprise. It is not clear why a night air attack should necessarily put into the mind of the enemy commander the idea that he is going to receive a raid from the sea at dawn next morning, but this was one reason put forward. A heavy air raid shortly before a landing must cause great confusion and will give the assaulting troops a chance to strike before the defenders get really set again. St. Nazaire should have proved the danger of taking on German coast defences without a proper air bombardment.

The naval force commander, Captain J. Hughes Hallet, had always insisted that a capital ship should have been employed to lend fire support to the assault. There is no doubt that the comparatively light naval losses support his view. A 6-inch cruiser such as H.M.S. *Kenya* which supported us at Vaagso might have made all the difference at Dieppe. The main German defences enfilading the beach were concentrated in the two headlands and it should not have been impossible for 6-inch guns firing at the cliffs to have brought down whole portions of them, besides destroying houses and barricades along the waterfront. The troops attacking on the main beach at Dieppe were invited to assault without proper covering fire.

Some people assumed, in view of the heavy casualties, that the enemy had warning of the raid in advance. Against this I can only say that we found the defence posts on our cliff-top near Belleville-sur-Mer unoccupied. Would the Germans have neglected these points if they had expected a raid?

We heard later that even the news of the action with the coastal convoy at night had not reached the German private soldiers, while the lighthouses at Dieppe and the Point d'Ailler (near Varengeville) remained burning until our landing-craft were close.

To sum up the results of the Dieppe raid, one can only say that if we made a mistake in attacking such a strong place without adequate fire support, at least the enemy were lulled into a sense of false security. Thereafter, they pursued a policy of coastal defence which was to be their undoing in 1944. In war the right things often happen for the wrong reasons.

.   .   .   .   .

No. 3 Commando had one hundred and forty casualties at Dieppe. The reinforcements who arrived to replace them were a very remarkable body of men. More than ninety of them were policemen who had volunteered to join the army. So much for the myth that the Commandos were full of gangsters and cracksmen! Several won commissions, many were decorated and nearly every one of them became an N.C.O. Their influence was most marked in the years that followed, particularly in 5 and 6 Troops, which had suffered grievous losses at Dieppe. These two old troops were able to rise from the flames and reproduce their old form because the old hands had this good new material to mould. Conscientious, fit, self-reliant, the policeman has much to offer when he takes to soldiering.

.   .   .   .   .

A few weeks after Dieppe I was sent to Inveraray for a fortnight to be attached as an instructor to the United States 168 Combat Team, who were undergoing combined operations training. Here, for the first time, I met Derek Mills-Roberts, under whom I was to serve in Normandy, and learned from him the details of 4 Commando's exploit at Varengeville. Derek had served with the Irish Guards in Norway and was always full of ideas on tactics and training. He had also been sent to help the Americans.

No. 168 Combat Team were National Guards from the Middle West, from such places as Des Moines and Council Bluffs. They were training under the supervision of a team headed by Brigadier Mike O'Daniel, a veteran with much battle experience from World War I, known to his followers as "Iron Mike". After a short period he tired of his rôle as Chief Umpire, dispensed with the services of the Colonel Commanding and took over the reins of power himself, a decision which Derek and I wholeheartedly endorsed! He was a delightful and energetic commander, who described his brigade as consisting of "corn-fed country boys".

This Combat Team, or brigade, was training for an operation which turned out to be part of the North African landings. It was at that time extremely inexperienced; the men had a rooted objection to performing any evolution at the double and thought us distinctly eccentric in trying to make them do so.

Derek Mills-Roberts, who had recently won the M.C. at Dieppe, was then aged about thirty-five, a good-looking, clean-shaven officer, whose hair, already grey, lent him an air of distinction. He was little above medium height but strong and active. He had a fierce glint in his eye, but a smile lurked in the corner of his mouth. His language was violent, forceful and explosive, though fortunately the Americans had no interpreter. Stern and resolute, he was a fine tactician; daring to a degree, but never lavish with his men's lives.

．　　　．　　　．　　　．　　　．

After this interlude I returned to the Commando and to the usual round of running courses and setting exercises. We now moved to Weymouth, a good area for billets and for most forms of training, but not for shooting.

Nothing very remarkable took place during our stay there. We made numerous attacks on the various defences on Portland; 6 Troop frequented a pub where they used to play a record of Bing Crosby singing *You are my sunshine* and this they sang forever after, as well as their ruder favourite of former days—*O'Reilly's daughter*. At length, one day the Colonel made us a speech in which among other things he said, "We've got friends in high places"—then we knew that something was going to happen, probably unpleasant. And so one night we moved out, parading at the station at 11 p.m. with everybody present, even if some were dragged there and propped up in the ranks. George Herbert, raging, paced furiously up and down in front of 6 Troop telling them they were a useless collection of recruits and that he, though as drunk as any of them—which he wasn't —could still stand up—which he could.

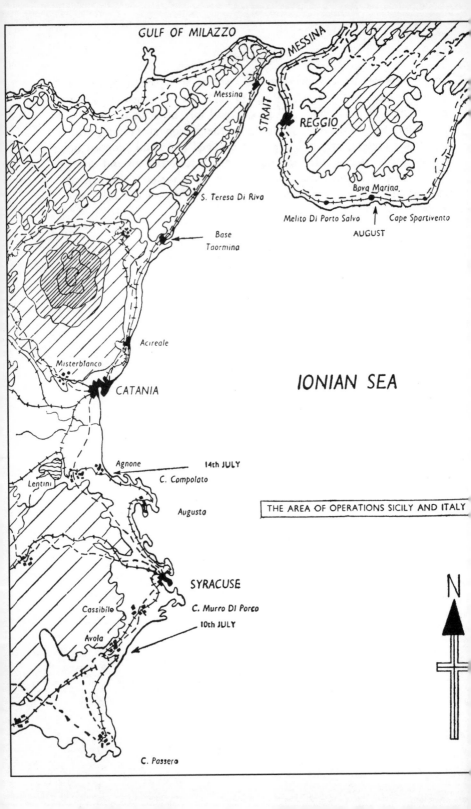

GULF OF MILAZZO

STRAIT of MESSINA

Messina

REGGIO

S. Teresa Di Riva

Bova Marina

Base
Taormina

Melito Di Porto Salvo   Cape Spartivento

AUGUST

Acireale

IONIAN SEA

Misterblanco

CATANIA

Agnone   14th JULY

Lentini   C. Compolato

Augusta

THE AREA OF OPERATIONS SICILY AND ITALY

SYRACUSE

Cassibile   C. Murro DI Porco

                          10th JULY

Avola

N

C. Passero

PART TWO

THE MEDITERRANEAN

CHAPTER V

THE FIRST LANDING IN SICILY

IT was on 18th February 1943 that the Commando embarked in H.M.T. *Letitia* at Glasgow, but not until 12th March did we reach Gibraltar, having called at Oran, for some obscure reason, on the way.

We were only about six weeks in Gibraltar. During our stay the garrison boxing tournament was held, and men like Corporals Dennis and Dowling made short work of the local talent. Though the garrison was not less than 15,000 strong, we won five championships.

. . . . .

On 10th April we sailed for Algiers in the *Princess Emma*, arriving on the 14th.

When, as occasionally happens, somebody asks me where I got the Africa Star I tell them at Fort de l'Eau, hoping that this will conjure up for them pictures of a heroic and desperate siege. It was in fact the Algiers transit camp. I cannot remember any good of it, except that we were made very welcome by the other units there because of the good name 1 and 6 Commandos had won in North Africa. These two units were about to return to England after fighting all through the winter with 1st Army. Derek Mills-Roberts, who was commanding 6 Commando, and Ken Trevor, the Second-in-Command of No. 1, were already old friends and I was to serve with both of them later in the war, the one in Normandy, the other in the Arakan.

We were not sorry when the time came to leave l'Afrique du Nord for Egypt.

After a short time in camp near Alexandria we moved to Suez, where we were to complete our training for the assault on Sicily. Here we were joined by Walter Skrine, a major belonging to the Headquarters of Combined Operations. He had tired of his desk and attached himself to us for the operation. Walter came from the depths of the bogs of Ireland; beneath a mild and courteous exterior he was a terrible old fire-eater.

.   .   .   .   .

The key to the island is Catania, or rather the Gerbini airfields nearby. If we could land there and push north we might prevent the arrival of reinforcements via Messina. Otherwise the enemy would be able to reinforce the garrison more rapidly than the Allies could land and supply their troops over open beaches; the ports were all strongly defended and, with Dieppe in mind, appeared impregnable to direct assault.

The R.A.F. working from bases in North Africa, and even from Malta, could not cover landings north of Syracuse. Thus once again the limiting factor was the range of fighter cover. It was decided that General Montgomery's Army should land by night in the south-east corner of Sicily. The American Task Force was to land simultaneously on the southern and western coasts. The early capture of airfields was vital, so that our aircraft would not have to go all the way back to Malta or North Africa to refuel and rearm.

Every harbour from Syria to Morocco was now a potential invasion base. It was skilfully put about that we intended to attack Greece and the Dodecanese, and I personally became convinced, for some reason, that Rhodes was the objective.

No. 3 Commando was in the 8th Army, under command of General Dempsey's XIII Corps, and had two targets: a coastal battery near Cassibile and the defences of one of the beaches where the 5th Infantry Division was to land.

.   .   .   .   .

The Commando and most of the infantry of XIII Corps were encamped on the stony, dusty plain of Ataka, between the Gulf of Suez and the rocky range of hills about three miles inland, and there during June we carried out our rehearsals. The wind got up most days before noon and the dust penetrated everything we had, particularly the food—with mortifying effects upon most people's insides. It died down about five o'clock every evening when we usually went swimming.

We started to rehearse our respective plans. John Durnford-Slater was going to attack the coastal defence battery with 4, 5 and 6 Troops, while the remainder were under my orders for the assault on the beach defences. On the plain near Ataka we had courses marked out of the exact size and shape of our objectives. Times without number the soldiers ran over this ground both by day and night; sometimes as a drill, sometimes as a field firing exercise, until everyone became perfectly familiar, not only with his own job, but with the tasks of the other groups.

On 20th June we went on board ship; John's party and a few of mine in *Prince Albert* and the rest in *Dunera*—a very pleasant change from the dust and flies of Ataka, for the accommodation in a modern troopship like *Dunera,* built not long before the war, was princely compared with our bivouac ashore. Indian stewards were still serving in the officers' dining saloon. We shared clean cabins, the ship had fans and there were few flies. We were able to do a little boat training, to practise the flotilla in navigation and to make the soldiers, many of whom had not been on an operation before, familiar with the assault landing-craft.

General Dempsey came down to have a look at us and watch a rehearsal. After it was over, he asked me to come and explain my plan, and we sat in his car with the map and air photographs of Beach 44 and its defences. My party, carried in six landing-craft, five from *Dunera* and one from *Prince Albert,* were to go ashore at a rocky place, half a mile north of the main beach. There was a prominent rock on the shore called the *Scoglio Imbiancato,* which appeared to be a reasonable landmark to find at night. We were to break through the wire with Bangalore torpedoes and divide into three parties. There were machine-gun positions on the headland and some suspicious-looking roofless buildings by the shore in which we expected to find pillboxes. On the far side of this beach was another headland and more pillboxes, but those were to be attacked by a company of the 6th Seaforths. Inland of the beach there seemed to be two strongpoints, one of them a farm. Nearby were more machine-gun posts and some trenches in a quarry.

The General said that he approved of my plan for taking these positions, told John Durnford-Slater that he was pleased with everything he had seen of the Commando and made a short speech to the men, welcoming them to XIII Corps and saying that he had heard all about their experiences: that they looked fit and that he had given them the most important single task of the whole operation. After this he took leave of us, shook hands and said: "I congratulate you both."

There was another meeting with the General, to discuss final points about the plan. This took place on 26th June, aboard H.M.S. *Bulolo*, the Headquarters Ship, where he and his staff were established with Admiral Troubridge, the Naval Force Commander. The General showed us various photographs, which we examined through an Italian stereoscope. He promised a late set of oblique air photographs, which would be useful for a last-minute check on the beach defences and would at the same time help to identify points inland. Various details were discussed. He was convinced that the roofless buildings on the point were important.

"You guarantee me that?" he said. "I don't think it will be difficult . . . two machine-guns . . . twelve men . . . that's what I should do myself."

He asked if three men of the Royal Engineers, who were to be attached to clear a gap in a suspected minefield, had arrived. "Are they 'Alamein men'?"

"There's nothing in the olive groves," he went on; "the whole position is so ridiculous that it must have been made for training; there are not many places in the area where troops could train under semi-peace conditions. They ought to have made proper positions under the trees. It may well turn out to be a dummy position."

Then he looked at me closely and said slowly: "Object: to get 17 Brigade ashore. Object: to get 17 Brigade ashore without casualties!"

He added: "If you do that it may make all the difference to our chances of taking Syracuse on the first day."

Arising from all this there were many visits to be made to units of the assault brigade, all in different ships. We had to make sure that we would not shoot each other up in the dark.

·   ·   ·   ·   ·

We moved up the Canal to Port Said, which offered an incredible spectacle. *Dunera* had moored at right-angles to the quay and we stood on deck in the sweltering sun, watching liner after liner, crowded with soldiers, come up the Canal and secure more or less alongside us. Not far off was a group of hospital ships, gleaming white and with large red crosses amidships. There was the *Monarch of Bermuda,* a four-funnel luxury liner with the 2nd Royal Scots and the 1st In-niskilling Fusiliers aboard, both battalions due to land on our beach and make for Syracuse. There lay the *Duchess of Bedford,* a tall ship with older and less rakish lines, carrying the 17th Infantry Brigade Headquarters and the 2nd Northamptonshires; *Sobieski* with the 6th Seaforths; *Prince Albert* with the rest of our Commando, much smaller and dazzle painted for camouflage, with sharp bows and a single squat funnel. Low in the water, with her almost destroyer-like appearance, her lines suggestive of speed, she looked ideal for the business of raiding.

·   ·   ·   ·   ·

On the morning of 5th July we sailed. The mysterious cipher, M.W.F. 36, by which the convoy was known, turned out to mean Moving West, Fast Serial, Number Thirty-six. There were lines of ships, a considerable distance apart, steaming at twelve knots. Ahead was an anti-aircraft cruiser, and Hunt-class destroyers circled continually. Our course lay within twenty-five miles of the African coast, which was often in sight, so there was no difficulty about air cover.

Ours was only one of the many convoys converging on Sicily from east, south and west. A slow convoy of thirty M.T. ships carrying the assault vehicles and equipment had preceded us. It had been loading up for weeks past at Alexandria, Beirut and Haifa and was to be joined later on by fifteen tank landing-craft from Tripoli, three small tankers from Malta, a crane ship and another strange vessel designed to hold the special landing-craft in which lorries and the like would be ferried ashore. We were timed to come up with this convoy somewhere east of Malta and to land five hours before it arrived.

We felt that something was brewing when on 7th July an unknown aircraft was seen making for Crete. But if the enemy were going to put in a torpedo attack it would have to be done that very evening, for by the following morning we would be out of range of Crete. Nothing happened.

While we cruised along in the sun from day to day our chief occupation was the briefing. Groups of men were taken in turn to

79

the model-room to study the beach and its defences so that everyone could visualise the objective and the route from the landing-place. It was one thing to brief people on the model, but quite another to make sure that everyone had taken it in, so we had frequent sessions and all were tested. The method employed was to make each man describe the plan and to have him corrected by others until he knew it by heart.

Good briefing is undoubtedly a tonic to the morale of the men; even so, there were some odd notions about this operation. Christopher, my orderly, told me that since Tunis had fallen two months earlier than expected the Italians were backward with their defences in Sicily. So far so good, but he also informed me that the lads were displeased with Mr. Churchill, who had given the position away by saying, according to the B.B.C., that he expected some heavy fighting in the Mediterranean before long. Christopher was greatly distressed by this breach of security!

On 7th July we had some more intelligence from *Bulolo*. There was one German division, probably the 15th Panzer. Their tank-assault regiment was supposed to have 150 tanks, including about forty Tigers. The Germans, about 16,000 strong, included elements of the famous Hermann Goering Division. The four Italian active divisions which had been identified were Livorno, Napoli, Assietta and Aosta. General Guzzoni, aged sixty-six, was their Commander-in-Chief. We understood that he had retired from the Army twice already but had been brought back. At the ripe age of twenty-eight I found it difficult to understand the Duce recalling an officer who was obviously thirty years too old for the work.

On the morning of 9th July, when we were near Malta, we caught sight of the slow convoy. Some of the tank landing-craft were having a rough time in the heavy swell which had now begun to trouble us. By the afternoon the sea had risen so much that we wondered if the operation would have to be postponed. Lowering landing-craft from heavily rolling ships would be a hazardous business. As night fell the wind began to drop. We could see nothing ahead in the darkness but the red glow from the top of Mount Etna, impressive but forbidding.

The convoy turned north, near Misurata, and passing to the east of Malta headed for Sicily. We heard that the Gerbini airfields had been raided nineteen times during the day. The port of Palermo was already out of action.

About 11 p.m. our troops began to get dressed, and when we joined them on deck they were grouped ready to make their way to the boat-deck and embark. They were in tremendous form, singing at the top of their voices. The ship was blacked out and there was only a dim light between decks, hardly enough to see people's faces.

Because of the weather we stood in closer to the land than originally intended and we were about seven miles from the coast, when a little after midnight we filed along to our boat stations and were lowered in five landing-craft, each carrying about thirty-five soldiers.

.　　.　　.　　.　　.

Even after the lapse of fourteen years I cannot look back upon that night without chagrin. From first to last everything went wrong. We were in the hands of the R.N.V.R. officer commanding our land-ing-craft flotilla, who, if he knew his job, did not mean business. Perhaps he was merely incompetent. Conditions were not easy, with a strong head wind, a heavy swell and a black night.

Suffice it to say that we never met our sixth craft, immediately lost one from *Dunera,* and soon after that a third broke down. Next we lost the motor launch that was guiding us. More time was wasted asking for a course from the *Duchess of Bedford.* North 53 West, we were told—precisely the same as the course given at the briefing.

We crept towards shore; found ourselves to port of the flotilla con-taining the Royal Scots Fusiliers when we should have been to star-board; politely passed astern of it; missed the sonic buoy and decided we did not know where we were. In fact we were not far from Beach 44, which we had failed to recognise.

We cruised about until Walter Skrine and I identified Murro di Porco Bay, and not until we had actually entered it were we able to persuade our boat officer to put about. Next we got shot up, though without any loss thanks to our armour plate, by the observation post at Torre Ognina and went straight out to sea at full speed.

Having persuaded our friend not to return to the *Dunera,* we altered course and picked up twenty men from a sinking glider. Then just as it was getting light we found ourselves once more at the entrance to Beach 44, just as the last shell from John Durnford-Slater's battery landed on a headland to our right. Instantly our lieutenant started to go out to sea again, but we got him to join another craft which was already there. In it was Brigadier Tarleton, who was not a little surprised to find us *behind* him.

"We will go in together," he said, and we all landed unopposed at the right end of the Cassibile Beach and took up a defensive position along the railway line.

There was firing and intermittent mortaring from the direction of Cassibile village, but such defences as we could see did not appear to be very formidable and on the whole things were going well.

Cassibile fell after considerable resistance and 17 Brigade pushed off towards Syracuse. The village was our appointed rendezvous with the rest of the Commando, and there we waited for the rest of the day.

Such was my first landing in Sicily.

．　　　．　　　．　　　．　　　．

John's flotilla, commanded by Lieutenant Holt of the *Prince Albert*, had found the *Scoglio Imbiancato*, not without considerable difficulty, and had come under fire a couple of hundred yards from the shore. From a pillbox some Italians were firing with a machine-gun; from the seven craft twenty-one machine-guns returned the fire, and it took only a few seconds to convince the garrison that they were doing no good. The Commando struggled through a mass of barbed wire, ran up the beach and struck off inland, ignoring the beach defenders. They could hear the moans and cries of the wounded. The enemy machine-gun positions, seven in all, were mopped up by Ned Moore, the Medical Officer, who went after them with a tommy-gun. It was a bright moonlit night and, led by John Pooley and the Colonel, the Commando, in a long double file, set off across country at a good speed. They carried out the approach drill as practised near Port Tewfik, with the leading troop marching on compass bearings and counting the paces. At one point a farmer fired his shotgun at 6 Troop. This act proved fatal—to him—but, as Curly Gimbert remarked, "He had the right spirit."

Then the battery began to fire. The Commando was still not in position and John Durnford-Slater, who had promised General Dempsey that he would do the job in ninety minutes, was racing against time. From a dry watercourse in front of the battery he sent a party to harass the Italians with rifle fire and a 2-inch mortar. Exactly on the flank of the guns and about 400 yards from them he placed a 3-inch mortar and four Brens under Roy Westley, a tough and aggressive officer from the Hertfordshire Yeomanry. They dropped a 3-inch mortar bomb into an Italian ammunition dump, which went on exploding for some time. Most of the soldiers carried two 3-inch mortar bombs suspended by cords round their necks. As they passed the position of 2 Troop they dumped their bombs with loud clanks and sighs of relief.

By this time the Colonel had formed up three troops, two forward and one back, in rear of the battery. They illuminated the battery with flares, and by their light the assaulting troops poured in a heavy fire. Charlesworth, the Colonel's batman, sounded the *Advance* on his trumpet and in they went, blasting the wire with Bangalore torpedoes. The Italians had been firing back with a number of automatic weapons, but when the final assault came in with the bayonet most of them surrendered. One machine-gunner, made of sterner stuff, was killed.

In this charge, in which John Pooley and Brian Butler particularly distinguished themselves, the Commando only had three casualties. Within eighty-five minutes of the landing and after firing only about twenty rounds, the guns and all their ammunition had been blown up.

Of all the operations in which I took part, I enjoyed this the most, John Durnford-Slater wrote afterwards, and well he might. Yet, brilliant though it was, this exploit was not nearly as dangerous as his adventures at Vaagso; nor was it as important as his part in the battle of Termoli—which still lay in the future. At Dieppe he had had a series of misfortunes, whilst I had been lucky. This time the boot was on the other foot.

Torre Cuba

On the next morning General Dempsey ordered John to send a fighting patrol to clear the area between Torre Ognina and Cassibile. In his book *Commando* John refers to this incident:

Peter Young . . . was in a bad mood, as his landing-craft had been indifferently handled and had put him ashore late. . . . There were some Italians holding out in a fort nearby and I gave him permission to capture this place. He came back in the evening much more cheerful.

For this mission I took 3 Troop under Captain John Lash, who was keen to distinguish himself. My old ally, George Herbert, who had been commissioned when we were in North Africa, was in this troop. We pushed off up the road to the north, and after a time came to a road and railway junction.

Here men of an R.A.S.C. company told us that there had been firing during the night from a place called Torre Cuba. However, all had been quiet during the morning and they assumed that the enemy had either withdrawn or surrendered. Nevertheless I told Lash to deploy when we were still a good distance from the farm, which was just as well.

Torre Cuba was fortified, with high walls and strong buildings. We approached from the west, well spread out; to the right of the track was Lash with his H.Q., Lieutenant Nicholas and his section, and Sergeant Knowland's sub-section; to the left was Lieutenant Buswell with his section. For my part, exercising the divine right of commanders, I was walking along the track with several orderlies. Christopher was riding a bicycle alongside me, when suddenly a Breda about two hundred yards ahead opened up straight down the track which ran between two walls. Without more ado I fell flat on my stomach; Christopher leaped over the wall on the right of the track, apparently without even setting a foot to the ground. This first burst hit a soldier a little way behind us. Lash crawled forward in bounds towards the concrete machine-gun post at the south-west corner of the farm. Every time he advanced George Herbert leapt up and plastered the post with a Bren fired from the shoulder—a favourite trick of his. Some Italians near a glider three hundred yards away to the right kept firing, but ineffectively. Lash arrived within grenade range of the enemy and hurled a bomb. It missed, but the Italians took to their heels; in the confusion Lash, Herbert and Trooper Underwood rushed into the farm firing like mad. They wounded eight Italians and a British prisoner, who ran out to welcome them— he was not seriously hurt. Almost simultaneously Buswell and Sergeant Shaw broke in at the north end of the farm.

The engagement had lasted about ten or fifteen minutes. The bag was two officers and fifty-one men of the 206th (Italian) Coastal Division, under Capitano Covatto. One British officer and ten men, prisoners taken from the nearby glider, were set free. We had one casualty.

The position was very strong, a square farm with strong walls and buildings, all loopholed. At each corner was a Breda machine-gun, and in a tower was another. Across the farmyard ran a trench no less than twelve feet deep! There was a telescope on top of the water-tower, which was about sixty feet high, and with this the Italians had seen us when we were still about three-quarters of a mile away. They had already beaten off three other patrols, but some of them said that they would not have fought if Covatto had not forced them to.

The Italians, though not unduly anxious to do battle, were stoical about their wounds. One poor fellow had had a foot blown off by a bomb some time on D-Day, yet made no complaint.

The airborne troops and a handful of our men took the prisoners back to Cassibile, but I kept the captain with me, for our task was not yet done. There was still a garrison on the cliffs at Torre Ognina. Covatto and I had no common language, for he did not speak French, but I was able to invent enough Italian to explain that I was summoning Torre Ognina to surrender. I explained that if the enemy wanted a fight they could have one, but in that case I should see that they were all put to the sword. If, on the other hand, they laid down their arms their lives would be spared. What words I found to convey this proposition I do not remember, but after a good deal of ham acting (drawing my forefinger across my throat!) the Captain got the idea. We set off, still deployed. As we approached Torre Ognina we passed an evacuated strong-point and reached the wire without a shot fired, Covatto leading through the obstacle and no sentries in sight. Rounding a huge rock we came on the enemy in a group all huddled together and had no difficulty in persuading them to give themselves up, but whether the Captain delivered my summons in due form I cannot say. Another officer and sixteen more men were made prisoners.

CHAPTER VI

AGNONE

O N 12th July the Commando was ordered to move to Lo Bello, a farm near Syracuse. We had left all our transport in the Middle East, but we managed to conjure up a small car for the Colonel, a disreputable lorry and a couple of farm carts. With our heavy equipment—such as it was—loaded in this makeshift transport column we set off, the men marching. It was hot and dusty, but the farm proved a pleasant, shady place set amongst orange groves.

Not far away in an orchard was General Dempsey's Tactical Headquarters, a simple affair, one or two tables, a wireless set, a jeep and a couple of trucks. Walter Skrine and I wandered that way and watched the great ones from afar. Dempsey was talking to Brigadier John Currie, the renowned commander of 4th Armoured Brigade. They were joined for a few minutes by the Army Commander, in his usual buoyant spirits. Seeing Walter sniping at him with his camera, Monty waved to him in an affable way, calling:

"Come here, come over here. Take a photo if you want to!"

That evening the Commando was still resting in the lemon grove at Lo Bello, when General Dempsey strolled over and talked quite informally to some of the men. Corporal Pantall knew there was "something in the air" because the Corps Commander, with a twinkle in his eye, had said to them:

"We've got something good for you this time!" This was the first we heard of XIII Corps' plan for the advance to the Primosole Bridge.

That night we received orders to embark at Syracuse in a landing craft (Infantry) and transfer to the *Prince Albert* in the Bay of Avola.

It was a calm and sunny morning as we left harbour and headed south to join the invasion fleet. Moored alongside the quay we saw a captured Italian submarine, which, unaware of our arrival, had returned to base and surfaced only to be hit by a minesweeper, whose crew, though doubtless surprised, had quickly got their one gun into action and put a shell into the conning-tower!

An air attack was going on as we came alongside *Prince Albert*, but nevertheless some of the crew gave us three cheers, which we returned.

There were more raids by fighter-bombers during the day and the Luftwaffe pressed home their attacks in the teeth of a formidable barrage. Every ship was pumping shells into the air—Bofors, Oerlikons, all the lot—but still two or three vessels were hit and a tanker brewed up in a dense black cloud of smoke and flame. *Prince Albert* escaped these attentions.

We still had no idea whether the projected operation was "on" or not, when at about 3.30 p.m. John Durnford-Slater was summoned to a conference at Admiral Troubridge's Headquarters in Syracuse. The Army Commander and General Dempsey were both present. It transpired that the 50th (Northumbrian) Division, now leading the advance inland, had been checked by enemy positions on Monte Pancali overlooking the road to Lentini; a commanding position but believed to be occupied, not by Germans, but by Italians.

In order to hasten the drive for Catania it was decided that the 50th Division would attack that night and capture Lentini.

During the night one airborne brigade was to be dropped close to the Simeto River to capture the Primosole Bridge and hold it until relieved by ground troops next day.

Simultaneously 3 Commando was to land on the coast at Agnone and capture a bridge called the Punta dei Malati, over the Leonardo River, three thousand yards north of Lentini and about five miles from the coast. We were to prevent the demolition of the bridge and to cut off the enemy withdrawing from Lentini.

There was an enemy coast defence battery on a headland and four or five pillboxes on the beach; however, the Italian general commanding the Napoli Division had surrendered and had ordered the coast defences to do the same, so that there was no reason to suspect that our landing would be stiffly opposed. A Hunt-class destroyer, H.M.S. *Tetcott*, was to lead us in and bombard the coast defence battery during the landing. As there were only eight landing-craft, the landing was to be made in two flights.

It was late in the afternoon when John returned to *Prince Albert*. He arrived in the wardroom rather breathless, a roll of maps under his arm, summoned all officers and announced that we were going to do an operation that same night. This caused some consternation.

I felt quite sorry for the troop commanders, who were not going to have much chance of briefing their men and little enough to complete their administrative arrangements. Yet in many ways this was better than all our painstaking preparations for the first landing which as far as my party was concerned had gone so lamentably astray.

John gave out his orders. The first flight was to consist of the main body of the Commando. The second flight, under John Pooley, was to be 5 and 6 Troops. Part of 2 Troop were to guard the landing-place until the second flight came ashore. The troop commanders went off to pass this on to their men.

Walter Skrine and I studied the map to find a route which we would have a reasonable chance of following in the dark. Fortunately, there was a railway which ran directly inland from behind the beach and this was obviously going to help us for part of the distance, though after a few miles it disappeared into a long tunnel; I did not care for the idea of following it beyond that point. Walter, a regular officer of the Royal Artillery with a good deal of service, had been to the Staff College before the war, a thing practically unheard of in the Commandos! He had provided himself with an impressive-looking compass from a wrecked glider. I felt that if we left the route to him we would be in good hands; and, relieved of this burden, I turned my attention to the next problem: to try and select, off the map, defensive positions in the area of the bridge.

Soon after dusk *Prince Albert* was steaming at high speed. There was a moon and the weather was fine. Below decks the soldiers, busy with their final preparations, did not know that an E-boat had made an attack on us and that Lieutenant-Commander Peate, by going full speed ahead had evaded the torpedo, which passed close under the stern of his ship.

The officers gave their men as much information as they could. Everyone had a look at the map of the area, but still the contrast with the arrangements for the first landing was most marked. This time there were no models, no air photographs and only about an hour and a half in which to make all the preparations. Reveille had been at 3 a.m., and many of the soldiers felt like a good night's rest rather than an operation! In our former landings we had worn steel helmets, but this time we decided to wear berets. Each man carried a ration of chocolate, biscuits and either bully or sardines. Boats were lowered

88

about 9.30 p.m. and as we embarked sailors handed each man a packet of sandwiches.

The craft set off in the moonlight, closely followed by H.M.S. *Tetcott*. As we drew towards land there was much activity, particularly towards Catania, which was under bombardment from the sea or air or perhaps both. There were explosions on land and in the air, which lit up the coast-line momentarily and gave us a good idea of direction. Very lights and tracer could be seen to the west and south, and an anti-aircraft barrage over Syracuse. To the north-east star shell and flares were being fired in some naval engagement off the coast of Italy. Two aircraft were seen to fall into the sea in flames.

Just before the dim outline of the headland came into view some twin-engined aircraft flew over, very low, and passed over the coast. They looked like Dakotas—the airborne boys making for Primosole. They were not fired at as they crossed our beach. Straight ahead all was quiet and still: it was a tense moment in this eerie night as we saw the land ahead in the moonlight. Our flotilla opened out into line abreast and crept in dead slow so as not to arouse the beach defences. Could they see us?

We were not left long in doubt. When we were about a hundred yards out the coast defence battery and several light machine-guns opened up on us. The destroyer *Tetcott* immediately opened up on the battery, while the pillboxes were taken on by twenty-four machine-guns—three mounted in the bows of each landing-craft. Every fifth round was tracer and the noise as well as the streams of bullets converging on the pillboxes was most encouraging, but the best thing of all was the way the destroyer came right in close to the headland and gave us fire support.

In my craft the machine-gunners stood up in their exposed gun positions firing incessantly.

I was standing looking out for targets and trying to get the lay of the land. There was a good deal of stuff flying about. A searchlight flicked on for an instant, but it drew a great deal of fire and the crew quickly switched off again. The craft ran slowly in—far too slowly, I thought, for once the guns began to fire it would have been better to go flat out, as the machine-gunners and the others kept up a steady volume of fire, and there was a good deal of fire coming back. Suddenly a rain of blows struck my chest; clearly I was being riddled with bullets. I wondered why I did not fall—there was no pain, a sure sign that I had been too badly wounded to feel anything. It was a few seconds before I realised what was happening. I was being hit by the stream of empties which were pouring from the Lewis gun and flying straight at me!

The boats were supposed to strike the beach simultaneously, but they were not in proper line. The Colonel with the flotilla officer, Lieutenant Holt, was in the fourth craft from the right; I was in the right-hand craft at least two lengths behind him, and so he touched down first, as was his custom. The ramps went down and there was a momentary lull in the enemy fire as we ran across a sandy beach not fifty yards wide. Charley Head, in the left-hand craft, got ashore to find himself looking at an Italian machine-gun. He began to pull out his pistol, found it took too long, ran up to the emplacement and kicked the gun over to the astonishment of the crew, who promptly surrendered.

The plan was to blow the wire with Bangalore torpedoes and so I ordered the men to take cover until this was done. There was a low bank, crowned with wire, at the inland edge of the beach and under this the soldiers lay. To the left all was tumult and confusion. Grenades kept going off, and there was a good deal of shooting. The soldiers from the port craft were crowded together under the headland. They were suffering casualties and began to edge in our direction. Suddenly quite a large group of shadowy forms approached. I did not like the look of it.

"Where the hell d'you think you're going?" I shouted. "Line that bank!"

Farther along John Lash and George Herbert were seconding my efforts. With a good deal of cursing I restored some semblance of order.

It was at this critical moment that someone away to the left discovered a gap in the wire and shouted out this welcome piece of intelligence. I decided to forget about the Bangalores and take a chance on the gap not being mined. It turned out to be quite wide; I shouted to the soldiers to follow and they began to file through. The enemy were still hurling down grenades; luckily few of them burst among the soldiers bunched in the gap, though I saw one poor man dragging himself away on his hands and knees. Walter Skrine, with his runner, pushed off down the track leading inland towards the railway station. We went along a little path with a hedge on either side and ran inland, past an enclosure where there was some sort of hut or barracks.

The soldiers moved off from the beach in a ragged column, without many casualties, though Buswell told me that one of his Bren teams had been wiped out by a grenade. We hurried up the path.

John Lash came up and said we were going too fast for his men to keep up. I told him that I wanted to get clear of the beach defences and ordered him to get his advance guard out in front, which he did. I followed them with my orderlies. We had not gone far when we ran into about ten Italian prisoners coming slowly towards the beach with their hands up. They stopped and began milling about in the path and chattering. The soldiers with me halted. We were wasting time and I shouted to the men to clear these people out of the way. We had no interpreter, and in the darkness and confusion the Italians were slow and stupid. I remember hitting one of them with the butt of my rifle; I was not in a very good temper. They got out of the way and I had just passed them when some imbecile, thinking no doubt that they were attacking him, fired. A volley of shots followed and the whole column came to a standstill.

"Cease fire!"

After a few caustic comments they did so. Meanwhile the advance section also had halted and clearly had not the least intention of going on.

We pushed on, but had not gone far when firing broke out ahead. Walter Skrine, who, not without reason, was anxious because of the slow progress we were making, had pushed on.

Suddenly a motor-cycle and sidecar with a machine-gun in it came down the road towards him. His runner, Cox, put it out of action with a well-aimed hand grenade.

Another machine-gun and some riflemen opened up on our leading section which went to ground; in the ensuing exchange both Walter and Cox were severely wounded.

John Lash was just behind them and sent Nicholas and the advance guard round the enemy's left flank, while the rest of his troop engaged them from the front.

Captain Leese now came up with 1 Troop. I sent him round to get in the rear of the enemy by following and reinforcing Nicholas' small party.

There was still a lot of firing. Two men of Lash's troop were hit; one of them wounded in the knee, was clinging to the trunk of an olive tree a few yards from me. We were being shot at from the

railway line on our left and could make out a certain amount of movement. I called for a Bren gun and Corporal Dowling of 1 Troop ran
up and started firing. He was not quite on the target; I took over
the gun and fired four or five magazines. George Herbert came
up and began spotting for me. The Bren is a lovely gun. I was enjoying myself when the Colonel came up. By this time the enemy on
the railway line had packed up.

The Colonel suggested that Lloyd of 4 Troop might try and outflank
the enemy by going to our left, but I was against this, fearing that in
the dark they would fall foul of Leese's troop. The delay was maddening and it was a great relief when suddenly we heard Lincoln Leese's
hunting horn in the distance, straight ahead. Hearing him behind
them the enemy melted away. We rose to our feet and surged forward.

Almost at once I came across Walter Skrine lying beneath the trees.
Near by Ned Moore was attending to the wounded. He handed me
some morphia and told me to give it to Walter, who, not wishing to
delay me at such a time, refused to take it. After a few brief words
I went on.

No. 3 Troop needed time to sort themselves out, and so I told Bill
Lloyd to pass through them, which he did, pushing inland at a good
speed. I was walking along with their leading sub-section when I heard
George Herbert's voice asking for water. He was sitting on a bank,
holding his head. This was a loss indeed.

"How are you, George?" I asked.

"I'm getting weaker all the time," he replied.

Christopher gave him some water, which evidently had magic
properties, for soon after he got up and went forward with his section.
A grenade had concussed him, giving him a minor wound in the ear.

We were following the general line of the railway now and Bill
Lloyd asked me whether it would not be better to walk along the top
of the embankment. I agreed, and the men went along in file on
either side of the track. A little later I was leading along the left-hand
side when Lloyd called out to know which sub-section we were.

"All right. It's me, Bill," I said, or something equally ungram-
matical.

"Don't let the Second-in-Command's party get in front of you,
4 Troop," he called out. "Get out in front."

Very thoughtful of him. Sergeant Coaker doubled his men past us
to act as an advanced guard.

Not long after, we reached Agnone Station. Against the wall stood four Italian prisoners, and sitting with his back against it was Lincoln Leese.

"What's the matter?"

"I can't see. I'm sorry. I've lost an eye. It was a grenade. My Sergeant-Major's dead."

He had done enough; I told him that Veasey must take over the troop and that he must make his way back to the beach.

Once past Agnone Station, we had evidently broken the crust. There were still occasional shots, but the soldiers were steady now and had given up plunging into the ditch every time there was a shot fired. No. 4 Troop, in the lead, were going well, and wasted no time searching for shadows in the houses we passed.

Arriving at the tunnel, the Colonel held a conference with the troop commanders. We checked up on casualties. We still had at least 160 men with us, not counting John Pooley with the second flight and the men guarding the beach.

It was a very brief meeting. John rapped out his orders in a tone which invited no questions:

"We'll continue the advance, with 4 Troop leading, then 3, then 1. Headquarters will move in front with you, Bill. For God's sake don't straggle. We're going to cover about three miles of real rough country before we hit the bridge. We've got to get on fast to make it before the enemy retreat."

With this he dismissed the troop commanders.

.   .   .   .   .

Aboard *Prince Albert* 5 and 6 Troops, the second flight, had at least an hour's wait before them. The landing-craft took longer than expected and it was after 1 a.m. when the soldiers, who by now were waiting on deck, saw their dim shapes coming back across the moonlit water. They could smell burnt cordite as the craft came alongside.

H.M.S. *Tetcott* came up to port and a voice hailed:

"*Prince Albert! Prince Albert!* First flight has got ashore all right in spite of opposition. Since they landed the enemy has put an anti-tank gun four hundred yards to the right. Do you want us to shell the beach, or to lay down a smokescreen?"

Commander Peate replied: "Don't shell the beach. Troops are holding it. Put a few smoke shells on top of the cliff."

The landing-craft were hauled up on the davits to deck level, a number of wounded were carried off to the Sick Bay, and 5 and 6 Troops embarked. From the boat crews they learned that the first flight had met with a good deal more opposition than expected.

When the flotilla was several hundred yards from the shore *Tetcott* opened fire and put down a number of smoke shells on the cliff ahead. Ashore the vegetation was soon ablaze. As the craft were forming up in line abreast for the final run in, with 6 Troop to starboard and 5 Troop to port, the enemy, who had probably been reinforced, opened fire with their anti-tank gun and numerous automatic weapons; nevertheless, owing to the low silhouette of the craft they did not do very much damage. Arthur Evans, of 6 Troop, a former policeman, was in a craft which was actually pierced through and through, presumably by the anti-tank gun, but happily nobody was hit!

The destroyer giving fire support ran so close inshore that the soldiers who saw her looming high alongside felt sure she would run aground, but at the last moment she stood out to sea. Almost at once some of the craft beached, a few came to within twenty or thirty yards of the shore and quickly retracted, leaving the soldiers to wade.

On the left Tony Butler's boat got stuck on the rocks under the headland and, despite the efforts of Holt, the Flotilla Officer, it could not be got off.

From the cliffs one hundred feet above, the defenders were firing machine-guns and rifles and hurling Red Devils,[1] which burst in the water all round the stranded craft. The 5 Troop men replied with the Lewis guns belonging to their boat and one of their Brens. There was a terrific din, but the people in the boat kept cool. Holt tried in vain to get it off the rocks, apologised for putting them there and suggested that they should swim for it. The steel doors opened and Tony Butler led his men out. Corporal Pantall, the fourth to go, saw the man in front of him disappear just before he jumped in himself. Down and down he went, fifteen or twenty feet; weighed down with his rifle, ammunition, grenades and heavy boots, he wondered if he was ever going to surface again. As he came up a burst of machine-gun fire splashed up the water about a yard away and he struck out hastily for the shore some twenty yards away and crawled out on to the rocks. His watch had stopped at 2.5.

Donald Hopson had been left to guard the gap in the wire and to

[1] Italian hand grenades.

signal the second flight ashore. Not the least remarkable fact about that eventful night is that he succeeded in doing so, though his small party was surrounded on all sides by the enemy, who as we now know included quite a number of Germans, and was encumbered by about thirty Italian prisoners and a number of wounded. It was an unpleasant ordeal for a couple of hours, but we could not have chosen a better man for the job. We had many dashing characters in 3 Commando, but nobody was cooler under fire than Donald; self-possessed and efficient, he was quite a different type from the usual scatter-brained subaltern.

Passing through the gap in the wire, Pantall caught up with Tony Butler. Of the twenty-eight men in the boat, only nine had found their way through the defences, for the others, cut off in small parties, had gone off to the left. Sergeant Smith succeeded in scaling the cliff with some of them and capturing a good many prisoners and weapons. Considering their position, stuck on the rocks and completely overlooked, their casualties had been astonishingly light. Unhappily they included Holt, the Flotilla Officer. The other half-dozen craft did not suffer so badly.

The beach was still under fire as 6 Troop, now Ruxton's, came ashore on the right; grenades were thudding into the sand. Evans, who had seen no really serious fighting before, thought it must be impossible to cross, but since there was no other course he ran after Paddy Quinn to the shelter of the cliff and, looking round, saw to his amazement that the whole section had arrived unscathed. He saw a lot of prisoners too, and he could hear someone hailing the boat crews to know if they could take off the wounded.

Sergeant Darts, a young giant well known to me since Dunkirk days when he was in the Pioneer Platoon of the battalion I had served in, was in command of the rear section of 6 Troop. Reaching land, he called the roll and found that his No. 1 had lost the Bren and magazines. What he said to Trooper C—— is nobody's business. Lincoln Leese, who had got back to the beach with his batman and was guarding some of the prisoners, came up to Darts, said he was blinded and asked where the craft were. Darts replied that the firing had been too severe for them to stay long on the beach and pushed on, leading his men through the wire.

Once clear of the beach, John Pooley, who was in command of the second flight, formed up his column, pressed forward to the railway

line, and, climbing up the embankment, moved off along it, Tony
Butler in front. The party had not gone far when an Italian soldier,
sitting in a tree overhead, challenged; then, hearing someone talking
English, he threw down a Red Devil. Before it burst the soldiers were
lying on their stomachs on the side of the embankment. It exploded
harmlessly; a tommy-gun riddled the Italian, who crashed heavily to
the ground. Before the men could get to their feet again a German
voice barked an order and a machine-gun opened up at short range.
Firing back, 5 Troop quickly crossed the line and put the embankment
between them and this new enemy. Corporal Pantall, the last man of
Tony Butler's section to cross, heard a burst hit the rails beside him.
Woyevodsky, whose section came next, lost one of his tommy-gunners,
killed.

According to John Cummings, who was following, the enemy gun
was firing straight down the track. No. 6 Troop, which so far had lost
nobody, all turned right, dashed across a field and reassembled on the
other side. John Pooley soon had things under control and, re-forming
his column, led them back on to the railway line, followed it as far as
the tunnel and then struck off along the route we had followed earlier.

Just as daylight was appearing Pooley's party reached the road about
half a mile from the bridge. In the distance they could hear firing and
then a terrific roar as a German ammunition truck went up.

A few minutes later John Pooley came up to the Colonel and reported the arrival of the second flight.

$$\cdot \qquad \cdot \qquad \cdot \qquad \cdot \qquad \cdot$$

To return to the first flight, after we left the tunnel we struck off to
the right and found ourselves in the most infernal country imaginable
—undergrowth, walls, rocks, and every sort of obstacle to speed and
good order; the officers and sergeants had the greatest difficulty in
keeping the men closed up. It was not long before we were checked
by a wide stream, unfordable where we struck it, a fact Bill Lloyd
discovered for us in the most practical way—by disappearing in it.
Leaving the column, I made a cast to the left and soon found a shallow
place where there was a ford—perhaps a rough dam. Christopher
trotted off to guide the others and we splashed through, to find ourselves in a veritable jungle of reeds. We fought our way through this
for what seemed a very long way to find ourselves in a valley overlooked by a low ridge on our right.

The going was a bit better now, but it was getting lighter. We pressed on at a desperate pace, anxious not to be caught by the dawn. Bill Lloyd kept his men moving fast and since Walter Skrine had been knocked out, I navigated. At last we came to a country road which we knew must lead to the bridge. It was easy going now, and it was not long before we reached the edge of the enemy position.

Here there was a hedge to the right of the road and beyond it an orchard. The leading section of 4 Troop went on down the road and I took a party into the orchard. We soon found ourselves face to face with a pillbox sited just inside the hedge so as to cover the road. It was only a few yards away, but everybody stopped and looked at it, whilst on all sides people began giving orders and calling for grenades. I had no grenades, but, seeing that there was no wire round the pillbox, I ran up to the middle loophole and fired my rifle through it two or three times. Inside an Italian began shouting, evidently in a state of wild alarm; almost at once he ran out into the road. Brian Butler, advancing at the head of his section, threw a Mills bomb at him and killed him. Craft came running up and gave me two hand grenades.

There were more explosions, and then Brian Butler of Lloyd's Troop dashed past shouting:

"With me, Movement Group!"

Nobody appeared and he began to curse. I told the men with me to come on and we ran round to the other side of the pillbox. There was nobody else in it. Looking around, we could see another work, a wall shaped like an arrowhead, about thirty yards away. We ran up to it, but there was nobody there. We went on to the north end of the bridge, to find that Bill Lloyd was there already. There was another large pillbox to the north-east; running up to the door, we threw in a bomb, but the garrison had already left.

And so the bridge with its small garrison, about a platoon, under a be-ribboned Italian captain, fell into our hands. There was no wire round the place and so we just overran it. We may have had some casualties in doing so, but not more than one or two.

The Colonel had ordered me to co-ordinate the defence of the bridge, and so I went round to have a look at the positions the various troops had taken up. Lloyd's troop at the north end of the bridge was well posted except that they had a Bren actually on the road, altogether too exposed. Erskine said that there were still enemy on the other side and so I ordered John Lash to take 3 Troop over the river and form a bridgehead at that end. No. 1 Troop was posted to watch the road to the north and Headquarters was near the first pillbox we had taken. Altogether it was a considerable area. Returning there, I tried to interrogate the Italian officer. It appeared that the Area Commander at Lentini was a friend of his, but I completely failed to put across the idea that he should proceed there and persuade this individual to surrender.

For about a quarter of an hour there was a complete lull, except for a burst of fire from the direction of 1 Troop. I felt very tired and almost fell asleep. All the time it was getting lighter. Then in the distance we heard a heavy vehicle coming slowly towards us from the south. A tank? There were PIATs posted at the north end of the bridge, but we did not really know what these new weapons could do. Slowly this monster, whatever it was, rumbled across the river. The suspense was intolerable, but at last with a roar one of the PIAT men, who had held his fire with most praiseworthy self-control, struck the enemy vehicle amidships. It was an ammunition truck with a trailer, which blew up and went on exploding for many minutes, thousands of rounds of ammunition flying in all directions to the discomfort of friend and foe. It was still dark, and we were fairly well spread out to the north of the bridge.

Now things began to happen with bewildering speed. Lash's batman arrived to say that 3 Troop were held up *under* the bridge—though they had at least removed the leads so that the demolition charges could not be exploded. When I asked if they wanted fire support from mortars or PIATs, I was told that they did not. Things began to look a bit ugly.

The Colonel spoke to me and said he had received an alarming report, untrue as it turned out, that hardly a man remained unhurt under the bridge and that the enemy were working round our left flank. I suggested taking a party from Headquarters to hold a house which flanked the bridge, but at this moment the second flight arrived.

Pooley's men had no sooner joined us than someone shouted that he could see a tank. Corporal Pantall, looking through the hedge, could see a large German Mark VI Tiger tank facing us from the other end of the bridge, no more than two hundred yards away. Almost immediately it opened fire with a heavy machine-gun and began spraying the corner of the field 5 Troop were in; there was no cover and in open formation they dashed for a wall on the road side. In doing so many were wounded and some, including Tony Butler, were killed outright. Some took cover in and behind a huge stone pillbox, but it received a direct hit from the tank and crumbled like a pack of cards causing many more casualties.

The Colonel ordered Pooley to occupy a house just east of the bridge. They crossed the road and an open field, moving well though under heavy machine-gun fire, and took up position behind the farmhouse, which itself received several direct hits from the tank. The Commando replied with its two Vickers and with Brens, but they could do little against armour. By this time more tanks could be heard coming down the road and the one already in action was scoring direct hits on each pillbox in turn. Both Vickers were quickly put out of action. Charley Head had just put one in position and was walking away when he heard an explosion and, looking round, saw it and its crew dashed to pieces.

At Headquarters there were a number of wounded, one a German officer, and a group of prisoners. The enemy were not more than two hundred yards away and we had little cover but a cactus hedge. The pillboxes were proving deathtraps as became only too plain when some men ran up dragging a wounded man on a mattress. It was Bill Lloyd, who had got a broken ankle besides other injuries when a shell hit the pillbox north-east of the bridge where he was taking cover. The two Bredas, or Spandaus, which were playing on the area were the least of our troubles.

The Colonel held a quick discussion with me. We still had about 350 men, but very little cover and none of us had digging tools. The best chance was to withdraw into the hills to the east and re-form there. There was no time to lose.

"Peter, do you think one of your runners can get word to 3 Troop to pull out from under the bridge?"

If he went fast enough an active man would have a chance of getting through. I chose Christopher, who played football for the Commando and was very fit. He listened to my orders and dashed off without batting an eyelid, found 3 Troop and got back again unscathed.

"Peter," said the Colonel a little later, "have you a good runner who you can send to tell 1 Troop to retire?"

I said I would go myself and set off accompanied by Clark and Christopher. The enemy had got a mortar into action by this time.

John had already given orders for the withdrawal and we met parties of men, mostly from 2 Troop, moving off with their wounded. They were going too far north-east so I pointed out their proper route. As we neared 1 Troop's position a man came up and said:

"Sir, the Adjutant has been hit!"

Charley Head was sitting propped against a tree, badly wounded in the leg. We spoke a few words to each other and then he asked us to leave him. This didn't seem a very good idea, so I told Corporal Clark and another man to carry him out of the firing.

Then we found Veasey. I ordered him to withdraw to the eastern hedge as soon as the orchard was clear of our men.

"I expect you to make it a classic example of what a withdrawal should be."

He smiled.

When the rest had gone we fell back and 1 Troop moved off as if it was on a field day. We passed a wounded N.C.O. being carried along, making a lot of noise. I told him to be quiet; unkind perhaps, but necessary. A man of a different stamp was Corporal Hopkins, M.M., a regular soldier from my own regiment who had been with me at Vaagso and Dieppe.

"I've lost my hand," he said calmly as he walked by.

Ned Moore and his medical section, Sergeant Spears and the rest, had been doing their best for the wounded, but the casualties were mounting too fast for everyone to have his wounds dressed.

At the end of the orchard we found 3 and 6 Troops and told them that the fire was only coming from a couple of tanks, which was perhaps an understatement. The rest of the Commando were already making their way back towards some orange groves. I sent off 3 Troop telling 6 to hold on a little longer to cover the rest. Looking round the end of the hedge, there was no sign of pursuit. Ruxton had already been slightly wounded so I sent him off with the leading section when we began to thin out. Then, giving 1 Troop a bit of a start, we moved slowly back in extended order, ten paces between each man, across the field.

With proper intervals this is a most useful formation; it is good for control, for developing fire and for avoiding casualties, particularly under shell or mortar fire. For this reason we had practised it again and again, and the men did it extremely well, keeping their dressing by their sub-section commanders, not hurrying and not bunching. One reads in old books of men under fire moving as steadily as on parade; for once in my life I was actually seeing it. It was good to see.

When we reached the orange grove the Colonel was waiting in the corner by the road.

"There's a party of 4 Troop in those cactus bushes," he said, pointing to a place a little way off. "We've given them orders to retire on two blasts of the whistle."

Charley Head had got this far—about four hundred yards—on the shoulders of Sergeant Darts, a tremendously powerful man. Sergeant King, a regular soldier of the Rifle Brigade, now came up to John and reported that the Adjutant was on the edge of the wood to our right. The Colonel asked John Cummings to take care of Charley and he and King carried him a few hundred yards farther. Cummings then detailed four men to carry him and they used a gate as a stretcher. It was very heavy so John Cummings roped in a few civilians to lend a hand. They were most reluctant and Cummings, no mean heavy-weight, encouraged them by clouting one of their number and firing his pistol over their heads—much to the indignation of a newly-joined officer who told John he should not make these people help as they would get into trouble with the Germans.

"That won't break my heart," was all the answer he got.

Sergeant Coaker, a cool young N.C.O., was in command of the party of 4 Troop who were covering the withdrawal. We could hear a German tank moving towards us, perhaps a quarter of a mile away, but it had not yet come in sight and, looking at the soldiers, Leyland, Mallett and the rest, it was plain that they were not unduly impressed by this machine.

The tank did not appear, so we fell back in a leisurely manner to the orange grove. We reached a place marked on the map as *Tenta Principe,* whatever that may mean. Here we made a rough road block with rocks and some shells which we found in a box beside the road, thinking this would be sufficient to make some of the crew dismount. On one side of the track were orange trees, on the other the hill where the rest of the Commando were regrouping. On the lower slopes was a low stone wall, and under cover of this we awaited the tank. We had a smoke grenade ready, and half the party were to fire at the slits while the others rushed it. The tank, however, failed to put in an appearance, and so after waiting for a time we went up the hill and rejoined the Colonel. He had a number of men with him drawn up in

line facing towards the bridge and taking cover behind rocks and
boulders. The position was being shelled and mortared and there was
some machine-gun fire, but not very severe.

The country to our front was pretty bare, but still it was hard to
make out where the mortar was firing from. In the distance I could
see a house in a small rectangular enclosure. It seemed to me the
only possible place that the mortar could be firing from. To see what
would happen I got down behind a rock, set my sights at two thousand
yards and took a shot at the house. It does not seem a particularly
likely tale, but, believe it or not, the mortar did not fire again—I can
produce witnesses!

Still, this exploit did not improve matters much. There was still an
88 firing at us, and from time to time bursts of machine gun fire swept
the ridge. I had hoped that when we were reorganised we would
advance and attack the bridge from both sides, but, with tanks about,
this would have been to invite destruction in such open country. In
the hills we would be comparatively safe from the Panzer troops. John,
therefore, decided that our best course was to split up into small bands
and make our way across country to Augusta; so, calling for the troop
commanders, he gave out his orders, speaking quietly but quickly
as he always did:

"Yeah, well, it's obvious that 50 Div. can't reach us. There's nothing
more for us here. We must get back to Augusta. Our only chance is
to split up into small parties. Lie up where you can during the day and
make your way back into our lines tonight."

Then he gave them a compass bearing—164 degrees—and away
they went.

This plan would probably have succeeded one hundred per cent but
for the unsuspected presence in these hills of the 3rd Battalion of the
Hermann Goering Parachute Regiment, which seems to have been
flown in on 13th July, only just before we arrived.

No. 6 Troop, who had been ordered to cover the withdrawal, had
hurriedly taken up fire positions on the hillside with only a few large
stones for cover. When their turn came they followed the rest of the
Commando into the hills, passing me and George Herbert. We gave
them their orders and the compass bearing.

For some distance, two miles perhaps, I went along with the Colonel.
Brian Butler was with us and about a dozen soldiers. After a time
John Cummings met us. *I remember,* he wrote, *noting how grim*

you looked and you said: "Cave and Tony Butler are dead." The Colonel said: "This is a day that will give you a lot for your book, Peter"; and I remember you saying: "It's the biggest day yet." I recall this incident perfectly and particularly the fact that in spite of all our adventures John Durnford-Slater was still in excellent spirits."

"Yeah, well, Peter," he said to me as we worked our way along the hillside, "you always wanted to do this Bonnie Prince Charlie stuff," and he began to laugh.

We were keeping a shoulder between us and the German tanks, but farther up the mountain we could see other parties retreating in good order. A shell struck one man a direct hit, but the men were so well spread out that those on either side of him were not wounded. They were Woyevodsky's men from 5 Troop.

We were all pretty tired by now and, coming to the head of a re-entrant where there was cover among some olives, the Colonel decided to lay up. We all sat down on the hillside. The party was rather large for concealment, so I suggested that I should push off. Taking Christopher, who alone of my orderlies was still with me, I crossed the ridge to a farm called Pagliarazzi. We rested, had a bite to eat and watched our people shelling a high ridge the other side of Lentini. This was 69 Brigade attacking Monte Pancali, though I did not know it then. It showed that it would be some time before the British reached the Punta dei Malati. The inhabitants of the farm were friendly, but I could not understand much of their talk and I did not want to stay there. After pondering for a bit it occurred to me that it is not every day that one finds oneself behind the enemy lines and that we ought to do something about it.

"Christopher," I said, "it seems a pity that we haven't got a few men with us."

"Why, Major?"

"If we had we might go back to the bridge. There are sure to be soft-skinned vehicles going up and down the road."

We discussed the question, and the more we thought about it the better it seemed. After all, in due course the 50th Division would come stumping up the main road and we could join them. The hills stretching away towards Augusta looked pretty bare. While we were talking we heard footsteps approaching. We took cover in a barn, shoved our safety catches forward and waited. Into the yard strolled a young subaltern who had joined the unit just before the operation. He was foraging. I asked him whether he had seen any others of our men nearby. He said there was such a party, and so I told him to lead us to them. In the wood not far from where I had left the Colonel we found Ned Moore, John Budd, the Signals Officer and Clive Collins with ten men. Budd was wounded in the leg and another man in the foot. Ned himself was very footsore and could scarcely walk. One of the men was only armed with a pistol, while another was a medical orderly. I decided to leave these two and the wounded with the Medical Officer and divided the rest into two small sections under Lieutenant Collins and the new subaltern. We could see vehicles moving north along the main road. I went over to tell the Colonel my plans, but he had moved off, so I sent Underwood to bring up the rest. There was a long delay. When they eventually arrived I asked the newcomer what had held him up and he said he had thought it better to come a long way round by some trees.

"I don't see what alternative you had," I retorted, "but to come the way I told you to."

From his looks it was evident that he didn't think that very reasonable, so I added:

"You might as well realise that I'm in charge of this party. If you've no confidence in my leadership, you can go off on your own." It would have been better if he had.

We set off for the bridge, going downhill through the trees with an interval between the sections, and then advanced along the valley of the Leonardo, taking cover in the numerous orange groves. We collected a few shrivelled oranges—better than nothing.

After a time we came upon Charley Head, who was lying in some bushes on the banks of the river. He had with him two wounded men and Lance-Corporal Abbott, M.M., who was unhurt. He had been with me at Dieppe and I was glad to have him with me. Ned Moore had given Charley a shot of morphia, but he was still conscious. I gave him two of my rotten oranges, not a very handsome present. Charley told me that so far no enemy had disturbed him, and we pushed on towards the main road.

By this time it was very hot and, feeling exhausted, we took a short rest in an orchard. I fell asleep for a little while and woke much refreshed. Late in the afternoon we came to a house. I put most of the party under the new lieutenant in the building while Clive Collins,

Trooper Leech and I climbed an embankment nearby and took a good look at the main road.

There were troops moving north along it and armour was manœuvring along a hillside about a mile and a half farther west. We felt pretty certain that the 8th Army had arrived. At this moment a soldier ran up and reported that a party of the Northumberland Hussars had contacted us. I went to meet them and found my precious lieutenant had left his post and was gossiping with them. I ordered him to return. . . .

The Northumberland Hussars were very friendly and said they would provide rations. Leaving my party in the house, I walked down the road to see the Battery Commander and find out the form. In my absence a patrol of about eighteen German paratroops approached the house. Sergeant Veasey, who spoke Italian, very nearly succeeded in luring them into the open at short range, but one of the men stupidly gave the show away by calling out in English. After a brisk exchange of fire the Germans fled, leaving some of their equipment.

A liaison officer from 151 Brigade came up and promised to send ambulances. We spent the night in a house called Sanciolo, about a quarter of a mile south of the bridge—which was still intact.

.   .   .   .   .

The Colonel reached the British lines in the early hours of the morning, after a series of adventures. John Pooley, John Cummings and George Herbert broke through with him.

.   .   .   .   .

A number of the soldiers never got the Colonel's order to make for Augusta.

A party of twenty or thirty, including Bill Lloyd on a bicycle, and Pienaar, a South African, made for Agnone beach hoping to find landing-craft. The party moved along in good order, the wounded in the centre, and as more men kept joining them they were thirty or forty strong by the time they neared the beach. Here they came under mortar and machine-gun fire from the high ground to the south. In the confused fighting that followed Bill Lloyd was killed and Pienaar captured. This whole group was split up, but a number escaped in ones and twos. Troopers Dix and Jennings lay up under the cactus bushes and in the evening tried to go inland again along the railway.

Lots of ditches and odd noises so we took it steady . . . Later *We opened up our Emergency Rations (without permission of an officer) and ate well.* Next morning, while they were hiding under a bridge they heard footsteps. *We looked out and saw three Germans, so we got back under!* Not long after they joined "Knocker White's Task Force."

White, who had won the D.C.M. at Vaagso, was by this time T.S.M. of 4 Troop. He had seized the Italian Headquarters near the beach. *This was a very heavily defended building held by a dozen or so of our people, and about a dozen wounded, and an M.M.G. Section of the Parachute Regiment. There were machine-guns everywhere, and lots of grenades. Best of all, there were some clean clothes—Italian K.D. uniforms.* This fortress was eventually relieved by the York and Lancaster Regiment, who sent ambulances and food, and the Commandos, mostly wearing blue Italian shirts, went back by truck to Syracuse.

Sergeant Taylor and Corporal Pantall with six men attacked a party of Italians in a farmhouse. Creeping forward to a wall, they approached the building and there before their eyes they saw two 3-inch mortars standing unattended in a well-camouflaged position amongst some shrubs. The mortars were trained on the beach and in an adjoining shed were piles of ammunition. Rushing into the courtyard with fixed bayonets, they surprised the two sentries and disarmed them. In an outhouse they found nine more Italians having a meal. They removed the sights and put the mortars out of commission. They put a total of forty-four grenades and the bolts of all the rifles down the well, locked the prisoners in one of the buildings and made for the hills.

Two nights later they made for the British lines. Hearing vehicles and the tramp of infantry, Taylor and Pantall crawled forward to reconnoitre. From behind a wall, they heard a voice say:

"I'm f—— browned-off with all this!"

Then they knew all was well. Once more it was the York and Lancaster Regiment.

.   .   .   .   .

Ruxton's troop were told to withdraw on the blast of a whistle, and on hearing the signal began to fall back in the direction of the beach, still followed by the enemy's fire. Mapplebeck led his men down the side of the hill and soon got out of the fire, but later they were shot at by an enemy tank and took to the hillside once more. Soon after Ruxton came along and took charge. Peter Long joined them and they began to advance in extended order across the open towards a "wadi". Suddenly, when they were only a hundred yards short of it, they came under heavy fire from the front and both flanks and went to ground shooting back. Mapplebeck, who had a Bren on each flank of his sub-section, called to his men in turn to see if they were all right and then, finding the right Bren-gunner a bit windy, took over his gun himself. He succeeded in knocking out a German machine-gunner who was shooting up that flank. He then ran back to his old position in the centre, where about five minutes later he was hit in the foot.

"Buck" Ruxton now decided to charge and, ordering the two Bren guns to give covering fire, leapt to his feet and ran forward, followed by his men. It was indeed a forlorn hope. They were met by a withering machine-gun fire, and Ruxton fell with several wounds. His men went to ground again and continued firing.

"The next thing I knew," said Mapplebeck, "was that we had surrendered."

The enemy, who, as it turned out, greatly outnumbered them, dis-armed our men. The wounded were carried down the wadi to a cave, where they were looked after by Corporal Walsh, the Irish Guardsman, and others.

Ruxton's party appears to have run into the Headquarters of a German regiment, probably the 1st Parachute Regiment.

Mapplebeck asked where the Captain was and, on being told that he had refused to be brought down, insisted on his being carried into the cave, where, though well cared for by a German doctor, he died two hours later. Walsh and his men buried him. He was a gallant and aggressive officer and a great leader.

When the Germans fell back the wounded were left behind, and next day a Bren carrier belonging to the King's Own Yorkshire Light Infantry came along looking for them.

．　　．　　．　　．　　．

The surprising thing about this operation was not that so many of our officers and men were cut off and captured, but that so many escaped. Of ten officers taken prisoner nine escaped by one means or another, though one, Pienaar, was unhappily killed before he could get clear. Some of the other ranks also succeeded in eluding their captors.

In the morning, about thirty hours after the landing, I sent Clive Collins' section to the bridge, where they buried Lieutenants Tony Butler and Cave, and four others, three so burnt as to be unrecognisable. The other section I sent to bring in Charley Head. Since the lieutenant knew exactly where to go I did not think this presented any undue difficulty; however, I was careful to give him precise orders, knowing his tendency to "reason why".

When the ambulance arrived from 151 Brigade I took it along the tracks north of the River Leonardo to where some of our wounded had been located.

At Sanciolo, on our return, we found Donald Hopson and Aubrey Moody, who had arrived with three ambulances and five Bren-gun carriers to clean up the area. The carriers had a brief skirmish with some German parachutists in an orange grove just east of the road, and while it was going on General Dempsey drove up in a Jeep. He spoke to me for a few minutes and said he was pleased that the bridge had not gone up. I told him that there was a shooting match going on just down the road, but this did not impress him and he shot off up the road towards the Primosole Bridge.

We drove off in the carriers to try and make our way to Agnone and find Walter Skrine and the other wounded. During a halt I stopped a Sicilian who was coming down the road towards us, and by an extraordinary chance he turned out to be carrying a note from Walter. This man had somehow slipped through the lines, but we found it impossible to reach Agnone, for between us and that place 15 Brigade was still fighting a pitched battle with the 3rd Battalion of the Hermann Goering Regiment.

Meanwhile my lieutenant, having found Charley Head, had thought fit to push on to contact Ned Moore. The only consequence of his disobedience was that he fell into the hands of the Germans, and so did Charley Head, though both escaped later on, or were left behind when the enemy fell back.

. . . . .

The operation had been a tough one, certainly our toughest so far, for Vaagso had been much shorter. Taking into account the strength of the enemy, we felt we had not done too badly. At least we had achieved our object, though had the opposition turned out to be as

expected we might have achieved our end with many fewer casualties.[1]
The 50th Division afterwards said they had identified in the area between the bridge and the beach :

904 Fortress Battalion.
Three battalions of Panzer Grenadier Regiment Koerner from
Catania.
S.P. guns of the Hermann Goering Division.
Tanks of the 101st Italian Tank Battalion.
An unspecified number of Italian infantry.

The majority of the survivors after a few square meals and a couple
of nights' rest began to look forward to the next battle. If anything
morale was higher after the operation than before; the men felt that
they had proved themselves in a really tough action.

What did the operation achieve?

The arrival of 3 Commando from the sea not only prevented the
enemy destroying the important bridge over the River Leonardo, but
caused much confusion in the enemy rear and induced him to move
large forces to the coastal area—or to leave them there—so that the
main attack by the 50th Division was not seriously delayed.

The Germans evidently expected further landings on the beaches
south of Catania and overestimated the forces we *did* land.

General Montgomery gave orders that a stone bearing the words
3 Commando Bridge should be let into the masonry of the Punta dei
Malati—and, in due course, this was done. It was still there in 1948. It
is on record that General Dempsey told Brigadier Laycock after this
action :

"The men of No. 3 are the finest body of soldiers I have seen anywhere."

[1]The Commando went into Agnone about 350 strong. Of these five officers and
twenty-three other ranks were killed, four officers and sixty-two other ranks were
wounded, while eight officers and fifty-one other ranks were missing, mostly prisoners
of war, a total of 153 casualties.

CHAPTER VII

BOVA MARINA

A FTER Agnone there were about 270 officers and men left in the Commando. Of these about twenty had proved unsatisfactory and were sent back to their units. As there was no immediate prospect of reinforcements, the unit was temporarily reorganised into Headquarters and four troops.

We remained camped at Lo Bello, where we made ourselves quite comfortable. When we had cleaned up a bit we began to do some training, but, not knowing what our next engagement might be, we did not work the soldiers very hard. About this time I left for a fortnight's attachment to XIII Corps; I was to act as Liaison Officer between that Headquarters and the Special Service Brigade, not a very exacting task. During my first night there I was awakened by a staff officer, who told me the news that Mussolini had resigned and that the King and Marshal Badoglio had taken over.

On 31st July we were told that 3 and 40 Commandos and the Special Raiding Squadron were to take part in Operation "Baytown", the invasion of Italy by the most direct route, across the Straits of Messina.

The next day John Durnford-Slater, who had commanded the No. 3 for over three years, was given command of a brigade formed from 3 and 40 (R.M.) Commandos and the S.R.S. In his own highly individual and robust way he had raised his Commando, selecting his own officers, and insisting always that it was to be "the greatest unit of all time". He had set high standards, and the men liked him for it and had confidence in his leadership. He was a good-tempered commander; and though he could be rugged and direct, he almost never used bad language. He enjoyed the good things of life, and this appealed to the soldiers; although he claimed that he had long periods when he lived quietly, he was certainly not against wine, women and song—he considered *Goodnight Sweetheart* to be the "greatest song of all time".

Now it fell to me to take over. I should have been sobered by the thought, but in fact it was one of the happiest days of my life. It had long been my ambition to command a unit, and to have the good luck to get the one I had served with so long was unusual good fortune. If John had been a casualty, I might have felt differently, but since he was being promoted I had no such qualms. He and I had always been firm allies and I was glad that I was still to serve under his command.

· · · · ·

In the middle of August I was sent for by General Dempsey. We were to carry out raids on the toe of Italy to reconnoitre the coast defences, before the invasion.

The objects were to take prisoners in the following order of priority: live German soldier; live Italian soldier; live Italian civilian; or, failing that, dead German or Italian soldiers. We were to look into Bova Marina to see if it was suitable as a landing-place.

On the night of the 24th, about 7.30 p.m., I sailed in the L.C.I. with two patrols under John Nixon and John Reynolds, but the weather was very bad and one of the craft—we had two landing-craft in tow— kept dipping her nose under water. There was no alternative but to go back.

By the next night the weather was calm again and at about 7 p.m. we set out again. When we thought we recognised Cape Spartivento one patrol transferred to the landing-craft.

The run-in took an hour and twenty minutes, because we were farther out than the Boat Officer had thought. We eventually landed at a place which none of us could recognise. Straight ahead was a tall chimney-stack which we had not seen on any photograph or map.

Nixon captured a railway worker named Celio Domenico. We had landed at a small village and we found him in the street, waiting to go on duty. Then we found from a signpost that the place really was Bova Marina and so we had made a perfect landfall. It was as quiet as the grave and apparently ungarrisoned—a strange state of affairs on the mainland of Europe before the invasion. Nixon laid a couple of mines where the road and railway bridge crossed the dry river, and we departed in peace.

General Dempsey now ordered that five parties, each with a powerful wireless set, should be landed in the neighbourhood of Bova Marina with the object of passing information back to a control set at Taormina. This operation was to start that night. There was not much time for preparation. The Commando had no wireless sets powerful enough for the job and it was arranged that volunteers should be made available from the 156th Field Regiment.

The patrols boarded the L.C.I. at last; it was nearly dark before the signallers, looking rather bewildered, arrived with their bulky No. 21 sets, which were an awkward load and required two heavy batteries apiece.

We got under way soon after dark and I gave the soldiers further briefing during the voyage. There were five patrols, each consisting of four Commando soldiers and two of the attached signallers.

We put them all ashore from a landing-craft in two different places. I discovered from some Italian civilians that the first was some three kilometres from Bova.

It was broad daylight by the time we left and we were fired on by coastal batteries; one craft was hit, but fortunately no one was hurt. On our arrival at Taormina I reported to XIII Corps.

General Dempsey ordered me to put a wireless set aboard another L.C.I. and speak to the patrols that night from a position five miles off Bova. Should they fail to reply I was to go ashore, contact Nixon's patrol and order him to light a beacon between two and three o'clock in the morning on the next two nights as there was a possibility of a British force landing there.

In due course we arrived five miles south of Bova Marina; the Signals Corporal could produce no results on the wireless set, so we decided to go in without more ado. This time the run-in seemed to take no time at all. Once more we landed unopposed, and once more in a strange place. After looking around ashore to find out where we were I came to the conclusion that we must be too far to the west and asked the Captain to cruise along close inshore until we should reach the chimney-stack. As soon as he tried to retract we discovered that the L.C.I. was hard aground!

While we waited to see if the sailors could get the L.C.I. off, the men lay in an arc on the beach, their rifles ready in case some patrol should come down to investigate. After a time we heard footsteps coming from the west—evidently only one man. When he drew near I challenged. It was Gordon Pollard, who had got cut off from his patrol. I told him that the L.C.I. was stuck.

"There's another force coming in tomorrow. You can remain here and guide them in with a light."

It was now about 4 a.m. All this time there had been very little sign of the enemy except one burst of machine-gun fire and one shell, both from the west, but neither very close. The Captain now told me that all attempts to refloat the L.C.I. had proved vain and he must abandon ship. I advised him to split his men into small parties, to take water-bottles, and gave him and his First Officer the same briefing that I had given to my own men. He apologised for running aground, saying that he thought I was in rather a hurry, and added that he had always been taught to touch down with his engine two-thirds ahead.

I set off eastwards along the beach, and soon came to the dry river-bed, followed it inland for about half a mile and then took to the hills. It was hard going, climbing in the dark, but I wanted to be well up in the mountains when dawn broke. For a time we made good progress, the men were fit and navigation was our only trouble. The country became wilder and more difficult, and as we didn't seem to be getting any higher I called a halt. We could see a fire not far off, but when it got lighter there was nobody about, and so, although there was no cover, we went on up the mountain. Suddenly crossing a crest, we came to a group of three little houses in a hollow. This, I thought, would be a good hideout. The doors of the first house, a two-roomed affair, were open and we walked in without ceremony. The room was practically filled by a huge double-bed on which, without more ado, I lay down. Dix mounted guard, watching the mule track by which we had come. Rob Waldie and two men installed themselves in the highest of the three houses which was a good observation-post. From there one could see the little village of San Carlo on the other side of the wide, dry bed of the River Amendolea.

The Maffizi family proved willing hosts and welcomed us in the most kindly manner, bringing us eggs, bread, water, figs, cheese and *figua d'India.*[1]   .   .   .   .   .

After dark we went down the mule-track to Bova Marina. We had a look at the eastern end of the beach, but found no exits suitable for tanks. We made a great bonfire against the south wall of the factory, and this we kept well stoked up until three o'clock. We did not much

[1]Opuntia vulgaris or prickly pear. Commonly used in Sicily and Southern Italy for hedges.

care for doing this, but nobody came down to see what we were at, nor did any craft come in from the sea. On our way home we met John Nixon and three of his party. We took them back with us, for having found such a good base I had decided to collect as big a troop as I could, in case we should have an opportunity to harass the enemy.

The next evening we were seen by some of Sergeant Leyland's party while we were going down the dry river-bed, our route on the first night. They led us to Leyland, who was obviously enjoying himself. He said he had an excellent observation-post on a ridge overlooking the coast road.

As we now had five more men we arranged that Rob Waldie should light the beacon fire while I set an ambush on the main coast road. We agreed that my party would not open fire earlier than four o'clock in the morning so as not to alarm the neighbourhood before Waldie's task was done.

At midnight Waldie set off, and by 3 a.m. my ambush party was in position at the corner of the bridge at the western end of Bova Marina—the same bridge we had passed under on the night we came ashore. About half an hour later we heard men stumbling past up the dry river-bed and all the dogs in the neighbourhood began to bark. This I felt sure was not an enemy patrol but Rob Waldie returning from the Co-operativa—the factory with the high chimney-stack. Leech, who was one of Leyland's party, assured me that he had counted eight men—which was odd, as Waldie had only five. Perhaps it was an enemy patrol after all, but whoever it was had not seen us.

I told the men that the signal to open fire would be my first shot. We heard a lorry approaching from the west. When its headlights were about ten yards away I rose up behind the parapet of the bridge and emptied my Webley into it. It shot past, and as it went Leech gave it a magazine from his tommy-gun. The riflemen fired a volley. About fifty yards down the road it stopped; we could hear groans. It was not very bright of me, perhaps, but I had expected it to crash much nearer to us. It was still very dark and I could not make out how much damage we had done, apparently not very much; I decided to withdraw before the enemy could retaliate. Somewhere, I imagined, some Intelligence Officer must be plotting our activities on his map, and trying to calculate for his commander how many British troops had landed. This would give him something to put in his situation report. The L.C.I. could carry about a hundred, and he would know that others had landed the night before she ran aground. The more coloured pins he stuck in his map, the more men he would credit us with; the more men we were supposed to have the better.

. . . . .

During the morning two fairly well-dressed Italians with several armed followers appeared, obviously anxious for a parley. *Collaborazione* was to be the subject for discussion. One of the men was thin and nervous. He said that he had spent five years in prison because he was not a Fascist. The other looked more robust and alleged that he had killed a *Capitano Tedeschi*. They said that they had six hundred Social Democrats, most of them armed, at their beck and call, and that these people would do anything for us, if only we would tell them the date of the long-awaited invasion. It was now 31 August and I knew the landing was to be 3 September, but I put them off with such vague answers as *Subito* and *Dopo Domani*—my vocabulary wouldn't run to much more.

They said they had been looking for me for some time in order to offer their services, but when I suggested various simple tasks—such as reporting details of the garrison at the Amendolea Bridge—their eagerness evaporated. Eventually they left to fetch an interpreter. Since I did not altogether trust them I kept a hostage, one of their relatives, a handsome young Italian soldier of about twenty, who, his regiment being in Rome, had posted himself to Calabria—Private Angelo in reverse.

They had not been gone long when there was a sudden alarm. Two Germans had shown themselves in the little cutting where the mule-track crossed the rim of the hill about fifty yards south of Maffizi's house.

"Stand to!"

My party was ready first and, advancing to the cut, we peered cautiously over the edge.

Nothing to be seen.

Then Leyland said that he had caught a glimpse of a man, bent double, moving along the hillside to our right; we moved there fast, being joined by the others as we went. Corporal Jackson got a view of them halfway down the hill going in the direction of San Carlo, and we dashed down the rough winding footpath in hot pursuit. Now and again we saw them and opened fire hoping to pin them to the ground.

At the foot of the hill was an orange grove; Leyland, Jackson and Leech were still with me, whilst the rest of the party were covering us from the hillside above. We pushed on through the trees and almost at once Jackson found one of their rifles—Italian. They were obviously in a panic, so we fired one or two shots through the trees to make them think we could see them and ran down the track to the Amendolea. Some peasants admitted that two soldiers had gone by, but they were nowhere to be seen. On a steep outcrop of rock about a hundred yards to our left was a small square stone house, and just as we were thinking our quarry had vanished an Italian soldier stepped out of it. Leyland, who was still with me, took a shot at the man and sent him indoors. There was a window looking in our direction, and from the cover of a stone wall Leyland kept this under fire whilst I ran towards the house. The mound was steep and the path spiralled up to the front door which was on the San Carlo side. When I reached it I shouted *"Renditevi!"*; I could see seven Italian soldiers inside. I menaced them with my bayonet and shouted *"Renditevi!"* again, thinking that if they didn't surrender I should be able to shoot one, but wouldn't have time to reload. I should then have to start doing the haymaker's lift on the others with my bayonet; fortunately they decided to pack up. By this time Leyland, Leech and the others were coming up at the double. Rob Waldie flushed two Italians from a house just beyond, one of whom contrived to escape.

Gathering up our prisoners, their weapons and their belongings, haversacks and suitcases, we beat a retreat to our hideout on Monte Triolo.

In the captured Italian post we had found a map-case full of documents, including a map of Calabria showing the sectors of all the coastal divisions in the toe of Italy, and the locations of various minor formations. This information we were able to some extent to supplement by interrogating the prisoners and civilians. The question was how to get it back to XIII Corps, since we had no wireless.

Our first idea was to send one of the men in disguise towards Reggio, where by bribing a fisherman he might succeed in getting himself put ashore at Messina. Lance Corporal Thornton volunteered for this hazardous scheme; we disguised him as best we could and when we had done he looked exactly like a British soldier in disguise. I did not think he had a chance in a million of passing the guards at the Amendolea Bridge, or of getting through Melito di Porto Salvo. And so, much to Thornton's disappointment, I decided to abandon this project.

Corporal Edmunds now volunteered the information that he had seen a big boat on the beach at Bova and that it had sweeps and a sail. John Nixon was insistent that with twelve men he could man this boat and be out of range of the Melito battery by dawn. I thought it very doubtful, and in the event the sails proved to be rotten.

About 10.30 Allied planes came over and bombed Bova Marina. While this was going on the sentry reported that a truck had just driven into San Carlo, coming from the direction of the coast. Through the glasses I could see its tail sticking out from behind a wall in the yard of a building which, according to one of the Italian civilians, was a platoon headquarters. We could see people, apparently soldiers as well as civilians, leaving the village, going north. Perhaps the Italians were preparing to retreat. A quarter of an hour later Rob Waldie and I were still watching them with interest when a platoon of soldiers in extended order ran out of San Carlo, making towards Monte Triolo across the bed of the Amendolea. I was positive that there were twenty-four. From their businesslike manner I deduced that they were Germans, perhaps a reserve of lorried infantry from Melito or Catanzaro, sent out to round up parties such as mine. They were not making directly towards us, but if they kept going they would arrive eventually to the north of our position. Giving the order to "stand to", I told Rob Waldie to stay where he was and keep a look-out, and went to see if I could get a sight of them from the Monte Triolo side. Going about two hundred yards, I found that to approach from that direction they would have to come down a long slope and then cross a deep ravine. I turned back, feeling sure that if they came at all it would be through the orchards and up the path where we had chased the two Italians the day before. At this instant Jackson signalled from the observation-post. I ran up the hill to him. Stealing through the orange groves, and loping across the gaps between the trees, came the enemy platoon.

In the middle of the track, exercising the divine right of commanders not to take cover when the soldiers do, came two officers. One gave out an order and a runner, his rifle slung on his back, ambled back towards the river-bed. They were well deployed, and from the cool way they worked I felt they *must* be Germans.

Waldie told me that he had definitely counted between forty or fifty enemy. Since I had only seen twenty-four earlier, I thought for a moment that this might be an exaggeration, but then I considered that I already knew him well enough to realise that he was a hard-headed Scot and not likely to see double. In any case, we only numbered eighteen and we were not dug in. We could, of course, defend the three houses, which would be just too bad for the inhabitants. But the factor which weighed most heavily in the balance was ammunition. It was not eleven o'clock. We had nothing like enough to last until nightfall. In any case it is the job of guerillas to give battle when *they* choose and not when the enemy appears all eager for the fray. Without more ado I gave orders to withdraw eastwards; the peasants began to conceal any spare kit which, for the sake of lightness, we were not taking with us.

We ran down into the deep river-bed whose lower reaches we had followed several times in our earlier patrols. I reckoned that by the time the enemy had toiled up the hill, and perhaps wasted a little time questioning the inhabitants, we should have about a quarter of an hour's start. None too much, particularly as we did not know the country. I was determined to keep on the high ground and not let the enemy get above us.

We had not gone far when the aged Maffizi caught up with us. He was sixty-five and had fought in *la Guerra Mondiale* without being taken prisoner—unlike most of his contemporaries in the neighbourhood. His shoes were made from pieces of a motor-car tyre secured with string. If he wanted to come too I had no objection, but it seemed unlikely that he could keep up. Almost at once he started talking and gesticulating, evidently wishing us to go another way. I took no notice of him and kept on down the river-bed; a few yards brought us to a steep precipice, clearly a waterfall in the winter months. I decided that after all Maffizi knew best; from then on he was our guide.

Moving in single file, we made our way eastwards, always along gullies and always keeping a shoulder between us and our pursuers. We went fast, and after a time, more by accident than design, split into two parties, but this was all to the good.

Once we met an Italian soldier, suitcase in hand, toiling up a path into the hills. Whether he was a deserter or was going on leave I cannot say. We looked at each other without halting and then went our several ways. It was about this time that Maffizi bade us farewell and made off to see how his family had fared.

Next we met one of our collaborator friends, the alleged murderer, who regaled us with wine, water, bread and fruit. We did not stay with him, but eventually established ourselves in a house on a mule-track a little below Bova Superiore. Leyland, Christopher, Dix and Griffiths were with me, and here in the evening John Nixon and three others joined me.

We had no news of Waldie and the other party, but I felt confident that they could look after themselves.

By this time some of us were suffering from various ailments. Nixon's hands and wrists were covered with sores and bandages; I had cuts on my right hand which were beginning to go bad, whilst two of the men had trouble with their feet.

In the evening I climbed a hill near our new abode. In the distance, perhaps three miles away as the crow flies and some way below us, I could see the group of three houses, our old hideout. As I watched, the sinking sun glinted on metal. Peering through my field-glasses I made out our erstwhile pursuers, who were leaving to return to San Carlo. They marched slowly—disconsolately, I hoped—over the shoulder and out of sight, in all not much less than a hundred as far as I could make out.

We rested that night and all the next day. One man acted as sentry posted in the shadows outside the house with a tommy-gun on his knees. Each of us, except Nixon who was not well enough, was on guard for an hour at a time, and so as to avoid unnecessary movement sat on a chair with his back to the wall of the house.

During 2nd September Allied planes bombed Bova Superiore. There may have been a small garrison there, but I doubt it. The bombing wounded a woman who had brought us eggs on the previous evening. It caused my host grave alarm, as I found to my cost when I allowed him to give me a shave with his cut-throat razor!

* * * * *

During the next day we made our way back to Maffizi's house, arriving there well before the appointed hour. On the way we once caught a glimpse of Waldie's party, but met no enemy. Giuseppe, the fifteen-year-old son of the house, a youth chiefly remarkable because he had six toes on one foot, met us before we arrived and told us that our pursuers had been a company of Italian Parachutists, stiffened by a few Germans. They had arrived demanding the whereabouts of the

Inglese, and on being told *"Niente Inglese"* they were so furious that they had carried off everything from the three houses—blankets, mattresses, sheets, towels, clothes, crockery, everything they could lay hands on. One of them had fired four shots into the floor round Giuseppe's feet. However, they had got no information, and except for one field dressing they had got none of our kit. Despite the harm we had brought upon them, the Maffizi family greeted us on our return with the utmost cordiality.

. . . . .

Next morning we could make out a certain amount of movement near the Amendolea Bridge. We found a splendid place for an ambush where a steep ridge overlooked the path at close range. After waiting for some time we got bored and began to make our way towards the bridge. When eventually we reached the bridge it was to find that the garrison had decamped leaving it intact. There was Italian uniform and equipment lying about everywhere. A peasant came up to us.

"Inglese?" he asked.

"Si."

"Dove Signor Majore?" he asked.

"Io, Majore," I replied, tapping myself on the chest.

He looked disbelieving at first—our turnout had suffered during the last few days—but when we had convinced him he produced three Italian soldiers, who surrendered themselves to us together with two light machine-guns. There was a naval signal flag, red and yellow, lying on the ground, taken from the L.C.I. This I told Dix to take with him.

We learned that the garrison had marched off to take cover in the railway tunnel at Bova Marina, but that there was still a detached platoon between the bridge and San Carlo. I decided to attack it. Four men seemed plenty for the job on current form.

We moved across the dry bed of the Amendolea in open order, the peasant guiding us, and the three prisoners laden with water bottles, magazines and their two Italian machine-guns. I made them wear their steel helmets—it looked better. Rather to my surprise we were not fired on, and, reaching the other bank, we mounted the two guns and sent the civilian forward to summon the enemy to surrender. The enemy were nowhere to be seen.

Lieutenant Guidorossi, aged thirty-two, had twice won the *Croce di Guerra* and was a bemedalled veteran of Spain and Ethiopia. He now emerged from some trees, came forward and surrendered. He handed over his Biretta pistol—but not the holster, which he said was his personal property—and began rounding up his platoon. He had eleven men and Rosaria Cotroneo, a Red Cross nurse—*Honi Soit Qui Mal y Pense.* We gave them a few minutes to collect their kit, put on their helmets and fill their waterbottles and then set off for the Amendolea Bridge; I did not care to linger on the scene of this easy triumph; the country was very enclosed and there seemed a danger that we might be taken by surprise.

We marched along the road in file on either side of the road, two of my men in front and two in the rear, the Italians deprived of their rifles but carrying the automatic weapons. Guidorossi and I marched in the middle. His men obviously had a high opinion of him. He was *buono ufficiale,* particularly because when they had been sent to take up the mines laid by John Nixon he had let them remain at a safe distance and disarmed them personally. If he had not resisted, it was, I thought, rather because he had not much confidence in his men, for he was himself a stout-hearted officer.

On an eminence near the Amendolea Bridge stood the house of Cavalliere Rosetti, a large, pleasant person of about forty. Placing the three light machine-guns to command the road, we proceeded to shave and wash in peace. The nurse, Rosaria, patched up our various injuries for us and we began to think that it was not a bad idea to take pretty girls to the wars. Leyland went back with her to the position we had left and returned with two Italian Very-light pistols and a number of cartridges. I discovered that Dix had neglected to bring the signal flag with him, and so, feeling rather officious, for he was a most cool and conscientious soldier, I told him to go and fetch it. It was just as well, for not long after a British destroyer appeared to eastward cruising along the coast.

Cavalliere Rosetti had set off on his bicycle to see if the British had reached Melito, but even so the quickest way home was obviously to thumb a ride in the destroyer. We fired Very lights, and then Griffiths, the signaller, made a flag out of a field dressing and with that and the one Dix had retrieved started to semaphore.

According to Paul Lee, an Associated Press War Correspondent aboard the destroyer, the following exchange took place:

"Five of us have cleared this place. Two hundred disarmed Italians in railway tunnel down the road want to surrender. Can you send a boat?"

Lt. Commander R. F. Jenks, son of a former Lord Mayor of London, was the captain of H.M.S. Quail.

"Why do you want a boat?" came the reply.

"We have been here over a week and wish to report."

Jenks then looked at his watch and said: "Probably British Commandos. Anyhow, it's teatime, so let's bring them off for a cup."

Lee went ashore in the boat that ran in for us. It was commanded by Sub-Lieutenant Gillott, a suspicious-minded officer, for as it neared the shore I could see that it was bristling with firearms. Lee wrote:

As we arrived at the surf-lapped beach, a score of helmeted Italian soldiers . . . rushed down to the edge of the water.

Alert to the possibility of a trap, Gillott had the gun trained on them, but at that instant five weary men in khaki and green Commando berets sauntered down from the bushes.

Two herded the Italians into a single line, two others knelt behind the dunes with automatic rifles covering the road just behind the beach, while the fifth, who proved to be Major Young, came forward to greet us. . . .

I wanted Gillott to take off the prisoners as well as my own men, but there was only room for seven of them. Guidorossi himself, naturally, got a place, but there was not much to choose between the rest, and so we selected five others and Rosaria.

She was a cute but unwashed little brunette Red Cross nurse in Army shorts, assigned to his [Guidorossi's] outfit, wrote Paul Lee.

Sub-Lieutenant Gillott did not think much of the idea, but the Commandos all said:

"Bring her along. She knows how to look after herself and is a good sport. She volunteered to give us all a shave this morning."

Gillott agreed, and leaving eleven disconsolate Italians—or perhaps Sicilians—on the beach we went aboard H.M.S. *Quail.*

Commander Jenks, wearing a white sun-hat, received me on the bridge. We talked for a few minutes and sent off a signal reporting that he had picked us up. Then he said:

"Is there anything you would like?"

"At this moment," I said, "there's nothing I'd like so much as a bath." He gave me the run of his cabin and I had what John Durnford-

Slater would, under the circumstances, have called "the greatest bath of all time".

The R.Q.M.S. met me on the beach at Teresa and drove me to XIII Corps, where I reported to Brigadier Sugden, General Dempsey's B.G.S., Admiral MacGregor and John.

Guidorossi and his men were removed to a prisoner-of-war cage, but poor Rosaria, of course, was free to go where she pleased. There was a tearful scene, but since she could not go to prison, and was hardly suitable for enlistment in the Commando, we could only leave her to her own devices.

. . . . .

Of those who landed with me when the L.C.I. grounded on the night of 28th August all escaped except two of the Gunner signallers. Some of the crew of the L.C.I. returned, including the Captain and the Midshipman, but I cannot tell how many.

. . . . .

From Reggio I went to visit the Maffizi family and thank them for their kindness during our days in hiding. They were most reluctant to accept any reward.

I was feeling very fit, after a week on a starvation diet, and ran up the mountain to Maffizi's house, but next day I fell sick with malaria and was removed to hospital in Messina. The Commando went off to do a landing at Pizzo, which fortunately resulted in very few casualties.

After some days, being somewhat recovered, I went for a ride in a horse-drawn cab. Messina had been thoroughly blitzed and there was not much worth seeing, until on the return journey I came upon the vehicles of the Commando waiting to cross the Straits. I returned to the hospital, and suggested to the authorities that it was a good opportunity to get back to the unit, and they agreed without much difficulty.

It was a tedious and exhausting journey, but eventually I reached the unit at Scalea. Ned Moore, the doctor, came to see me when I arrived and announced that I had got jaundice. I retired to bed again, but refused to be removed to hospital.

Ned looked after me very well except that he insisted on carving fragments of a bullet out of my left ankle—they had been there since May 1940, doing no harm to anyone.

. . . . .

As a reconnaissance our expedition could scarcely have been a more complete failure. This our masters in XIII Corps never held against us, holding, as was really true, that we were the victims of our heavy and unsuitable wireless equipment. They preferred to recognise that "in circumstances of hardship, difficulty and danger" the men showed the quality of their Commando training.

CHAPTER VIII

TERMOLI

THE last action in which 3 Commando took part in the Mediterranean theatre, though it began with a landing in the traditional style, developed into a normal pitched battle in which the 78th Division and John Durnford-Slater's Special Service Brigade defeated the German 16th Panzer Division.

By the beginning of October the Germans had, in the words of Eric Linklater,[1] "determined to hold the doors to Rome". Termoli was the hinge of the outermost pair.

The little medieval fishing port of Termoli lies on the Adriatic two miles north of the River Biferno. If it fell the Germans, instead of holding the line of that river, would be forced to fall back and make a stand farther to the north-east.

The task of the Commando Brigade was to land west of the town, capture the port and join hands with the 78th Division, which was advancing by land. The brigade consisted of 3 Commando under Captain Arthur Komrower, who had recently rejoined; 40 (R.M.) Commando under Lieutenant Colonel "Pops" Manners, and the Special Raiding Squadron under Major "Paddy" Mayne, D.S.O.

The force sailed from Manfredonia on 2nd October. I returned from hospital in time to see them off, but John Durnford-Slater and Ned Moore conspired to prevent my going too on the grounds that I had not recovered from my attack of jaundice.

The plan was for 3 Commando to form the bridgehead, and at 2.15 on the morning of 3rd October the ramps went down: an unopposed landing in exactly the place selected. Fifteen minutes later the bridgehead was secure, and the success signal brought in the rest of the flotilla. No. 40 Commando and the S.R.S. moved through the bridgehead and 3 Commando became the reserve.

Before long Arthur Komrower was ordered to immobilise a railway train and sent 6 Troop forward. They captured the German driver

[1] *The Campaign in Italy.*

125

and fireman, who, though armed, decided not to argue and raked out the fire. Eight German soldiers were found asleep in the carriages. After this the troop was sent to support 40 Commando, held up on the outskirts of the town by a machine-gun post firing from a warehouse; this was too close for a mortar, too far for a grenade. Arthur Evans, the policeman, armed with a rifle fitted with a discharger cup,[1] stole along the railway embankment and put the gun out with his second bomb. This exploit put 6 Troop into great spirits and, advancing, they helped to clear the town. They covered Sergeant White's mortar section, who persuaded the crew of a German 75-millimetre gun to abandon their piece with three salvos of bombs. They surprised the German Commander shaving in the yard of his house and rounded up a few parachutists to keep him company.

Our men who had been captured by the Hermann Goering boys at Agnone had been well treated; some actually recognised their former captors among the Termoli prisoners and were able to return the compliment.

Two of the parachutists volunteered to act as cooks, cleaned out one of their field kitchens and produced breakfast. The prisoners were from the 1st Parachute Regiment. It is said that General Heydrich, the enemy Divisional Commander, had a narrow escape. He left the town on foot, leaving his 1939 Porsche behind him.

By 7.30 all was quiet. About seventy prisoners had been taken by the brigade. Upwards of fifty vehicles and much equipment fell into the hands of our men.

By eleven o'clock the 78th Division had contacted the S.R.S., and at two in the afternoon John Durnford-Slater ordered 3 Commando back into the town to rest, and the remainder of that day passed peacefully enough. At about midnight the Headquarters of 36 Brigade arrived in the town, and the commanders of 11 and 36 Brigades told John Durnford-Slater that the Special Service Brigade would be relieved by 8.30 the next morning.

.   .   .   .   .

Early next morning, 4th October, battalions of the 78th Division advancing to the north-west ran into opposition about three miles from the town.

Through some freak the telephone line to Guglionese was still intact,

[1] An E.Y. rifle.

although that town was behind the enemy lines. John Durnford-Slater, with the aid of an interpreter, spoke to the Mayor.

"There are hundreds of German tanks here," said the Mayor.

"Don't talk such bloody nonsense. There are no tanks nearer than Rome."

But the tanks were real enough; they belonged to the 16th Panzer Division from north of the Volturno.

. . . . .

At 11.30 John Durnford-Slater warned Arthur Komrower to be prepared to make landings on two islands to the east, but during the next hour the whole situation altered radically. At 12.30 Brian Franks, the Brigade Major, arrived and told Arthur that the unit would be going into the line, and by 2.45 the Commando, with a troop of the S.R.S. attached, was in position on the outskirts of the town astride the Ortona road. During the afternoon Komrower went into Termoli and saw Durnford-Slater and the Commander of the 11th Infantry Brigade. It was arranged that Lieutenant Colonel Chavasse of the Reconnaissance Regiment was to take over the whole force on the Ortona approach, including 3 Commando under Komrower.

Forward Observation Officers from a field and a medium regiment came up and established observation posts. On 3 Commando's front were four 6-pounder anti-tank guns, a 17-pounder and a section of three Vickers medium machine-guns all attached from other units. The afternoon was fairly quiet except for some shelling. During the night the Commandos dug in: they had no blankets and wanted to get out of the wind. It rained.

. . . . .

Back at Manfredonia, I felt disgruntled, bored, and rather lonely after the expedition had set off. On the 4th curiosity overcame me and so, as I was feeling much better, I set out in my Jeep for Termoli. George Herbert and Christopher were with me, Clark was driving. We were delayed by foul weather and many demolitions and spent an uncomfortable night in a house near San Severo. The bed was full of bugs.

Next morning we drove on and soon found ourselves in the back area of the 78th Division. There were signs along the side of the road with "This is a Battleaxe"—the divisional sign—and similar remarks painted on them.

"I don't want to tempt Providence, but you don't often see a German aeroplane nowadays," I said to George Herbert.

This was going too far. Soon after we found ourselves sitting in a traffic block waiting to cross a river; the bridge had been blown and sappers were hard at work on it. We had not been there long when some keen German airman came over and bombed us. . . .

As we neared Termoli the smell of cordite hung in the air. We passed half a dozen fresh graves decorated with German helmets. Once in the town we sought out John Durnford-Slater's Command Post.

"Hullo, Peter; you shouldn't be here, you know."

"I'm better. How's it going?"

"If Billy Hill, the bookmaker, was here he'd be laying evens."

John told me that Arthur Komrower had been doing very well with No. 3 and he wanted him to command them until they were relieved, but he consented to allow me to remain at his Headquarters and give him what assistance I could.

John told me that our battalions had not made much progress during the day. Indeed he had had a brush with a senior officer, and in an effort to "wake him out of his stupor", as he put it, he had tried to be rude to him. Asking how long one of the battalions was going to take about relieving 3 Commando, he had said:

"It might be two or three days, then?"

"Oh yes."

"It might as well be three years," John retorted, with, for him, unaccustomed rudeness, but he drew no response.

That night I slept peacefully in the Albergo Corona.

.   .   .   .   .

It was a fairly quiet night though there was some shelling, and at 6.45 the next morning a dozen enemy aircraft came over and attacked the town and harbour. By about eight o'clock the Germans, with tanks and infantry, were attacking the Argylls.

At 9.30 a brigadier called and told John that the enemy were infiltrating towards the town and that the situation had deteriorated considerably. He wanted the Special Service Brigade to be responsible for the immediate defence of the town and for suitable positions to be reconnoitred so that troops could take up a close perimeter if things got worse.

At 9.45 we heard the good news that eight Canadian tanks had

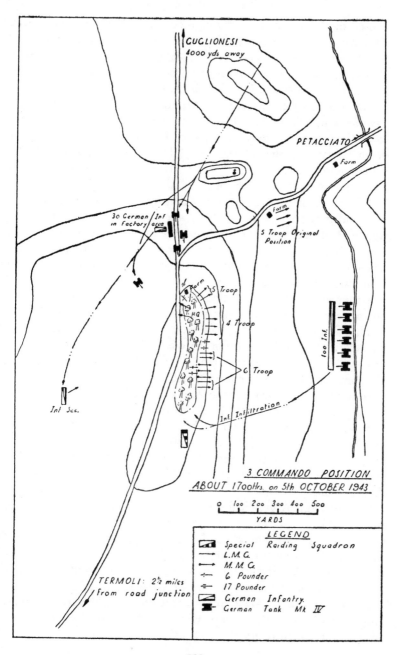

GUGLIONESI
4000 yds away

PETACCIATO

Farm

30 German Inf
in Factory area

Farm

S Troop Original
Position

Farm

S Troop

HQ

4 Troop

6 Troop

100 Inf.

Inf. Sec.

Inf. Infiltration

3 COMMANDO POSITION
ABOUT 1700hrs. on 5th OCTOBER 1943

0   100 200 300 400 500
YARDS

LEGEND
Special Raiding Squadron
L.M.G.
M.M.G.
6 Pounder
17 Pounder
German Infantry
German Tank Mk IV

TERMOLI: 2½ miles
from road junction

129

crossed the Biferno and that by nightfall there should be forty across. This was encouraging, but things did not look too rosy; units and formations seemed to have become intermingled. John sent Brian Franks back to XIII Corps to report progress and it was arranged that I should act as Brigade Major until his return.

Not long after I drove up to visit Arthur Komrower and rode straight past the unit, which was well concealed in some olive groves. Coming to a Y junction, we took the right fork and found ourselves going down a forward slope. Mortar bombs began to fall around us. This seemed wrong, somehow, so I told Clark to swing in behind a farm-house that stood on the right of the road. Behind the building were a few British soldiers. I asked them if they knew where the Commando was, and they pointed to a gully on the left. They added that there were no British troops ahead of them. We shot back up the road again, more mortar bombs falling around us as we went, and were not sorry when we were hidden among the olives. Here we found Arthur Komrower and Colonel Chavasse.

Arthur was quite happy. The men had no gas-capes or pullovers, but at least the food was not too bad. During the night R.S.M. Stenhouse and another man had been wounded by shellfire. There was still a little shelling, but on the whole the situation seemed to be in hand. I returned and reported to John, who left me in charge at his Command Post and went off to call on 11 Brigade.

Meanwhile on the front of the Argylls and the Commandos the day was becoming more lively. Five Sherman tanks of the County of London Yeomanry moved up the hill in support of the Argylls. One was immediately set on fire, and at about ten o'clock another withdrew to the road near 5 Troop. From this time onwards the Commandos' position came under heavy fire, receiving many missiles intended for the Shermans.

By midday the Argylls had suffered severe casualties and were forced to fall back to a factory near the Commandos' position. Leech of 6 Troop was surprised to see our forward troops withdrawing followed closely by the enemy. Through his glasses he could make out a Tiger tank covering the advance of nearly seventy men, about 1,400 yards away. He pointed this out to the Corporal commanding a Vickers section of the Queen's Westminsters, and a few good bursts of Vickers and Bren dispersed this group, which made no further attempt to advance for several hours.

Between eleven o'clock and 12.30 our own artillery put in some good shooting, but the enemy retaliated in kind, and at one time shells were landing on 6 Troop at two-minute intervals. John Reynolds, the Troop Commander, was among the first to be hit.

Back at the Command Post there was plenty of bad news. At about midday Lincoln Leese returned from a liaison visit to 36 Brigade to say that the West Kents, threatened by enemy tanks, had been forced to retire. The exact locations of the various battalions of the two brigades were, it seemed, far from clear.

About eleven o'clock the Germans had begun shelling the town with a couple of 88-mm. guns, which traversed a few degrees after each round. Two fell near our Headquarters, causing us to withdraw rapidly into the room farthest from the enemy.

About this time things took another turn for the worse. No. 5 Troop were in a rather exposed position, with both flanks in the air, and so Arthur Komrower decided to withdraw them about four hundred yards to a more favourable position in an olive grove. This move was carried out with only five casualties, all of whom were brought back, but unfortunately it coincided with a general retirement of all the forward troops, and in the disorder that followed about six men of the Commando fell back farther than they were meant to. Among the soldiers who withdrew were some of the anti-tank gunners attached to the Commando.

By two o'clock in the afternoon three enemy tanks were approaching the Y junction, which I had accidentally passed during the morning, and all the troops on the flanks of 3 Commando had withdrawn. One of the Forward Observation Officers had been wounded. Colonel Chavasse and some of his Reconnaissance Regiment and a party of the Argylls remained with the Commando. By this time the road between them and the town was being accurately shelled.

· · · · ·

About this time I left Headquarters and drove out to see Pops Manners and Paddy Mayne, who had now taken up positions to cover the San Salvo road. Manners and Peter Hellings, his second-in-command, were standing a few hundred yards from the cemetery outside the town. Over against its wall was a carrier platoon; as we watched, most of the men got out of the vehicles and ran off across the fields. There was no obvious reason for this, for the shelling was not severe. It was just panic. A few of 5 Troop appeared. They had no business to be there.

"Where the hell do you think you're going?"

"We were told to withdraw, sir." They had a good sergeant with them and so, satisfied that they had merely mistaken their orders, I asked Manners to let them attach themselves to 40 Commando.

Next a Bofors ack-ack gun appeared, going like hell. This we were able to stop and after a few well-chosen words the crew were convinced that there was no danger—at least none from the enemy.

Returning to Headquarters, I found that the house had received a direct hit; Lincoln Leese, who had lost an eye at Agnone, had been killed; and one of John's staff had been blown out of the window. Almost at the same time a shell had landed in a vehicle full of Mayne's soldiers, killing thirteen of the S.R.S. It was not until five o'clock that evening that some of our men found a German Artillery Officer, who had stolen into the town and was directing his guns from a church-tower. He refused to surrender. . . .

Meanwhile Brian Franks had returned having seen General Dempsey, who had commented: "I'm afraid Termoli's in for a sticky afternoon." Still, it was a consolation to know that the Corps Commander was fully *au fait* with the situation, and Brian reported that 36 Brigade should arrive during the night.

No. 3 Commando were now isolated about three-quarters of a mile in front of the rest of our troops, with both flanks exposed, but nevertheless things in general began to take a turn for the better. About 3.45 Peter Hellings appeared from 40 Commando and announced that he had seen twenty Shermans making for the high ground west of the town, and that, two miles down the road, fifty-two Canadian tanks were about to cross the Biferno Bridge. This had been swept away by the heavy rains on the morning of the 4th, but by truly heroic efforts the Royal Engineers had rebuilt it, despite continuous shelling. Hellings told us that a troop of 40 Commando was shooting up a German force that was infiltrating towards Paddy Mayne's position.

I said to John Durnford-Slater: "The news has been better this last hour, Colonel."

"Yeah," said he. "All the real bad buggers have buggered off by now."

. . . . .

But if things were beginning to swing our way, 3 Commando was still playing the part of Daniel in the Lion's Den. At 4.30 three enemy tanks were at the Y junction and a fourth had got on to the high ground close to their left. It swung its gun round towards Komrower's position.

"I could almost inspect the barrel!" said one of the soldiers.

Arthur Komrower reluctantly withdrew 2 Troop from the farm they were in, because after it had received a number of hits the hay-stacks caught fire. But this meant that he could no longer observe the road junction. Shortly after five o'clock eleven Mark IV tanks, followed by about a hundred infantry, appeared two thousand yards away coming directly towards the position. The Vickers guns hammered away and managed to delay this attack; the enemy disappeared into dead ground, and soon afterwards six of the tanks were seen withdrawing uphill.

The Vickers teams attached to the Commando had done their stuff, though in one case rather against their will. The crew had actually thrown away the cocking handle and started for the rear when Corporal Harrison of 6 Troop brought them back. A shell landed near, but his men could see him still directing the fire though his head was bleeding. Again the machine-gunners wanted to go away, but Harrison pulled out his revolver and they went on firing. Another shell landed and this time he was hit in the leg, but he still refused to leave or even to lie down. The shelling was getting some of his men down by this time, but this cool disregard for danger was a tonic.[1]

Leech was the right-hand man of the whole Commando by this time. He heard an unknown voice on his right say:

"Come on, Taffy! Let's bugger off from here!"

Not long after, in the half-light, the Germans came on. As they consolidated each forward bound they fired off white Very lights in the direction of the advance. The third of the series sailed over 6 Troop, who had deduced the meaning of these signals, and were waiting for them in line. Lieutenant Alderson, commanding 6 Troop, placed himself in the centre to control the fire. He waited until the enemy were fifty yards away and then let fly, causing many casualties. The Germans had three machine-guns and fired tracer, which gave away their positions. Leech, who was not firing tracer, was able to

[1]Harrison survived and was later an officer in 6 Commando.

silence each in turn with his Bren. It was noticed that the enemy were wearing their greatcoats; perhaps they thought the position had been abandoned.

In this fight Evans and three others were sent to cover the right flank. As they got up to do so a machine-gun opened up on them. By this time they were so furious that without bothering to take cover they just stood and fired back with their rifles, apparently with success, for the gun ceased fire.

·   ·   ·   ·   ·

Just before dusk John Reynolds, wounded early in the morning, went to see Arthur Komrower and tell him what was happening on the right flank. There was urgent need for more 3-inch mortar bombs, and Colonel Chavasse was about to send his jeep back in the hope that it would get through to Termoli. Komrower sent Reynolds with it to fetch a load of bombs. The jeep got through, but Ned Moore got his hands on John Reynolds and put him to sleep with a shot of morphia. I remember seeing John that evening in the big hospital in the middle of the town. He seemed to me to be at death's door, but I am glad to say that he is alive to this day and a major in the Worcestershire Regiment.

At about 6.30 contact had been lost with the troop of the S.R.S. Their last message was that they were under heavy fire. This compelled Arthur Komrower to pull 6 Troop back to face the right flank. To the front there were enemy no further than a hundred yards from Commando Headquarters and they could be heard talking. Komrower decided that he would be in a worse position if a fire-fight began and so held his fire.

When 6 Troop fell back it left Corporal Edwards, Evans and another man as a listening patrol. After a while a bareheaded, unarmed German sauntered into the trees. Evans and one of the others crept up behind him and prodded him back to the troop lines. He admitted that he was from the 16th Panzer Division.

At 8.15 the craft carrying 38 Brigade came into the harbour. The Brigadier[1] visited our Command Post, and as soon as he had heard the situation said he would disembark one of his battalions at once, ready for immediate action. From this time we felt that the battle was won.

[1] Brigadier Nelson Russell, D.S.O., M.C.

During the night Donald Hopson, with his batman, succeeded in making his way back to Termoli. He explained that the Commando was surrounded on three sides by the enemy at between fifty and a hundred yards. It was evident that unless they were withdrawn before dawn they would inevitably be annihilated. John Durnford-Slater sent him back with orders for the Commando to withdraw into reserve at Termoli. He reached them at one o'clock in the morning. Three-quarters of an hour later the Commando filtered back to the rear of the position and formed up in file. Donald Hopson led them back cross-country until they reached the position of the Lancashire Fusiliers. Colonel Chavasse with his scout car, and Arthur Komrower in his jeep, driven by Sergeant "Brigadier" Leyland, were the last to leave.

The Commando had no ammunition for the mortars and very little for the Brens. At 3.30, tired but in good spirits, they reached the town. Arthur came and reported at the Command Post. I asked him to billet the men and stand to at 5.15, at which hour he handed over to me.

Next morning I set up my Headquarters in the Albergo Corona. The unit was in position round the railway station and various buildings on the edge of the town. I found that the Commando was still 146 strong. It had lost one officer and two men killed, two officers and twenty-six other ranks wounded, and six other ranks missing during the fighting of the previous day.

At first light on 6th October the town was shelled fairly heavily, and at 5.30 enemy infantry thrust down the railway line, but were held by the S.R.S. until 38 Brigade moved into positions on the outskirts of the town. Enemy aeroplanes came over about 6 a.m. and bombed the town. The shelling continued, yet things still seemed to be going well. The Irish soldiers forming up outside the Albergo were a businesslike-looking lot. I remember seeing one section commanded by a fresh-faced young lance-corporal of the Royal Irish Fusiliers, with a D.C.M. on his chest and the light of battle in his eye.

Evans had been posted as a sentry on the railway line. The sun was up, but he felt wet, cold and weary, and so he sat enveloped in a blanket upon a rock gloomily watching his front.

Up came an Irish lad. "Have you come from the front line, now?"

"I have."

"And what was it loike?"

"Bloody awful!"

At this the Irishman gave Evans a hearty slap on the back. "Niver moind! We've been tould there's Commandos here!" he cried and went his way.

A pretty compliment coming from 38 Brigade.

. . . . .

At 11.30 in the morning the Irish Brigade advanced in great style and stormed the San Giacomo Ridge. By 3 p.m. the 1st Royal Irish Fusiliers were firmly established on its objectives. Two hours later the 6th Inniskilling Fusiliers were in position on their left and the battle of Termoli was won.

Once this attack was launched we had really nothing to do. Nevertheless, at midday, whilst I was at Brigade Headquarters, McGovern, John Durnford-Slater's batman, raised the alarm by saying the Germans were in the railway station. Everyone stood to arms. Bren-gun carriers rushed by. It is true that bullets were still flying about, but it seemed highly improbable that the enemy were really in our midst. At this juncture some Italians came up and said there were some Germans in a nearby cellar. This was too much. With a few men John dashed up to the building. He had something in his hand and was tugging at it furiously.

"Here, Peter! How the hell do these things work?" He handed me a 36 grenade. I straightened the pin with my teeth and dropped it into the cellar through a sort of fanlight. A most satisfying crash followed, but no yells or groans. I fear the casualties were wine bottles.

That evening we withdrew to Bari; Arthur Komrower took the main body by sea and I travelled ahead by road. The brigade was allotted the pleasant little town of Molfetta for billets, and from there, after a short stay, we set off on our journey to England and the Second Front—a tedious journey by way of Catania, Bone—where we spent a miserable damp November—and Algiers.

Before we left, General Dempsey came down to say goodbye and to inspect the unit, drawn up in the courtyard of a school, our temporary barracks.

He spoke to the men about our various activities in Sicily and Italy. Agnone, he said, had been most important; Bova Marina he described as a novelty, but also most useful; and Termoli had been of vital importance.

Next he told us the principles on which he used to employ us. The job must be worthwhile. We must be told the task but left to do the planning for ourselves. The Commandos must not be landed more than twelve, or at the most twenty-four, hours before the main force could reach us. And he himself was prepared to put in everything he'd got, up to a complete division, to get us out again. A raid must go in with a quick hard blow and then come straight out.

He told the men that he hoped that he would command them again. As he was leaving I suggested that he ought to go home and take us to the Second Front.

"We shall see," he said.

PART III

NORMANDY

CHAPTER IX

D-DAY AND THE MERVILLE BATTERY

IT was on 4th January 1944, almost exactly five months before
D-Day, that the Commando, about 280 strong, landed at Liverpool,
where we were met by John Durnford-Slater and Lord Lovat, in
whose brigade we were now to serve.

Without more ado we were sent off on leave, returning to Worthing,
which was to be our billeting area, on 24th January. There was little
enough time and we began at once to train for the ordeal that lay
ahead, but it was difficult to get things going before the arrival of
our reinforcements, which did not take place until 16th February,
when 165 men joined from the Commando Depôt.

It seemed too much to hope that we would receive reinforcements
comparable with the original volunteers of 1940, or the police intake
of 1942. The war was now in its fifth year. Africa, Sicily and Italy
had all taken a toll; the inexorable law of diminishing satisfaction
was beginning to operate. But once again 3 Commando struck lucky,
for this intake had a good nucleus of Guardsmen, forty-five in number,
from the Guards Armoured Division.

Charles Vaughan, who commanded the Commando Depôt at Ach-
nacarry, used to call the training troops after the names of Commando
Brigadiers and Commanding Officers. When recruits arrived from
the Depôt I used to interview them so as to decide how to employ
them. I asked one recruit, among other things, what troop he had
been in at the Depôt, and I was told:

"Young Troop, sir."

"And who was Young?"

139

"Oh, some officer who was up there at one time."

"And what was he doing there?"

"A refresher course or something."

"And where is he now?"

"I suppose he's been bumped off, hasn't he?"

I left him to work that out for himself.

.   .   .   .   .

Life began to get hectic now, with an endless round of exercises, general inspections and athletic events.

On 21st February, General Montgomery inspected the 1st Special Service Brigade at Hove. The soldiers were paraded at ten o'clock, the General arrived at midday. The brigade formed three sides of a square and waited.

When it came to my turn to be introduced Monty said: "Have we met before?"

"Yes," I replied. "Once at Suez and once outside Brussels in 1940, when I was a Liaison Officer to Brigadier Barker in 10th Infantry Brigade."

"Oh," he said, "Bubbles, Bubbles. Yes, the 10th Infantry Brigade were put under my command for that show."

When he inspected the men the General had them formed into a lane; they were allowed to "stand easy". Then he walked through the lines letting them have a good look at him. After this he mounted a jeep and the soldiers rushed forward and crowded round while he spoke to them. There could be no doubt of the enthusiasm and confidence he inspired.

Next day the Commando moved to the Combined Training Centre at Dorlin on the west coast of Scotland, where we remained until 10th March. There, far from the bright lights and from higher authority, we absorbed the newcomers into the unit. Shooting, training exercises, and work with landing-craft occupied our days until we returned to Worthing. By that time the new men had settled down and were beginning to know where they fitted in.

In the Second World War special forces, whether airborne or Commando troops, did not differ altogether from normal infantry battalions. The men and even the officers were very much the same. Where we had the advantage was in the quality of our N.C.O.s, who were in general incomparably better than those of the field army. By 1944

3 Commando was particularly fortunate in this respect. The men who had survived Vaagso, Dieppe, Agnone and Termoli, few in numbers though they were, had developed into experienced and war-wise leaders. To me nothing in my job seemed more important than the selection and training of N.C.O.s. This had long been an *idée fixe* with me, but now I really had something to work on. The candidates for promotion had been under fire, not once but several times, and had had the opportunity to prove their worth. A unit commander usually has his officers thrust upon him, but he has only himself to thank if he promotes dud N.C.O.s. If he does he might as well look for some other form of employment. I am deeply conscious that 3 Commando was well served by its officers and men, but it owed its successes more than any single factor to its peerless N.C.O.s.

So much for one of the bees in my bonnet. Another one is fire-power. In the Commandos we were supposed to have five Brens in a troop; an infantry company, which had about twice the number of men as a rifle troop, had nine Brens. It seemed to me that we should increase our firepower so that one of our troops could at a pinch do much the same job as an infantry company. We worked this out and decided that eight was the ideal number. We then indented for the extra guns, through the usual channels, and, lo and behold, they quickly appeared. Things happened fast in the early months of 1944. The office and administrative staffs were going down the ramps on D-Day at the same time as everyone else. Every fourth man in Headquarters carried a Bren, and so we were really going into action with seven troops, all with teeth, as opposed to six troops and a long and harmless tail.

We were told that one of our troops was to be trained in parachuting. A number of men volunteered and the pick of them became the new 3 Troop under Roy Westley, a keen, hard officer with a touch of the gambler in him.

On 17th March we were inspected by General Dempsey. The unit was drawn up in review order on Broadwater Green, Worthing, and when at 12.15 the General arrived we received him with a General Salute. He came forward.

"Slope arms. Let me take you by the hand. How are you?" he said, and started to go round the ranks, talking to those men who wore the badge of the Royal Berkshire Regiment, his own old corps, and to those whose medals told him that they had served under him in Sicily and Italy.

After the inspection the parade marched past in column.

"Very excellent," he said.

The officers were introduced. He shook hands with them all and spoke for some time to Gordon Pollard and John Nixon, whom he knew of old. Then he asked me:

"How much do you know of the next affair? Do you know enough to be able to train your horse?"

I told him I was supposed to be ready by the end of May.

"That's about right."

.   .   .   .   .

When the end of May came we went into a "concentration camp" near Southampton, where, behind barbed wire, we were to be briefed and to wait for D-Day. The men were not allowed out except in formed bodies under officers, and by the time we had been there a day or two we were ready to face death in practically any form rather than go on living in boredom where we were. The amenities of the camp were few, though there was a cinema in a marquee. This, strangely enough, was staffed by American G.I.s. I heard one say to another:

"When I get back home my kids'll say to me: 'What did you do in the Great War, Daddy?' And all I'll say is, 'I showed *Claudia* to a bunch of goddam British boys waitin' to go over to D-Day.'"

.   .   .   .   .

When the Commando left Molfetta we knew that we were being withdrawn to go to the Second Front, and we rejoiced, for naturally enough the soldiers wanted to go home again, to see their families and friends, and to tell unlikely tales of their prowess in Sicily and Italy. The greatest invasion of all time lay ahead, with its promise of wounds and death, but for a few months at home it seemed well worth it.

We were now in the 1st Special Service Brigade under Brigadier the Lord Lovat, D.S.O., M.C., a formation consisting of four units, 3, 4 and 6 Army Commandos and 45 (RM) Commando. 45 (RM) had not previously been in action; 4 made its name storming the Varengeville Battery at Dieppe; 6 had fought with distinction in Tunisia.

Throughout the Normandy campaign the brigade was under command of General Gale's 6th Airborne Division. In this we were fortunate. The Corps Commander, General Sir John Crocker, afterwards wrote: "No British division was ever given a more momentous task than the 6th Airborne Division which landed from the air in Normandy before dawn on 6th June 1944, to seize the vital ground on the eastern flank of the Allied seaborne invasion. . . ."

It is easy for us who wore the Green Beret to look back on that far-off campaign and consider the operations of our brigade, as it were, *in vacuo*. That is to make the whole campaign meaningless.

General Gale's tasks were to seize, intact, the Benouville Bridges over the Canal de Caen and the River Orne; to silence the Merville Battery, which could fire on the sea approaches and the beaches where the 3rd Division was to land; to destroy the bridges over the River Dives and delay German reinforcements coming from the direction of Le Havre and the River Seine towards Caen; and, lastly, to seize the seaside towns of Sallenelles and Franceville Plage and to clear the coastal strip between those places and Cabourg. It was for this last task that the 6th Airborne Division was given Lovat's Brigade, the Cabourg sector being the objective of 3 Commando.

"The tasks," wrote General Gale, "were in all conscience varied and formidable enough. In fact they involved our first seizing and then dominating an area of some twenty-four square miles."

We were told a good deal about the enemy.

The 711th Infantry Division, perhaps 14,000 strong, held a short sector of coast between Le Havre and the River Orne and had the support of a number of well-sited heavy coast artillery batteries.

The 716th Infantry Division, mainly west of the Orne, had its Headquarters at Caen. Two of its eight battalions were said to be Russian.

The 352nd Infantry Division was available for counter-attack, while two armoured divisions, the 12th S.S. Panzer (Hitler Jugend) and the 21st Panzer, each about 20,000 strong, fully equipped and mobile, could reach the area within twelve to twenty-four hours.

In varying strength the Germans were holding the coastline from Narvik to Bayonne. In Norway alone it is estimated that they had 300,000 troops locked up, a thing most desirable from our point of view at a time when we were about to invade France! Those of us who had been to Lofoten and Vaagso—few enough by June 1944—

could feel that to some extent our earlier efforts were making our present tasks easier, for Hitler had proved sensitive to these harassing raids.

.   .   .   .   .

The 1st Special Service Brigade was to land over the beaches at la Brèche. Therefore, with the exception of 4 Commando, whose main task was to capture a battery at Ouistreham, the brigade had a long way to go before reaching its objectives. However, since they were using the same beach we could take advantage of the 3rd Division's fire-support plan. The coast defences east of the Orne were even more formidable than those at la Brèche, and so it paid us to land there, despite the longer approach march.

In his plan Lord Lovat laid down that 4 Commando was to land on the heels of the 8th Infantry Brigade, the assault brigade, and, wheeling left, to assault its battery. No. 6 Commando was to blaze the trail inland and join hands with parachutists at the Benouville Bridges. Nos. 3 and 45 were the follow-up Commandos, landing at H + 90. Instead of being thankful for small mercies, I felt vaguely insulted that my Commando was not to go in at H Hour.

The first three days of June were almost entirely devoted to the briefing. With models and air photographs we went through the operation, time and again, until every man knew by heart what he had to do. If there were casualties among the officers and N.C.O.s everyone knew who was to take over. Most important of all, every man knew that our main object was to get to the bridges and to join up with the 6th Airborne Division. Confusion was to be expected; all sorts of details might go wrong, but as long as they kept this aim in view all would be well.

On 4th June there was a Church Parade for all ranks and creeds, and on the morning of the 5th Lord Lovat addressed the whole brigade, saying as he ended, for the benefit of the two French troops attached to 4 Commando: *"Demain matin on les aura."*

.   .   .   .   .

At about 2 p.m. we embussed and drove to Warsash, where while waiting to embark 3 and 6 Commandos played each other at soccer.

At 4.30 p.m. the Commando embarked in its five landing-craft, and as we went on board an Embarkation Staff Officer handed each man some kind of label or ticket. He did not say who was supposed to collect these at the other end. At 5.30 p.m. the craft moved out to an anchorage in Southampton water, where the array of ships and craft was truly impressive. At 7 p.m. we moved down to Stokes Bay, where great flotillas of assault-craft, all moving in formation to a carefully timed programme, were gradually assembling; the Commando Brigade in the van.

At 9.30 p.m. Force S, of which we formed part, received its sailing orders; troops mustered on deck, and I made their actual destination known to them. Down below troop commanders gave out the maps, and in the dusk the armada set out. Once clear of the Isle of Wight the wind freshened. The storm which had already delayed us for twenty-four hours had not yet abated. All through the night our small craft pitched and rolled. I found it impossible to sleep; most of us were seasick, flung about by the crazy pitching of our craft; it was a miserable night. Breakfast for me was just a mug of cocoa, which went straight over the side, but otherwise I was not unwell.

Half-past eight the next morning found us hove-to about two miles off the Normandy beaches waiting for H+90 and our turn to run in. Sporadic shelling by the enemy was being answered by warships and a monitor, their great broadsides slamming away in reply to the occasional flashes from the shore. Most impressive.

Before the time came for us to go in I heard the news that the assault brigades were ashore, and these glad tidings were quickly spread among the men.

. . . . .

Dawn. Dawn of the day that the whole world has been waiting for for two years. Now the flotilla is steaming ahead, 45 Commando to starboard, 3 Commando to port, the craft leaping about like young lambs. Ahead big guns are flashing, but as yet not a sound comes back to us from them. Gradually the dawn brightens and the mist begins to clear, ahead big ships are silhouetted against a gloomy sky. Time to make ready.

Now we are moving among the great warships roaring out their broadsides, cruisers first, then the battleship *Ramillies* belching forth 15-inch shells—a sight to remember. We put on more speed, the soldiers forget to be seasick, and then suddenly, with almost magical precision, the columns of craft form into line abreast.

Land ahead now—a hundred yards away a column of water shoots into the air. Away to port a tank landing-craft burns fiercely, ammunition exploding as the crew go over the side. Ashore is a line of battered houses whose silhouette looks familiar from the photographs. They must surely mark our landing-place. On the beach a few tanks creep about and fire occasional shots at an unseen foe. Ouistreham is not much more than a thousand yards to port now. Somewhere on the front are the guns that are shelling us; the flashes are plainly visible every few seconds. The craft slows down.

"What are you waiting for?"

"There are still five minutes to go before H + 90," the Captain, a young R.N.V.R. officer, replies.

"I don't think anyone will mind if we're five minutes early on D-Day."

"Then in we go."

Another shellburst almost overhead. This time a splinter hits the front of my jacket. Someone ducks and his helmet clangs on the deck. Another flash from in front of Ouistreham. This time the next craft is the target—a near miss, or a hit, maybe. The craft shies like a horse. Our craft is to port of the rest, which somehow makes us feel more exposed. The beach at last! The ramps are pushed out and hang for a moment above the water. My weight on the starboard gangway submerges it and I find myself in five feet of water splashing ashore as Michael Woyevodsky rushes down the port ramp. Ahead the sand is marked by the track of one of our swimming tanks which has safely crossed the beach—enough to explode any mines that may have been there.

"Follow me! Single file!"

The soldiers troop across. It is 9.5.

.   .   .   .   .

But not all have got thus far. Three of our five craft are hit, including my own struck at the moment of touchdown. Christopher struggles up from below but not before the water is round his neck....

6 Troop is hardest hit. The shell explodes some 3-inch mortar bombs carried by many of the troops. T. S. M. Shaw and Paddy Quinn are among those killed. About a third of Douglas Johnston's section

remains operational. With blast injuries to the legs, he is dragged from the flooded troop space and helped ashore by Sergeant Leech M.M. who, with Lance Sergeant Evans, saves many other wounded from drowning. John Alderson, in full equipment, swims ashore with a lifeline, but another craft is steered alongside and acts as a bridge to the beach.

.   .   .   .   .

No. 3 Troop comes ashore in grand style and almost unscathed. In the bows Troopers Osborne and Jennings make mock of the German gunners: "Put your sights up, Jerry!" "Down a little." "Give her more wind-gauge", and much nonsense besides, as each shell flies past and, as luck would have it, misses their craft—except for the wireless aerial. The first man ashore is Slinger Martin, our veteran Administrative Officer, whose first campaign in France lies thirty years in the past.

.   .   .   .   .

At the back of the beach there is wire, not very difficult to cross but too much for some of the assault brigade.

"Don't touch the bloody wire, it's mined," shouts a young lad from a Yorkshire regiment.

Taking no notice of him, Martin, R.Q.M.S. Smith and their storeman leap over the wire.

"Good, Slinger. All off?"

"O.K.," he cries.

"We are going forward now. 3 Troop will have to get off as best they can."

We move up into the dunes and among the houses, while Westley's troop struggle to get their bicycles off the L.C.I., which has also taken a direct hit by this time.

No. 4 Troop comes squelching up, led by Brian Butler.

"Don't bunch!"

All round the houses are soldiers of the assault brigade. Inland lies level marshy ground—no cover; they don't care for the look of this, it seems. Most of the Commando are ashore and across the beach by this time. There's a little mortaring, nothing much, so the sooner we get going the better.

"Advance!"

147

We trot down the inland side of the dunes, dash across a road and a tram-line, and hurl ourselves over a wire fence, no great obstacle. The soldiers come swarming down the slope. Away to the left a quick-firing gun opens up. A shell smacks into the soft ground behind us, and something like the kick of a mule hits me on the right shoulder-blade.

"That was a near one," shouts R.S.M. Stenhouse.

"Near one be damned, it hit me!"

This marsh is not the place to linger in. We push on. Progress is slow, floundering and leaping across deep slimy ditches. But the soft ground minimizes the effect of the German shells. Even so Lieutenant Cowieson, of 5 Troop, has a nasty wound, and Sergeant King takes over his section. No. 3 Troop has lost Sergeant Dowling, wounded by a shell that landed within a yard of him.

At length we reach the forming-up place. Except for 6 Troop the Commando is still more or less intact. Donald Hopson comes up and reports. Then Cowieson appears, assuring me that he is all right, but he seems to be pretty hard hit and I tell him to go back. John Pooley, my Second-in-Command, has also been hit. He soon appears, however, not much the worse for a near miss, though he has a gash on his lip. I move my right arm about and find that it is still in working order; a clod must have hit my equipment.

Near our forming-up place a company commander of one of the assault battalions sits under a hedge with his C.S.M. and two others, waiting for his men whom we last saw digging-in on the beach a thousand yards behind him. . . .

Suddenly there comes an unearthly, blood-chilling, bellowing noise like a gigantic cow in agony and six bombs land in the next field in a cloud of back smoke—our first meeting with "Moaning Minnie", the German six-barrelled mortar.

"Ah, *Nebelwerfer*," says Donald Hopson in his usual cool manner, as if it were some sort of military curio that he has been wanting to add to his collection.

Taking a quick look round to check whether everyone is present, I see Captain Martin again.

"All up, Slinger?"

"Aye, aye, sir."

"Good. *Vörwarts!*" and the advance begins again.

·   ·   ·   ·   ·

148

It was now about ten o'clock. We were in touch with 45 Commando in the brigade's first forming-up place, but progress was delayed by minefields, confining the brigade to one track which had to be followed in single file. No. 6 Commando was ahead, but the advance was still maddeningly slow; and so leaving John Pooley and Donald Hopson to bring on the main body of the Commando, I pushed on with Sergeant Leyland, Corporal Christopher and a few others to get through to the Benouville Bridge and find out what was going on. Our rear-link wireless set had broken down.

We passed through 45 Commando in Colleville, where, except for a little small-arms fire, all was quiet. Along the road to St. Aubin d'Arquenay we met no resistance, though there was desultory sniping at the far end of the village where we met some of 6 Commando escorting prisoners.

Beyond St. Aubin the road was clear of troops. It led downhill to Benouville; we covered the distance at the double. Entering the village, my party passed a post manned by airborne troops, obviously delighted that they were no longer isolated.

The bridge over the Orne was under rifle fire from a château on the west bank of the canal, about eight hundred yards to the south. A number of dead Germans lay sprawling around an abandoned glider within thirty yards of the road, while the bridges, still intact, bore witness to the success of the airborne *coup de main*.

Here I saw half a dozen men of 3 Troop, who had dismounted from their bicycles and were taking cover under the low bank to the left of the road.

"What are you waiting for?"

"They're sniping the bridge, sir."

"Well, get on your bikes and go flat out; you'll probably get away with it!"

They leapt to their feet. One man fell shot clean through the head. The rest reached the other side. Now it was our turn. We ran across the bridge as fast as we could. On the other bank in a ditch beside the road sat a row of German prisoners. Almost at once Lord Lovat appeared and told me that our advance on Cabourg was off. The airborne troops had dropped over a far wider area than had been intended. The Commando was to move into Le Bas de Ranville, so as to protect the Headquarters of the 6th Airborne Division, and to block any enemy advance from the south.

By 3.30 p.m. most of the Commando had crossed the bridge and was taking up defensive positions. Ten minutes later the Transport Officer got through with the first of our Jeeps, piled high with reserve ammunition—a good effort.

When we had been in position for less than two hours four German tanks were reported on the rising ground to our south. They were engaged by 3-inch mortars belonging to the Airborne Division, and withdrew. At the same time H.M.S. *Serapis* fired twenty rounds into some German infantry who had been seen digging in the forward edge of a wood.

. . . . .

No. 3 Troop, carrying their parachute bicycles, with cases of 3-inch mortar bombs strapped to the handlebars, had toiled across the swamp, with some loss. But when they came to the road leading to the Orne the cyclist troop came into its own. Ordered to press on with all speed, they did so, running through a fair amount of sniping before they reached the bridges. According to Keith Ponsford, when they arrived there they were the leading troop of the brigade. However this may be, Lord Lovat, who had no other troops available, sent them to support Lieutenant-Colonel Otway of the 9th Parachute Battalion, who with eighty men had captured the Château d'Amfreville, after clearing the Merville Battery.

The village of Amfreville stands on a low ridge east of the Orne and overlooks a great part of the lodgement area. It was essential that this ground should be firmly in our hands on D-Day. If not the German artillery would have observation posts there and life in the beach-head round Ouistreham, and, indeed, much farther west, would be intolerable.

Otway suggested that he, Westley and Ponsford, the surviving officers of 3 Troop, should go forward and reconnoitre the village. This they did from the area of the château—later to be my headquarters.[1] It was arranged that the parachutists in position south of the building would give our men covering fire. Lovat now arrived on a bicycle and ordered Westley to attack the village without delay. In consequence 3 Troop went straight up the road leading into the village from the west, and came under heavy fire at a place where the road ran between high stone walls.

[1] The Château of Monsieur Leboucher. This had been a German battalion H.Q. until that morning.

At once Westley was hit in the arm; Abbott, who had been my Bren-gunner at Dieppe and Agnone, and two other men were wounded. Sergeant Hill, Troopers Osborne, Barnes and Jennings returned the fire and the casualties got away. As they withdrew a bullet made a neat parting down the Sergeant's scalp!

While Westley was having his wound dressed Ponsford took command. He ordered the Sergeant-Major to reorganise the troop, while he made a quick reconnaissance round the right flank and found a covered approach. After clearing some houses which overlooked the village square, Ponsford put one of his sections in position to give covering fire. Here the 2-inch mortar proved invaluable, for its high-explosive bombs, fired at a low angle, did much to demoralise the German garrison.

When he judged that his men had got the better of the fire-fight Ponsford charged across the open to capture the school, the main centre of resistance. Seizing this, the troop then swept through the village, killing six or eight of the enemy and capturing more than twenty others besides several horse-drawn vehicles. In this dashing assault the troop lost not one man. They then took up a position in the hedges east of the village, where Roy Westley, his wound bandaged, rejoined them.

No. 6 Commando had now arrived in the southern end of the village, and Ponsford, who did not know where 3 Commando was, went off to place his men under the orders of Derek Mills-Roberts.

While Ponsford was talking to Mills-Roberts the latter ordered his Bombardment Officer to bring down naval gunfire on Breville Wood. The first 15-inch shell landed between them and the wood so the gunner gave a correction. The next shell arrived with a deafening crash about fifteen yards from the group, making a massive crater and tearing branches from the trees above their heads. The air was blue with Derek's language: the shoot was over.

Once the village was in our hands the Germans began to shell it.

.   .   .   .   .

From the Bas de Ranville we could see fighting west of the Orne, where the Germans were counter-attacking the 3rd Division. This was about seven o'clock.

At about 8.50 gliders, hundreds of them, flying very low, steadily and gracefully, began to come in, with overwhelming fighter cover.

When they were more or less overhead the gliders slipped their tow and came down in the open fields between Ranville and Amfreville. It was an astonishing sight, very encouraging to us. There was a considerable barrage of ack-ack fire, but it was not very effective. The Germans began to mortar the landing zone, but they had little success and the 6th Airlanding Brigade alighted with very few casualties, a welcome reinforcement.

During the night we handed over to the Royal Ulster Rifles and concentrated in an area south of Brigade Headquarters. About 1 a.m. there had been some activity on our front, enemy tanks and infantry being reported. No. 1 Troop had three casualties, but by 4.30 we were in the new position as ordered.

At nine o'clock the Brigade Intelligence Officer came along and reported that two anti-tank guns were to be placed under my command, and a quarter of an hour later the Brigade Major arrived with their commander. We went off together and sited them where they could cover the open fields between Ranville and Amfreville, fields now covered with gliders.

The morning passed peacefully. We were well hidden in a little valley and had no casualties, but about 1 p.m. a message arrived from Brigade Headquarters:

2 i/c with two troops to support 45 (RM) Commando in their attack on FRANCEVILLE-PLAGE.

For this mission I gave John Pooley 4 and 5 Troops.

. . . . .

The Merville Battery

No. 45 Commando was now commanded by its rugged Second-in-Command, Nicol Gray, for its Colonel, Charles Ries, had been wounded on D-Day. Nicol gave out his orders in a field not far from Sallenelles, and I went along to see what task was to be given to my detachment, and to ensure that, so far as possible, they had everything they needed for the job.

While 45 Commando were clearing Franceville-Plage, John Pooley was to clear the Merville Battery. This had been captured by Otway's battalion on D-Day, but it was thought that one of the guns had been brought into action again and had been shelling the beaches. This may have been true, but it does not seem particularly likely.

Halfway through Nicol's orders the Germans began to mortar our group, which was rather large. At first he took no notice, but after a few salvoes he said lightly: "The Bad Men are getting more accurate" —to him the Germans were always the Bad Men—and we withdrew to a neighbouring ditch.

When the orders were done I had a few words with John Pooley before he set off. It was obvious that if there was a gun to be de-molished they would need some explosives; and as it seemed possible that the Brigade Engineer Troop might be able to produce some, I made my way to Brigade Headquarters to see what could be done. It was an unprofitable visit. No explosives were forthcoming.

The Commando was still in reserve, and so, leaving Donald Hopson in charge, I set off for Merville after Pooley to see how things were going. I wanted to get an idea of the country and the route to the battery. From the map it looked as if our detachment was going to be "out on a limb", and so it proved. Accompanied by Ned Moore, Sergeant Spears (the Medical Sergeant), Corporal Christopher and a wireless operator, I started out to follow in Pooley's footsteps. We made our way through Hauger and round the outskirts of Sallenelles, and eventually, after moving along a rough track hedged in by high trees, came rather unexpectedly on the rear of 4 Troop.

A message came through from Hopson to say that the enemy were attacking Ranville with tanks; nevertheless, I thought it best to see Pooley again before I returned.

No. 4 Troop, who had already had a few casualties, looked far from happy, and did not seem to know the exact position of 5 Troop, but not long after they appeared charging into the battery from the south-east. I went forward to join them. The place was surrounded with wire and a deep minefield; an anti-tank ditch covered it on one side, at least. We discovered a narrow path through the minefield, which had obviously been used by the garrison, and through this we threaded our way—not without misgivings. We had just got in when John Pooley ran past—a German stick grenade in his hand. I called to him and he described his assault. While 4 Troop gave cover-ing fire he had led 5 Troop, which he had formerly commanded, into the attack. Confronted by the minefield, he had led the men straight through it, a cold-blooded decision to take if ever there was one, but it had paid, for they got through with only three men wounded.

There were not many Germans in the battery, but those few were very resolute and held out for some time. John ran on to direct the mopping-up and the reorganisation. I signalled to 4 Troop to come up and join us; and when Brian Butler arrived I told him to push on to some houses, which could be seen on the far side of the battery, to clear them and consolidate there.

At this moment someone ran up and said: "Major Pooley's been killed, sir."

There had been a few shots, but all serious fighting had seemed to be at an end. However, in one of the heavily concreted gun positions one lone German with a Spandau had hung on, and when John was a few yards from him he had opened fire. I found Alan Pollock, a small dark young subaltern of 5 Troop, attacking this position on his own, a Gammon bomb in his hand. Angry and distressed, as we all were, at the death of John, he was exposing himself fearlessly. Getting up close to the gun, he hurled in his bomb. Still uncertain whether the defender was dead, some of us got on top of the grass-covered casemate and dropped Mills bombs down the air vent.

The two troops reassembled in a lane on the north-east side of the battery. The place was very enclosed, and I told Brian Butler, who was now in command, to send out a fighting patrol to reconnoitre the gardens to the east. There was no sign of 45 Commando, who were fighting some way off in Franceville-Plage, and it was obviously only a matter of time until 4 and 5 Troops, who had already had a number of casualties, were surrounded and overrun. So far from our own lines, it would be almost impossible to feed them or to replenish their ammunition. There was nothing more they could do to the battery. The best thing I could do was to get them out again, and so, leaving Brian Butler to consolidate, I set off to explain the situation to the Brigadier, whom I found at his Headquarters at Ecarde. He listened to what I had to say and at once agreed that the detachment must be withdrawn.

The two troops lost far more in the withdrawal than in the approach and the assault. The fighting patrol which went out under Lieutenant Williams ran into trouble, for he was knocked out and Corporal Underwood killed. Sergeant Port and a private were cut off, and though they hid for some hours were eventually captured. The rest of the patrol split up, and in making their way back to our lines yet another man was shot in the stomach and gravely wounded.

The Germans had now brought up two self-propelled guns, and, supported by these, they counter-attacked. Firing at short range, these guns caused many casualties, and before long the ditch by the road where the two troops were was full of wounded. The men of the medical section, as always, did a magnificent job, but most of the injured fell into the hands of the enemy.

Brian Butler decided to withdraw his force into the woods west of the battery, but on the way ran into a deep minefield, where many more men were wounded. Michael Woyevodsky had an extraordinary escape when the man in front of him trod on a mine. The canister full of steel balls hurtled past his head but failed to explode. To add to their difficulties the two troops were shelled and mortared as they went, and when at last they reached our lines neither mustered more than forty men. Gordon Pollard's section of 4 Troop, which went into action twenty-three strong, came out with eight men.

It was difficult, if not impossible, to dispel the idea that the whole operation had been useless and doomed to failure from the start. Hurried into the fight with only the sketchiest briefing, 5 Troop had done remarkably well in storming through the minefield, only to lose a loved and trusted leader in the moment of victory. If any of the guns were still in working order, which seems doubtful, they could not be destroyed without explosives, which were not forthcoming.

Not since Dieppe had the Commando met with such a misfortune. Nevertheless, it is not possible to make war without setbacks of this sort. One must merely be thankful if they don't come too often.

· · · · ·

Round about three o'clock, while I had been visiting the detachment at Merville, Hopson had received a report:

Tanks seen in numbers on ridge SOUTH of RANVILLE.

When stragglers were seen coming from that direction towards the Commando's position things began to look serious, and farther down the road Lord Lovat was posting the men of Brigade Headquarters in a defensive position round the houses at Ecarde.

No. 6 Troop astride the Sallenelles-Ranville road had a grandstand view of the German tanks and infantry advancing to the attack, though they were too far away to be engaged with small arms. Some 17-pounders, without an officer, put in an appearance; John Alderson stopped them and pointed out this target. They were quickly in action, scoring several hits. Reggie Wills's Jeep had a .55 Browning mounted on it and from its position, concealed under a glider, caused some consternation among the enemy infantry. It was not long before this particular attack collapsed and the Germans departed—less a couple of tanks. South of Ranville, which was still held by the Airlanding Brigade, four more tanks could be seen burning where the Airborne had broken up another enemy advance.

CHAPTER X

THE BATTLE FOR THE RIDGE

D + 1

IT WAS about eight o'clock in the evening when the Commando was ordered to move to Brigade Headquarters. Lord Lovat sent Donald Hopson to take over from Otway's battalion, and at about nine o'clock 4 and 5 Troops, now at about half strength, rejoined from Merville.

By ten o'clock that night we were in position at Amfreville. No. 1 Troop, under Clive Collins with a Vickers machine-gun, was posted to defend the château, while 4 and 5 Troops, exhausted by their action of the afternoon, rested in the garden. The position was covered by 6 Troop at a crossroads where roads branched off to Sallenelles and the Bas de Breville, whilst to their right 3 Troop were posted between them and 6 Commando.

During the evening I walked over to see Derek Mills-Roberts' and to ensure that there was no gap between us. I found him in an orchard where his front line was sited so that its precise position was practically impossible to locate and, therefore, to shell. His men, in pairs, were dug in at about fifteen-pace intervals. We both agreed that life would be altogether too complicated if there were pockets of enemy in our rear. In this country of thick hedges, banks and ditches a continuous line was to prove the best defence.

At midnight George Herbert took a patrol through the orchards along the Longuemare road, returning at four the next morning to report that there were no enemy to our immediate front.

Except for some desultory bombing and shelling the night passed quietly. Stand-to was at 4.30.

D + 2

Back in England I had tried to forecast in my mind the course that events were likely to take. It had always seemed to me that the enemy

¹No. 6 Commando.

commander, having seen the general pattern of our landings, would have his forces ready for a counter-stroke by the morning of D + 2. This was the day. From past experience it seemed that at first the Germans would come tapping along our line with their fighting patrols, looking for soft spots, and then when they thought they had found one they would make a thrust at it. Clearly the ridge which Lovat's Brigade held was an attractive objective: the Germans would like nothing better than to get their observation posts established on this high ground.

By this time I had in reserve only 4 and 5 Troops, with, as a last resort, Headquarters. The longer I could keep my reserve intact, despite the requests for its assistance, which were bound to come from the front line, the more likely we were to hold. The ball was in the Germans' court. It was now simply a matter of waiting.

Nothing much happened for more than five hours, and then at 9.45 we had a message from Brigade Headquarters warning us that a battalion attack was imminent. The enemy were forming up in the general area of Le Bas de Breville, exactly opposite my position. Half an hour later 6 Troop reported that enemy infantry were advancing astride the Longuemare road, and John Alderson, its commander, who had been forward to reconnoitre, asked for artillery support.

A Bombardment Officer, with H.M.S. *Hunter* at his disposition, had already joined 6 Troop. We now sent up a Vickers machine-gun, and also a sergeant to observe for the 3-inch mortar section, though we had not enough mortars to do much damage. Five minutes later one of our own field regiments was ranging on the area in front of 6 Troop's position.

The enemy did not come on very fast, and it was not until about eleven o'clock that they came within close range. The Germans, moving through the orchards and gardens on either side of the Longuemare road, arrived within eighty yards of our position and occupied two houses. No. 4 Commando on our left was also engaged. Since its losses during the landing 6 Troop was less than forty strong and it would not have been surprising had its commander asked for the support of one of the reserve troops. But, so far from demanding reinforcements from me, John Alderson was consulting his section commanders as to how best they could beat off this onset. So as to give the Germans a false idea of his strength, he decided to attack, hoping to catch them on the move in the open.

The plan was to advance in extended order on either side of the road, with 12 Section under George Herbert on the left, half of 11 Section under Sergeant Evans on the right and Troop Headquarters and the rest of 11 Section under Sergeant Leech moving up the road in the centre. They moved off through the farm of Monsieur Picard with Herbert's section leading, followed by Troop Headquarters and 11 Section. They had not deployed when someone shouted:

"There's the bastards. In that house"—indicating the house of the late widow Berton.

This may not have been a proper fire order, but it was quite effective; fire was returned and at the same time a couple of grenades exploded.

The Germans were on the move, and 6 Troop had an immediate success when they met enemy riflemen advancing along the road. They began to surrender almost as soon as our men opened fire.

A machine-gun in a downstairs room of Madame Berton's house opened fire on Herbert's section, wounding his batman. Sergeant Leech crept forward under cover of the low wall surrounding the house and lobbed a grenade into the window, knocking out the machine-gun crew. Beyond the house was a second gun. John Alderson threw a phosphorus smoke grenade amongst the Germans and in the confusion his Bren-gunner wiped them out with a burst.

Alderson's runner ordered Evans to take his section into the orchards to the right of the road and advance in open order. They doubled up the ditch past several cottages, and over a German with his intestines spread round him, who was still sufficiently alive to groan when any-one stumbled on him. Once in the orchard, they were immediately fired at from the next hedge. However, everyone was in good form and returned the fire, silencing the enemy, who could be seen running along the hedge to the road, where they fell into the hands of John Alderson and were disarmed. Everyone was enjoying the battle; rapid advances, short pauses to put down a withering fire, including that of the 2-inch mortar used pointblank with its base plate rested against a tree—probably just as dangerous to our own side as the enemy, but the effect on the Germans' morale made it worth the risk.

Meanwhile George Herbert, passing the wall of the Château de la Rue, led his men down a track, so as to get in rear of the enemy, when they came under fire from Madame Berton's house. The track turned to the right, veering towards the Longuemare road, where

Alderson was already engaged. Herbert's immediate opponents were in an orchard to his left, lining a ditch on the far side and keeping up a rapid fire through a gate. Further progress seemed impossible, but meanwhile Alderson had moved farther on down the road, dealing out severe punishment as he went. Fully a dozen Germans were killed actually in the road, but on Herbert's front the affair hung in the balance, and with an officer of lesser calibre than George the section might well have remained where it was, pinned down. But in that commanding way of his he yelled out:

"Come on, we'll go in!"

Armed with a Bren and flanked by Forsyth and another man, he charged through the gate, firing bursts from the hip at the enemy in the ditch ahead.

Evans meanwhile had led his men through the orchards and across two hedges, to find himself in a large field of grain, just ripening. The enemy were withdrawing in the direction of Gonneville, and Alderson now swung his line that way. It was at this instant that he was hit in the knee. Leech shouted to Herbert to tell him that he was now in command, and George called back:

"Carry on as you're going!"

Almost at once, while pausing to change magazines, George Herbert was himself shot by a German, who stood up and took deliberate aim at him. The bullet cut the ribbon of his Distinguished Conduct Medal. He fell forward on his face, killed instantly.

The enemy were now in full flight, but one, concealed behind a tree, shot Leech through the arm at about three yards range, and was immediately riddled by his Bren-gunner. Someone bound up the Sergeant's wound and he carried on. Soon after Alderson sent word that the troop was to withdraw.

In this attack Gimbert, now the T.S.M., did yeoman service, "whipping in" and gathering up the prisoners, who numbered not less than forty-five. They were from a company of the 346th Infantry Division, and although they were routed they were a very smart lot of men, many of them armed with Schmeissers and other automatics. They seemed bewildered at their defeat, particularly when they saw the small number of their assailants. Our men, moreover, had not, I regret to say, in every case shaved themselves and many had smeared mud or greasepaint on their faces by way of camouflage. No doubt to the well-appointed Teutons they looked a ruffianly crew.

The prisoners were herded into Monsieur Picard's farmyard and were then brought back to Commando Headquarters, where their arrival caused a considerable sensation. I hope that Brigade Headquarters were equally impressed when they received this bag shortly afterwards.

The Germans lost perhaps thirty killed, including an officer, and at least as many more wounded. There can't have been much left of that company after 6 Troop had done with it.

In this brisk affair our losses were one officer killed and one wounded, besides two sergeants and five privates wounded. If our losses were small it was because of the speed and dash with which the attack was delivered and the shining example of the two officers and of the senior N.C.O.s. The distance covered was small, but after the charge the men came back feeling terribly tired and having completely lost the excitement, which had acted as a spur when they first advanced.

I went to see John Alderson, who had a painful wound in the knee. He was deeply distressed at the loss of George Herbert, as we all were. I had known him all those long years and had first chosen him to be a corporal. Nobody in my old troop had given me more wholehearted support. He was one of the outstanding leaders in the Commando.

.   .   .   .   .

By midday 6 Troop had withdrawn and reorganised in its original position, where I went to visit them. Our line was intact. Going over the ground where they had charged one saw dead Germans on all sides.

Patrols from 1 Troop went out during the afternoon, but there were no longer any enemy in contact with our front.

George Herbert's body was brought in by Donald Hopson and some of 6 Troop, and at about 5.30 we buried him in the garden of Château Amfreville. Lord Lovat arrived to visit us just as the brief ceremony was about to begin and stood with us at his graveside.

D + 3

Stand-to was at 5.15. Again the morning was quiet for several hours until at nine o'clock H.M.S. *Ramillies* began to bombard the enemy in Gonneville.

During the day there were continuous attempts at infiltration; the enemy were trying to locate the brigade's front line. About 10 a.m.

45 Commando, having withdrawn successfully from Sallenelles, moved into defensive positions south and south-west of Amfreville, and, although the men were very tired, by midday they were well dug in. This completed the perimeter round the high ground from Hauger to Le Plein, although the Commando Brigade was still rather isolated from the Airborne troops holding the bridgehead at Ranville. It was still quite possible for the Germans to advance between 4 Commando and the sea and to turn our left flank.

At 10.30 the Bas de Breville, where the enemy had formed up for their assault on my position on D + 2, was heavily shelled, with some success, for civilians later reported that the Germans had pulled out, taking two lorry-loads of wounded. Franceville was bombarded by rocket ships.

About four o'clock in the afternoon Sergeant Leyland borrowed my Jeep and drove towards Breville—I think with no more warlike object than to buy bread. He arrived near the village and was told by the inhabitants that there were two hundred Germans in the area of the church. He came back faster than he went, and this information was quickly passed to Brigade Headquarters. Clearly the enemy were forming up for an assault on 6 Commando, an assault which, oddly enough, did not materialise until next day.

Things were quiet on my front, thanks to John Alderson's fight the previous day, but on both flanks the Germans were very active. No. 45 Commando was sniped while it was digging in and sent out numerous small patrols to clear the buildings and orchards in their neighbourhood. From the direction of Hauger there was also a lot of firing, and in the evening I sent Gordon Pollard with a patrol of 4 Troop to investigate a report that Germans had infiltrated through 4 Commando's lines, west of my Headquarters. Though the report proved false, our front from Hauger westwards along the main road to Sallenelles was being probed by snipers. Pollard met some of 6 Commando, who after suffering a number of casualties had been forced to retire from a house near Sallenelles.

Towards dusk, about 9.30 p.m., there were further reports of infiltration from the east, where it was thought that thirty or forty Germans had got into 4 Commando's area. I was ordered to send a troop to help in the defence of their Headquarters and detailed 4 Troop. In the failing light they marched down the track from Château Amfreville to Hauger and, to their surprise and indignation, were met on arrival by a sentry from a French troop, who challenged and fired all in the same breath! Nobody was hit and, although on the extreme left flank confused fighting, on a small scale, continued into the darkness, Brian Butler was not called upon to intervene. Pollard returned after the troop had left and so I kept his men near my H.Q. *Remained in defence positions supplemented by 6 Troop. Night very cold and miserable, and awfully tired,* he wrote, a laconic passage which probably describes the feelings of most of the subalterns of the four Commandos on the ridge that night.

With enemy mortars active in the Sallenelles area, we settled down to get what rest we could in readiness for any onslaught the morrow might bring.　.　　　.　　　.　　　.　　　.

From my own point of view the day had been a good one. John Durnford-Slater came to see me in the morning, his usual confident self, and, though much saddened by the loss of John Pooley and George Herbert, was delighted with 6 Troop's success and the way Westley and Ponsford with 3 Troop had stormed Le Plein on D-Day. I even had time for some office work—writing citations for some of those who had distinguished themselves.

The Longuemare road was really the only possible approach into 3 Commando's position, and, finding that so unprofitable, the Germans were now concentrating on the Commandos on either flank. We enjoyed a breathing space and on this day suffered no casualties.

Reinforcements, two officers and twenty-five other ranks, came up during the afternoon. By this time we had had 124 casualties, including nine officers, so these fresh men did not go far towards making up our losses. Commando Group managed to scrape up another four officers and forty-eight men for us later, but by that time we had lost a further four officers and fifty-eight men.

D + 4

D + 3 had been the calm before the storm. On D + 4 the Germans put in a three-pronged attack with at least two battalions in a determined effort to drive the Commando Brigade off the Amfreville ridge.

At about midnight a strong fighting patrol, Michael Woyevodsky, Alan Pollock and thirty men of 5 Troop, went down to Sallenelles to spy out the land, and returned at five in the morning to report that there were no Germans to be seen. On the other flank a fighting patrol from 45 Commando went into Breville and reported that the enemy were still there in force.

It was about eight o'clock when the enemy began to mortar 6 Commando's position, and this fire spread gradually along the whole line until it reached 4 Commando, who received a heavy concentration which caused many casualties. At 8.15 the Germans launched a strong attack against 6 Commando, but they appeared where they were most expected and lost a great number of men. At the same time they were probing strongly along the whole brigade front, and at 8.30 the Major who was now in command of 4 Commando was compelled to ask once again for support.

Back on the Ranville road Slinger Martin, our Administrative Officer, was running the gauntlet from the supply point, with the vehicles of the whole brigade loaded to the roof with ammunition of all sorts. Salvoes of four mortar bombs were landing on the crossroads at Ecarde as the 15-cwt. trucks and Jeeps pelted by, a 400-yard interval between each. When his turn came Slinger's Jeep was nearly caught by a salvo which pitched on the opposite side of the road. The blast blew him from one side of the Jeep to the other, blew off his beret, ripped his uniform and covered the Jeep and its crew in a cloud of acrid smoke. The spare tyre was torn to shreds; but with the whole Brigade Administrative Staff watching their progress with bated breath, all sixteen vehicles got through.

By about nine o'clock small groups of the enemy could be seen moving across our front, and half an hour later a self-propelled gun was firing from Breville Wood. No. 2 Troop, the heavy-weapons troop, was immediately ordered to engage this piece with its 3-inch mortars, and a little later I asked the Bombardment Officer to take on this new target. I went up to the Château de la Rue and, climbing up into the roof, could, with my field-glasses, make out this gun. By this time we were beginning to suffer a few casualties and 6 Troop's position was being shelled.

Donald Hopson visited 4 Commando at 10.15 to find out how things were shaping, and about a quarter of an hour later the enemy came on in force against them.

The strongest part of 3 Commando's front was 1 Troop's position in the garden wall of the Château de la Rue which completely dominated the Longuemare road. The loopholed wall was a formidable obstacle, not unlike the walls of Hougoumont at the Battle of Waterloo. Clive Collins had no less than eleven light machine-guns, including captured Spandaus, and a section of 2 Troop's Vickers. I felt confident that he could hold out. Owing to the hedges the German artillery officers did not have a clear view of the wall, and for that reason most of their shells burst in the treetops. Nevertheless by 10.20 1 Troop had already suffered four casualties. In support they had 6 Troop, on their right was 3 Troop, and in the farm of Monsieur Maizès on my extreme right flank was a French troop which had been put under my command. My reserve was still the eighty men of 4 and 5 Troops.

By about 11.30 the Germans, thrusting against 6 Commando, were exhausted and the survivors fell back into Breville. Some who had got round the right flank of the brigade were accounted for by 45 (RM) Commando.

But the enemy were still pressing into 4 Commando's position, and by 11.15 were round the left flank in some strength. The situation was undoubtedly serious and Derek Mills-Roberts had been ordered to send a troop to relieve them. Meanwhile our own position was still coming in for a good deal of shelling.

At midday Donald Hopson went again to visit 4 Commando and found that the acting C.O. had been hit. It was at this juncture that I was once more asked to send a troop to assist our neighbours. Instead I suggested that I should take over part of their front, releasing one of their own troops to act as a reserve, which I thought would be more satisfactory to both units. This was agreed, and at 12.15 Clive Collins with 1 Troop took over the whole of the east wall of the garden of the Château de la Rue, and I moved up 6 Troop, now under John Nixon, into the building itself so as to support them. From that day the place became known as Château Nixon.

About this time 2 Troop reported an attack, during which they captured one Pole and forced the enemy to withdraw. This was confirmed when a little after three o'clock John Nixon came to Headquarters and reported that the enemy infantry in front of Clive Collins had packed up, though there was still a good deal of shelling. Whilst I was visiting 3 Troop a random shell mortally wounded Private Hodgson, who did not live to wear the M.M. he had won on D-Day. Lance Sergeant Edmunds, who had been with me at Bova Marina, was also killed and the troop was down to a strength of forty.

I went with Corporal Christopher to visit 1 Troop and inspect their new dispositions. As I arrived there was a quick burst of shellfire. It was soon over, and, expecting a lull, I walked along the wall to talk to Clive Collins. The shelling broke out again and this time we were in the thick of it. Not far away was a slit-trench whose sole occupant appeared to be dead. I got in the trench beside him. He had a mortal wound in the back of his neck and was unconscious but still alive. It was hopeless to try and get him away until the shelling ceased. Christopher had trotted off and was taking cover under a tree. Nobody else was in sight.

Most of the shells were bursting in the trees, but suddenly one hit the wall to our right, and part of it came down with a crash. There was a scream. Running to the place, we found a heap of rubble filling one of the slit-trenches. Christopher and I started flinging the bricks aside. It seemed to take a long time before we came to its occupant. The lower part of the man's legs were completely covered and I wondered what sort of a mangled mess we were going to find. It was a relief to find that, though much battered and choking with dust, the poor man was more or less intact. We pulled him out; he was very light, so I hoisted him on to my shoulder and carried him to the cellar of the château. He was the only genuine case of shell-shock I can ever claim to have seen.

No. 1 Troop was now only thirty-three strong, and Clive Collins had asked that a few men from 6 Troop should help to man the wall for the time being. Entering the cellar, I called for volunteers. The first to step forward was Walsh, the old Irish Guardsman, a very cool man under fire.

A little later I was called to Brigade Headquarters and told that two self-propelled guns had arrived and were to be put under my command. It was now about six o'clock, and what with one thing and another I had come to the conclusion that the battle was over and won, at any rate for the time being. The Germans were clearly back on their start line. It was agreed that we should patrol towards Sallenelles and Longuemare.

Halfway to the former place was an isolated house, which was in front of 4 Commando's lines. Thinking this might still be occupied by the Germans, I decided to send 5 Troop to raid it. We left about 9 p.m. I put the self-propelled gun on the track running down from Hauger, where it was concealed by the trees; Michael Woyevodsky crept up the slope about a hundred yards to our left and rushed the place. Not a shot! They were in.

There was a brief lull, and then down the road from Sallenelles came a German holding a white flag. This man was brought to me, and when questioned said there were a lot of enemy wounded on the edge of the village. The man appeared to be a medical orderly. Perhaps he was telling the truth. All was quiet. I decided to chance it and, with 5 Troop leading, and the self-propelled gun moving along behind, we overran the German position at the end of Sallenelles. There was no resistance, and the bag was one officer and seventeen men—many, but not all, wounded. Several Schmeissers were among our trophies. Why the Germans should have abandoned these people I cannot say.

It was now getting dark, but there was still time to have a look at Sallenelles. It was uncannily quiet. We searched everywhere, but there was nobody to be seen. According to our prisoners the enemy had abandoned the place about 4 p.m.

We went down on to the beach. There was still no sign of the enemy. I turned to Christopher as a thought occurred to me: "I suppose I must be the left-hand man of the British Army at the moment."

"Let's hope Monty won't shout 'Right Form!'" said he.

When we reached the end of the little village we could make out a pillbox, about three hundred yards away down an open stretch of road. The garrison, about half a dozen of them, had obviously seen movement, and were standing looking our way. We manoeuvred the self-propelled gun into position and gave them a couple of rounds and the fright of their lives. They did not fire back, perhaps because there was nobody left to do so.

A little after 11 p.m. we were back at Commando Headquarters. A dispatch-rider had just arrived to say that for some technical reason the shells belonging to my self-propelled gun were liable to burst prematurely!

Our losses during the day were six killed and twenty-three wounded, including two officers, Arthur Wardle and Reggie Wills. All these casualties were, I think, from shell or mortar fire.

$D + 5$

We stood-to at 4.30. Although on this day the Germans made no serious attack on the ridge there was heavy shelling and mortaring all along the brigade front. At about 5.15 the Germans, supported by self-propelled guns, made a feeble attack on one of the troops of 45 Commando, but they did not press home. The initiative had definitely passed to us, and at six o'clock the 5th Battalion The Black Watch (51st Highland Division) went in to attack Breville but were held up south of the village.

Donald Hopson went out at 6.30 with one of our self-propelled guns to make a diversion in their favour, but as he passed the gate of Château Nixon the gun went over a Hawkins grenade and one of the tracks was damaged. Donald himself was injured, but he remained at duty. Indeed, within the hour he went out with the other gun, covered by a patrol of 6 Troop under John Nixon, and shelled Longuemare Farm.

During the day identifications were found proving that elements of the Reconnaissance Regiment of the 21st Panzer Division had taken part in the attack the previous day, as well as the two regiments of the 346th Division already identified. No. 6 Commando brought in two 80-millimetre mortars and a 20-millimetre gun.

Michael Woyevodsky went to guide a fighting patrol from 45 Commando, which was sent out at 7.30 to clear Sallenelles. After a house-to-house search they returned at midday with a few German wounded, who revealed that some others had been evacuated during the night. One prisoner belonged to the 744th Infantry Regiment: his company had been sent from Villers-sur-Mer to support the 857th Regiment's attack on 4 Commando the previous day. They reported that the pillboxes north-east of Sallenelles were still occupied by the enemy, despite our visit the evening before.

No. 5 Troop went into the line, relieving 3 Troop which I intended to use for patrol work. Between 7.15 and 7.30 the Germans began shelling, causing several casualties in 4 Troop, and by 9.30, when 5 Troop took over, 3 Troop's old position was a pretty fair shambles.

During the evening I went to visit the 4th Special Service Brigade on our left. On my return I was met by Donald Hopson, who told me that during my absence Headquarters had been heavily shelled and our Signals Officer and three others had been wounded. Brian Butler and five of his men had been killed.

D + 6

D + 6 was to be another day of intense activity along the whole brigade front.

Although our Headquarters had come in for a good deal of shelling, the château itself, masked by tall trees, had never been hit at all. Our hole in the ground was not particularly convenient, and so I decided to move the Command Post into the building. This was a great improvement, for I now had a proper office, with my maps and air photographs always ready displayed on a table, and my bed in one corner. It was not only more comfortable, it was more efficient.

The morning passed fairly quietly, but at about 1.30 p.m. a message came from Brigade Headquarters ordering that "a fighting patrol of approximately the strength of a weak troop" should go out to the woods east of La Grande Ferme du Buisson and patrol vigorously until 5 p.m. This patrol was intended to act as a flank guard for the battalion that was to attack Breville during the afternoon. I sent Keith Ponsford to carry out this task, and he left my Headquarters at 2 p.m.

Moving out through Hauger and passing the lines of 48 (R.M.) Commando, he reached a T junction about two hundred yards west of La Grande Ferme. Here Corporal Grant climbed a tree and observed a small German patrol of one officer and three men approaching, up the road from the farm. Unfortunately these men saw Grant and began to withdraw. No. 3 Troop dashed forward, opening fire as they went. Other Germans could be seen among the buildings and Ponsford decided to attack them. While the Brens fired from the ditches, the men worked their way forward down the track. The 2-inch mortar opened up, firing low angle. There was a donkey tethered in the verge and the first bomb caught it fair and square on the backside. Beside it stood a little girl, aged about six, weeping bitterly at the loss of her pet, but taking not the slightest notice of the bullets which flew to and fro past her head.

One of the Germans, armed with a Schmeisser, covered the retreat of the rest. He was hit and fell in the ditch. No. 3 Troop cleared the farm and, returning to the wounded man, who seemed hard hit, carried him into one of the buildings. Ponsford sent a man to ask the

Marines to send out stretcher-bearers and pushed on, but by the time they arrived the man had vanished. I remember giving Ponsford a considerable rocket for letting this prisoner give him the slip, an error which he was to redeem very soon.

.   .   .   .   .

No. 3 Troop's patrol was a very minor part of the plan to capture Breville, which had been the jumping-off point for a number of German attacks. At about 5.30 the Commanding Officer and a Squadron Leader of the 13th/18th Hussars arrived to reconnoitre. They were to support the attack by the 12th Parachute Battalion that was to go in that evening. Donald Hopson went with them to help them find suitable fire positions for their tanks.

On my right flank, around La Ferme Maizès, were 2 Troop, under Captain Bartholomew, and No. 1 French Troop. The Frenchmen had suffered heavily in the Ouistreham fighting, and I decided that it was time they had a rest. They withdrew to Château d'Amfreville between 6.30 and 7.30, being relieved by 4 Troop, now under Gordon Pollard.

Meanwhile I was summoned to Brigade Headquarters, where Lord Lovat told me that I was to send three officers and a hundred men on a fighting patrol, which was to go that night towards Gonneville and create a diversion during the attack on Breville.

This was such a large proportion of my remaining rifle strength that I asked whether a smaller party would not do. The Brigadier pointed out that in North Africa 6 Commando had had very good results with their big patrols working in the Goubellat Plain. After some discussion it was agreed that the force should consist of three officers and sixty other ranks, under my own command. Besides making a diversion we were ordered to capture some prisoners.

For this mission I took a carefully selected party. Nixon and Ponsford went with me, and Clive Collins remained to take charge of the Château Nixon position. When Ponsford, whose men had already done one good patrol that day, told his men that volunteers were required to go out again the same night, the whole troop wanted to go.

The various contingents assembled at Commando Headquarters. We left at 9.20. The first move was to secure La Grande Ferme du Buisson, which I thought might very well have been reoccupied by the enemy. This was not the case and so I re-formed the patrol for the next phase, the move across the broad fields that stretch as far as the

Gonneville-Breville road. By this time we could hear the artillery pounding away over on our right.

I left nobody in the farm, although looking back I think it might have been prudent to have left a party of twelve to twenty men there as a firm base, and to secure our withdrawal. We set off in file wading through cornfields, which would give us some cover if we came under fire. But nobody did fire—it was perhaps an unlikely approach—and we soon reached a hedgerow within a hundred yards of the main road at a point about four hundred yards south of Gonneville. We could hear voices not far away. Nixon and Ponsford joined me and I whispered my orders to them. Nixon was to go about two hundred yards farther north and create a diversion, while Ponsford with half of his troop was to push on to the road and take some prisoners. One section was to stay with me ready to give covering fire if required. The three parties were to make their way back independently.

"Is that quite clear?"

"Yes, sir."

"Then off you go!"

For a minute or two all was quiet; the men were spread out along the hedge, with a few paces interval between each, eyes straining into the night. It was pretty black, despite the gunfire to our right, and occasional bursts of tracer far away behind us, where the ships were firing at intruding planes.

Then a machine-gun about three hundred yards away to our left opened up with a burst. Nixon's party replied for about half a minute and then all was still again. The enemy were evidently alert. Not much chance of getting any prisoners now, I thought. My calculations did not account for the strain of the past week. Some of the Germans in front of us were so tired that they slept through all this! Not long after, one of Ponsford's party came crawling back and said they had got a prisoner.

. . . . .

To go back a few minutes, Keith Ponsford had been creeping towards the road, his men divided into two squads with an interval of thirty yards between them. Ponsford and Corporal Lawrence, a German by birth, were leading. They stole forward by short bounds, whenever the occasional bursts of shellfire drowned the noise of movement. When the firing broke out on our left they made a big bound forward, which brought them within about ten yards of the road.

For two minutes they lay still and listened, and heard the footsteps of several men walking down the road towards Breville. On this they moved right up to the hedgerow, making for a gap, but it was boarded up, and being unable to get through without a great deal of noise, Ponsford stopped and listened once again. About two yards away he heard the deep regular breathing of a sleeping man. Signalling to Lawrence, he whispered to him to wake the German and tell him to come with him.

"Tell him that if he makes a noise we will shoot him."

Before Lawrence could move they heard footsteps again, and three men, no doubt those they had heard earlier, went back along the road, passing within a few feet. When all was quiet again Lawrence crept up to the sleeper and woke him. He made a quick grab for his M.G. 34, but Lawrence seized him and Ponsford caught hold of the weapon —he had a nasty moment when the muzzle was jammed against his stomach! Sergeant Synnott and Corporal Barnes helped to lift the man bodily from his trench. Obergefreiter Josef Czarkorsky was a Pole. At first he began talking rather loudly, but he soon decided to give no trouble—hardly surprising, for he was now standing with his hands up and several automatics jammed against his ribs.

At this instant steps were heard on the road once more.

"If you make any noise you will be shot," Lawrence hissed in faultless German.

The man was silent. A soldier walked by a few paces from where Ponsford was standing, but he suspected nothing, and immediately all was quiet again. They breathed once more.

Barnes was sent back with the prisoner and the captured machine-gun; Synnott, scouting around, reported another slit-trench a little farther to the left. From this they winkled out two sleepy young German soldiers, Obergefreiter Julius Haag and Gefreiter Hermann Lehmann, who made more noise than the first, but were quickly silenced. Sending word to me of his success, Keith withdrew as arranged, reaching Headquarters at 2.30 a.m.

· · · · ·

John Nixon advanced towards Gonneville, and, drawing near to the village, heard the voices of German soldiers talking; he deployed his men into line and opened fire. Besides automatics and rifles he had two 2-inch mortars. The Germans put up flares and replied to the fire, somewhat to the alarm of Ponsford's party who were by now making for La Grande Ferme with bullets whistling all round them. When he had expended most of his ammunition Nixon fell back in the direction of the farm. He reached Château d'Amfreville at 3 a.m.

When I judged that Ponsford and Nixon had had plenty of time to get clear I shouted the order to fire rapid at the enemy in the hedgerow to our front. The Germans replied with a desultory fire, and after a few more bursts I thinned out my section and fell back to La Grande Ferme. As we passed through we found some old peasants sitting in the house, who rewarded us for our night's toil with a present of half a dozen eggs! I reached my office at about 3.20, to find that all patrols were back safe, without loss.

We had certainly created a diversion; but since the Germans in Gonneville were hardly likely to go in the middle of the night to the assistance of their comrades in Breville, that perhaps was not very useful. But at least we had a clear identification of the 6th Company of the 857th Regiment.

.   .   .   .   .

Back at Headquarters I learned that the attack on Breville had been successful but that during the preliminary bombardment Lord Lovat and Brigadier Kindersley of the 6th Airlanding Brigade had both been wounded. A message had arrived from Lovat saying:

I have become a casualty, but I can rely on you not to take one step back—you are making history.

During the attack Donald Hopson had gone forward with the tanks and placed them in an orchard where they could bring fire to bear on Breville and the wood nearby. Gordon Pollard and Corporal White had also distinguished themselves. Seeing that the attacking battalion was suffering heavy casualties, they had gone out and rescued a number of the wounded.

.   .   .   .   .

Derek Mills-Roberts had also been wounded, during the day, but he refused to be sent to hospital and remained to command the brigade. During the day the Commando had lost two killed and six wounded, but the battle for Amfreville was over.

.   .   .   .   .

CHAPTER XI

AMFREVILLE AND THE BOIS DE BAVENT

FROM this time on the nature of the fighting changed completely. The Germans delivered no more attacks, but dug in more than a thousand yards east of us beyond the Breville–Gonneville road. It became a war of sniping and patrolling. In 3 Commando we made it our object to see that the enemy was confined to his own lines. This meant constant patrolling, but nobody minded that and many of the men treated it as a pleasant diversion.

On the very first day of this new phase there was a curious episode when, during the afternoon of 13th June, Sergeant Synnott and twelve men of 3 Troop occupied La Grande Ferme du Buisson. In the evening a party of forty Germans appeared and the Sergeant decided to withdraw, but finding that four of his men were missing he and Corporal Grant went back to fetch them. At that moment some British Marauders flew over and bombed the area of the T junction—probably by mistake. The Germans took cover, and in the smoke and dust our men, who had been lying doggo, escaped. Synnott sent a runner to report, and Donald Hopson sallied forth with 3 Troop and the French Troop which was then attached to the Commando. As he approached the farm a young French girl came running from it and showed him where the Germans had placed their ambush. Donald deployed his two troops and fired everything he'd got before he went in.

The Germans did not wait for this assault, but departed in a hurry, abandoning a considerable amount of equipment.

. . . . .

On the 14th I had further proof that the enemy on our front was now disposed to be cautious, or perhaps were tired and confused, for I was able to reconnoitre the area of Longuemare Farm and the crossroads near the Bas de Breville without a shot being fired. Going down the road towards Gonneville, a sharp-eyed soldier told me he could see movement ahead. Supposing this to be some enemy outpost, I sent word to Nixon, who was not far off with a fighting patrol and began to work round the right flank of the enemy under cover of a ditch. Progress was difficult because it was overgrown with grass, nettles and brambles, but after a long stalk we eventually found ourselves about a hundred yards from two German soldiers, a standing patrol, lying on a low mound watching the road to Breville. I had about half a dozen men with me, and I was just drawing a bead on one of the enemy, when they caught sight of Nixon's party approaching. The two of them jumped up and bolted for cover, raising the alarm as they went. We fired a volley, but though Nixon's men thought they scored a hit, I think it highly unlikely. It was a maddening end to a tedious stalk, but from then onwards we regarded the Longuemare Farm area as part of our domain.

It was on 15th June that we inaugurated the sniping season. We had selected and trained snipers when we were in England. The men chosen were the best shots, but this, oddly enough, did not work at all, for we soon found many of the best marksmen had not the temperament for the lonely work of a sniper. Many of the men who enjoyed sniping were by no means remarkable shots, but they would creep up so close to the enemy that they could not miss! In fact in this game stalking is as important as shooting.

An enterprising character in 1 Troop, Trooper Fahy, made himself a camouflage suit from denim overalls, hessian strips and odd pieces of material that came to hand. Then nothing would do but he must go off and try his luck. He and Trooper Leedham, a cool, resolute Irish Guardsman, similarly attired, showed me their suits and persuaded me to let them loose. I sent them down to the Longuemare crossroads and they were back within half an hour, having shot two Germans. The enemy in the Bas de Breville opened up with a machine-gun, but there was plenty of cover by Dead Horse Corner.

The snipers had a very good day on 25th June, when T.S.M. Edwards of 3 Troop and Corporal Osborne, M.M., went out together from La Grande Ferme about 12.30. For about two hours they crept about in the hedges and orchards, but they were quite unable to find any Germans and returned to the farm, where, about three o'clock, they met a sergeant of 4 Commando and decided to try again. Leaving by the east gate, they made their way along the hedges to a bomb crater. While the other two watched, Osborne moved out into the cornfield and proceeded to shout and wave his arms as if he was leading a section of men forward. After two minutes he reported enemy movement and the other two spotted a group of Germans watching Osborne's antics from a gap in a hedge. They fired together. Two men fell. An enemy machine-gun opened up, but the snipers returned to our lines unscathed.

The sniping went very well; indeed, our bag gradually increased to quite respectable proportions, and that without loss to ourselves. In 3 Troop Corporal Hanson and Trooper Hawksworth were the star performers; with T.S.M. Edwards and Corporal Osborne, M.M., they once accounted for five Germans in one day. After this the enemy became so careful that it was hard to find targets.

Patrolling, though it ensured that No-man's-land was clear of Germans, produced only negative results at this period, which is not to belittle the work of the officers and men who spent long and often tense hours between the lines. But since the Germans, if they patrolled at all, did not move out far from their own trenches, it was not possible to ambush them or take prisoners.

I spent a long time studying the maps and air photographs to discover a good approach to the German lines. Eventually it occurred to me that the numerous bomb craters in the corner of the cornfield near Gonneville would give excellent cover for a raiding party.

Ponsford, now a captain, was given this rôle. He divided 3 Troop into four parties. Two squads, each fifteen strong, were to give covering fire, while two more of six each were to make the assault. The support squads had between them five Brens and two 2-inch mortars. Going out through 4 Commando's lines, they reached La Grande Ferme without mishap. At a quarter-past one[1] they moved out through the cornfield until they came to a pond which was their check-point. Not long after they found several deep slit-trenches, some in the wheatfield and some in the sides of bomb craters, clearly the German day positions. The support groups under a young lieutenant called Thompson, who had only joined that day, now took up position while Keith Ponsford got forward to the road. Calling up the other assault squad under T.S.M. Edwards, he sent them along the road to a suspected machine-gun position in a hedge junction.

A few minutes passed, and then, hearing a cough, Ponsford and Corporal Spencer, who was a German speaker, went to investigate. They found nobody, and so after cutting a telephone wire they re-

[1]26th June 1944.

joined the rest of the squad and moved down the road going north. On each side were very deep slit-trenches and dugouts with thick head cover. These they searched, but they appeared to be empty. After they had gone about twenty yards they heard a few bursts of automatic fire from the area where Edwards was operating.

As Ponsford went forward to support his Sergeant-Major, machine-guns opened up on all sides, firing wildly and very high. The covering party replied engaging the German posts on each flank, and firing over the heads of the assault squads. Suddenly a German ran out of his dugout, came up to Ponsford and asked what was going on. Corporal Spencer replied. I asked him afterwards what he had said.

"Nodding, but you komming mit me," was his answer.

The German, drowsy and unarmed, realised that he had picked the wrong side and made no resistance. Ponsford sent his runner to tell Edwards to withdraw immediately, but the man ran into four Germans, shot at one with his tommy-gun but was fired on by the other three and forced to return.

Meanwhile Keith had ordered Spencer to tell the prisoner to direct him to the German Headquarters, but in the din that was going on he was probably misunderstood. The prisoner seemed to be trying to lead the party deep into the German lines, and as it was getting light Ponsford decided to withdraw. Several Germans were seen scurrying around in obvious panic, but, not wishing to draw unnecessary attention to his party, he did not engage them. Reaching the Breville road, they dashed across in a body and reached the covering party in one bound.

Hearing that Edwards was not back, Ponsford decided to wait a short time. The Germans began an accurate shoot with two of their light mortars, and one bomb actually burst in the crater where Ponsford and some of his men were taking cover, but nobody was touched. After about ten minutes they began to withdraw, doubling through the cornfield. It was a long trek, and as he went Ponsford remembered that I had told him the day before that about thirty yards of standing corn would stop a bullet—a maxim I had invented after Dieppe. Anyway, whatever the exact number of yards required, Keith Ponsford now had a good chance to see if it was true, for bullets were clipping all round him. But in fact nobody was hit, although by the time they reached the farm it was almost broad daylight.

In this raid, although we got a prisoner, we lost six men. T.S.M.

Edwards and his party were surrounded and captured, although he and Bennett both escaped later on. It seemed a poor exchange, but a policy of "live and let live" is no good when you are fighting against the Germans. If you leave them in peace they will take advantage of it, and the next thing you know they are beating you up in your own quarters.

Reinforcements, five officers and forty other ranks, arrived on 26th June. One of them had the misfortune to be captured the very next morning. . . . . .

Around the middle of July the sector east of the Orne was invaded by hordes of armour belonging to VIII Corps, which had concentrated north of Caen. Thin-skinned vehicles belonging to the armoured divisions parked themselves in the village of Le Plein ready to replenish their tanks when the offensive began. A group of three-ton trucks, noses pointing southwards, parked under the hedge about fifty yards from the drive of the Château d'Amfreville. The drivers little realised that our front line was not a hundred yards to their east. In the field west of the château more tanks and vehicles were laagered. We were able to point out places which had never been shelled so far, so that their crews could make their final preparations in peace. Still, we expected that all this concentration would bring some comment from the enemy, and 1 gave orders for further work on the defences.

Gordon Pollard noted in his diary:

July 18. D + 42. Offensive begins at 05.45 by 2000 bomber attack. Great sight. Planes flew quite low straight over our farmhouse.[1] *Bombing followed by shelling and then a great tank advance.*

Went with C.O. in evening and saw 100-odd dispirited prisoners.

This was the beginning of Operation Goodwood. It was a beautiful sunny day and we had driven down to Ranville in my Jeep, where we saw these prisoners in the cage. They were more than dispirited; they were shaken to the core. Little wonder considering the bombing they had been through. I remember one blond young German soldier, in dishevelled field grey and with no helmet; still trembling involuntarily —he looked as if he had been buried—and begging for cigarettes from his guards.

Good progress was made by VIII Corps on this day and I remember seeing our armour drawn out in the open rolling cornfields east of

[1] La Ferme Maizès.

Colombelles. There was no attempt at concealment, merely dispersion; as far as the eye could see there were tanks and more tanks, seemingly irresistible. Meanwhile the 3rd Canadian Division was storming the Colombelles factories, from whose great chimney the Germans had always had a commanding view of the 6th Airborne's bridgehead.

During the evening the Luftwaffe, stung into life by the new offensive, produced a few bombers and bombed our village. Unfortunately one bomb hit a blast wall, which I had ordered 4 Troop to build in front of the cookhouse in their farmyard. We had four casualties, including a sergeant who fell through a hole in the floor. The next day it began to rain, and on the 20th it rained very hard. *D + 44. Raining hard and farmyard flooded. Very miserable,* sums up the day quite adequately.

For us this was just one of the minor "horrors of war", but for VIII Corps, slogging its way southwards, the thunderstorms which broke that afternoon "drenched the battlefield and turned the sticky soil of Caen plain into a quagmire. That night Montgomery ordered his armoured divisions to withdraw into reserve. Canadian infantry kept up the pressure, but Goodwood was over".[1] It was, of course, a very considerable success, but its interest now lies in the technique employed. The Germans, according to Chester Wilmot, "had discovered that in open country like the Caen-Falaise plain a defensive system which was less than five miles deep could be breached at one stroke by armoured divisions advancing behind a screen of bombs".[2] For my part the sight of those German prisoners in the cage at Ranville is one I shall not easily forget, so utterly shattered and broken were they. A British soldier, officer or redcap, I forget now, strolled over to a group of Germans huddled under the apple trees. It was time for them to go back on the next stage of their journey. They got to their feet and ranged themselves in a shambling line. Suddenly a German N.C.O. began to rap out orders in rapid succession. Though no more impressive to look at than any of the others, he had these sheep in his grip. In an instant they stood before us, transformed, straight ranks quivering at attention, alert for his next command: Prussian discipline, it seems, can survive even two thousand bombers. The question therefore becomes: How long does discipline take to reassert itself after a shaking like this? This is a question that any soldier may

---

[1] *Struggle for Europe,* p. 360–1.
[2] Ibid., p. 364.

ask in these days of nuclear warfare, days when any battalion commander may be invited to command a unit which has had an atom bomb for its breakfast.

A German, Captain Von Rosen, has given a valuable picture of the effect of this bombing on his company of Tiger tanks:

We were located in the very middle of this bombardment, which was like hell, and I am still astonished to have survived it. I was unconscious for a while after a bomb had exploded just in front of my tank, almost burying me alive. I could see that another tank, at a distance of about 30 metres, had received a direct hit, which set it on fire instantly. A third tank was turned upside down by the air pressure. The Tiger had a weight of 58 tons. . . . All tanks were completely covered with earth, and part of them had to be dug out. The engines were full of sand and the air-cooling systems were not functioning. . . . Fifteen men of the company were dead, two soldiers . . . committed suicide during the bombardment, another soldier had to be sent to a lunatic asylum for observation. The psychological shock of these terrible experiences remained with all of us for a long time. . . .

Take your choice: which will you have? Ground Zero over your battalion which is well dug in and has thermal screens, or an experience such as Von Rosen survived? Your guess is as good as mine, but perhaps we are too prone to say that nothing in the Second World War could equal the horrors that await us in the Third World War.

. . . . . .

Word came that the battalions in the Beach Groups were being disbanded to provide reinforcements for units in the line. The Commandos were to be allowed to take volunteers from them; and hearing that the 2nd Battalion of the Hertfordshire Regiment was one of those concerned, I arranged with our Brigade Staff Captain that as this was a Territorial battalion of my own regiment all the volunteers from that unit should come to me. I went to visit them on 23rd July and found them near Ver-sur-Mer, commanded by Lieutenant-Colonel "Chang" Harper, who had fought in China and commanded Chang-Tso-Lin's bodyguard in the early thirties. He would have let me have every man in the battalion, but I was bound to explain to the men precisely what they were letting themselves in for. Most of them would have joined us had I been prepared to promise that they would stay in their original platoons. This I could not do, for our organisation in troops and sections was quite different. Nevertheless, by insisting on taking only the true volunteers, I feel sure I got the pick of the bunch and they came at a time when every man was needed. Such are the strange chances of war that these men, who must have thought their chances of survival pretty slim, suffered only one fatal casualty in the operations that lay ahead of them in France, Holland and Germany, though a number were hit.

Our time at Amfreville was now drawing to a close. July had, on the whole, been a quiet month: we had lost no more than three killed and twelve wounded, which, considering that we were in the line all the time and that our patrols and snipers were actively day and night, was not unsatisfactory.

Towards the end of the month Derek Mills-Roberts told me that we were going to move to another part of the line. I was sorry to leave Amfreville, which is a pleasant village. I had grown fond of the people and I looked on my sector with an almost proprietary interest.

The inhabitants of Amfreville were eager to help us in every way. The aged Monsieur Bernichon of Hauger, who kept the maps of the Commune, traced them for me so that I was able to mark in every section post in the greatest detail. One day in June I called on this worthy and found him drawing maps—for me, I hoped. I asked him what he was working on.

"I am tracing the tracks where your tanks went last week during the attack on Breville, so that we can claim for compensation."

Nobody was more helpful than Monsieur Alderic Picard, a farmer who became Mayor after the war and still holds that office. A true Norman, rugged and practical, he organised a band of labourers who carried out the necessary but nauseous task of burying the animals slain in the fighting. Unhappily they were numerous. Men who took all too little trouble to avoid a bullet steered clear of Dead Horse Corner, until a hot summer and the maggots had done their work. But that was right over the other side of no-man's-land; Picard and his unarmed corps could not be allowed to go so far afield. A good many animals were wounded. Once a patrol of 6 Troop discovered a wounded calf and put it out of its misery. They then cut up the carcase, placed it on a stretcher—a piece of equipment not normally taken on patrol, which with truly remarkable foresight they had provided—covered it with a blanket and retraced their steps towards our lines. Re-entering the position, they encountered a group of half a dozen Frenchmen, who, seeing the laden bloodstained stretcher, stood aside and reverently took off their hats.

One night during my stay at the Château d'Amfreville I was awakened from a profound slumber and, turning over, I saw by the dim light of a single candle a Bosche soldier, steel helmet and all, standing at attention not a yard from my bed. Tactically my position seemed hopeless, but I was just groping for my pistol when I heard some of my imbecile followers roaring with laughter. This character was a German deserter, who had come in to give himself up.

"We thought you would wish to interrogate him yourself, sir."

Bah!

.   .   .   .   .

During the morning of 1st August 47 Royal Marine Commando took over from us at Amfreville and we moved to our new position between Le Mesnil crossroads and the Bois de Bavent. We relieved the 13th Parachute Battalion.

Our advent was welcomed with a hail of mortar bombs. The lines were so close together that one could actually hear the bombs slithering down the barrels of the enemy mortars—and take cover. Perhaps under the circumstances it was impossible to conceal the activities surrounding the changeover.

Stung by the mortaring which had greeted us, we resolved to avenge ourselves by tormenting the occupants of Hind's Farm. Woyevodsky was hit at 2.10 p.m.; at 6.30 Donald Gurnsey, the Intelligence Officer, and a Forward Observation Officer from the Royal Artillery went up to our front line to have a look at the farm. An hour later I had settled the details of the shoot with our gunner. Our own troops were warned to take cover in case of retaliation. This first shoot was not very effective owing to bad visibility, but we had plenty of time, and a second was laid on for two o'clock the next morning. This, I thought, would depress the Germans at a time of day when they were probably not feeling their best anyway.

Our first night in the new position was uneventful. The morning was fair and clear, but there was a ground mist, so that once more our shelling was unsuccessful. At 1.30 p.m. we gave the wretched farm another going over, for it was the only clearly visible target on our whole front and it was known to be garrisoned. For the rest, the German front line—or rather their outpost line—was a thick double hedgerow which gave them complete concealment. Nevertheless, from what our predecessors told us of their habits and by study of the air photographs we were able to work out fairly accurately where their actual positions were.

During the afternoon there was some more mortaring but no harm done, and at three o'clock a really successful shoot was carried out against the farm. Our gunners scored many direct hits, and from 5 Troop's forward posts we had a first-class view. The farm buildings began to fall apart before our eyes. Somewhere in the ruins a man was screaming. But the Germans stuck to their unhealthy post and within the hour one of 5 Troop was shot through the neck by a sniper operating from it.

In the evening a gunner officer called to offer us naval gunfire and we studied the map for suitable targets. The hamlet of Le Prieure just behind the German lines seemed likely to be the billets of their local reserves. All this gunfire bore fruit. Towards midnight three German deserters, expecting an attack, came into our lines somewhere to our right.

•   •   •   •   •

Our 3-inch mortar platoon, located in a secure position behind a brickworks south of the Breville-Troarn road, were very active during our stay in the Bois de Bavent. The Germans never shelled our area, but they continued to mortar it. On 6th August, a typical day, more than 120 bombs from 50- and 80-mm. mortars fell in our area, mostly in the front line. There was no pattern, they just fell at odd hours throughout the day in batches of from eight to seventeen bombs. It was our policy to give them good measure and send back at least two bombs for the price of one.

No. 4 Commando, on my right, disagreed with this policy, saying that when they fired their mortars it only brought down retaliation on their own heads. This being their belief, I asked them to lend their mortars to me, which they did, thus doubling the strength of my battery. With mortars it is the first salvo that counts; after that everyone goes into his foxhole or dugout and there are no more casualties. Therefore the more bombs you get off at the same moment the better, and so, however good at rapid fire your crews may be, eight guns are still better than four.

As soon as we arrived in our new positions, on the morning of 1st August, the soldiers began digging and straightening up the mess the previous occupants had left. The men dug hard for three days, and by the end of that time the position had begun to look respectable.

A feature of our new position was the numerous notices with which some keen unit among our predecessors had plastered the whole area. Everywhere they had been nailed to the trees, putting tracks out of bounds because shells or bombs had landed there at some time in the dim past. Since there was no discernible pattern to the enemy mortaring which went on quite indiscriminately throughout the whole area we immediately made a bonfire of the whole lot.

On 7th August we received a draft of reinforcements, two officers and twenty-six other ranks, including Sergeant Leech, M.M.

On 8th August John Nixon, who had located a German post, attempted to raid it, but left it until too late in the morning. The Germans were on the alert, and in the ensuing scuffle John was slightly wounded in the stomach and had to go to hospital. Donald Gurnsey now became O.C. 6 Troop.

Meanwhile, far away on the right flank of the Allied armies the Americans were on the move, and on 12th August we heard the news that Trooper Bennett of 3 Troop, one of the men captured in the raid on 27th June, had escaped and, taking advantage of the fluid state of the German front, had made his way right round the back of their army and into the gap punched by General Patton. Bennett, who had been with me at Dieppe and Agnone, was a tough gunner. He had been a lance-corporal, but I had seen fit to take away his stripe for some reason or another. It now appeared that besides being a stout-hearted man, he was also a resourceful one. Soon after his return he came to visit us. He came to my dugout and described his adventures to Barty and me. To make matters even, I promoted him to corporal and suggested that as the Bois de Bavent was not the healthiest place in the line he would be wise to go off on leave at once, which as an escaped prisoner he was entitled to do. This suggestion did not appeal to him at all.

"Can't I stay a night with the boys, sir?" said he.

.   .   .   .   .

A few nights later Sergeant Leech, Corporal Ryan and two men were on standing patrol when, presumably owing to too much movement on the part of the men they had relieved, they came in for a fairly prolonged bout of shellfire. One shell landed altogether too near and covered them with dirt and clods, whereupon Paddy Ryan was heard to call out:

"Jack! De buggers are t'rowin' bloody stones at us!"

.   .   .   .   .

The Germans in the Bois de Bavent were by no means as placid as our old neighbours in the Bas de Breville, and on 13th August, taking advantage of a misty morning, about half a dozen of them attacked I Troop's listening post and killed Corporal Robinson. Trooper Furber shot one with his Bren and the rest made off. The dead German was brought in; he was the section commander.

On the 16th we received the code word Paddle and knew that at long last we were going forward.

.   .   .   .   .

I was not sorry; the Bois de Bavent was an unpleasant part of the line and our stay in there had cost us one corporal killed, two officers and thirty-three other ranks wounded.

CHAPTER XII

THE ADVANCE TO THE SEINE

THE Germans are an economical race and, not wishing to waste artillery ammunition which they had dumped in their forward areas, they fired off as much as they could during their last three days west of the River Dives. The increase in the amount of shelling and mortaring was so remarkable that it made me suspect that they were about to depart.

On 16th August we heard that we would definitely be going forward next day, as the enemy was now in full retreat, and during the evening I held a troop-commanders' conference in my dugout to give them their orders. Our objective was Varaville.

In the early hours of 17th August we began to advance. No. 4 Commando was the vanguard and we followed them and 6 Commando as far as Bavent. There was no sign of the enemy. It felt great to be going forward again.

Leaving Barty with the main body of the Commando in Le Plein Wood, I went forward with 4 and 5 Troops to try and make contact with the enemy, moving through Petiville towards Varaville. Not until we reached La Rivière did we find any Germans. Then a machine-gun opened fire on Gordon Pollard and 4 Troop. They immediately began to work round its flank, but were fired on by a second gun. Reconnaissance revealed much flooding on either side of the enemy position and so I decided to put in a full-scale attack with artillery support. It seemed to me that the least costly method would be to assault at about 8 p.m. when the setting sun would be in the Germans' eyes; this I felt would affect their shooting. I was not certain whether the Brigadier, Derek Mills-Roberts, would accept the delay involved, and while Barty concentrated the main body at Petiville I went to Bavent to see the Brigadier. He agreed with my plan.

During the afternoon patrols moved out to examine the enemy defences in detail. Meanwhile I assembled the troop commanders to explain the plan which Barty and I had concocted. No. 191 Field

186

Regiment were to lay down an artillery barrage on the village and then the Commando would attack with two troops on the right and two on the left, and the remainder in reserve. This was the general outline, but while the conference was still in session our patrols returned to say that the enemy had pulled out. This entirely altered the aspect of affairs.

There had been one or two explosions in the distance and I was anxious to prevent, if possible, the demolition of the Dives bridge. Our Gunner had a carrier, which he offered to lend us, and, leaving Barty to bring on the main body with all speed, he and I, with six or eight soldiers, set off for Varaville.

When we reached the edge of the village I halted the carrier and, deploying the men, advanced through an orchard on the right of the road. There were many hedges—a good place for an ambush. We found a German platoon position which had been abandoned, well-sited slit-trenches with good head cover and walls revetted with boards. We were now about a hundred yards ahead of the carrier, and so I signalled to the driver to move up to where we were, meaning him to halt there. We were moving forward when there was a loud explosion behind us. I could not make out what had happened and thought for a moment that it must be a shell. Looking back, I found that the carrier, advancing too fast and too far, had run into a minefield in the road. We ran over to the vehicle and found that a track was broken and several men were wounded. Trooper Fennessey seemed quite badly injured in the head, but he made light of it. This incident brought our expedition to an abrupt conclusion.

Not long after the Commando arrived and took the village. One Polish soldier had stayed behind to give himself up, but the rest of the enemy had departed across the marshes to the east.

The village had been completely ruined by weeks of naval gunfire, but a racing stables on the edge of it was undamaged. Here the enemy had a strong position, with bunkers inside the stables themselves. Here I set up my Headquarters. There was a water-tower, which made a good observation post. All round Varaville the country had been flooded, and the mosquitoes were even worse than in the Bois de Bavent.

Le Pont de Vacaville, 18th August

Having taken Varaville, our next task was to secure a foothold on the high ground east of the River Dives. Whilst other units of the brigade attempted to find a suitable crossing-place we were to discover whether it would be possible to get across le Pont de Vacaville—the bridge which I had intended to reach in the carrier the previous day.

It was approached by a long road, running straight as an arrow along a causeway and flanked on either side by flooded meadows. Near the bridge were several houses and beyond rose the Heights, overlooking the whole area of our operations. It was an easy position for the enemy to defend with a small rearguard and it seemed unlikely that we would be able to capture the bridge—if it had not already been blown up—without heavy losses. To be precise, the map showed two bridges. The 6th Airborne Division had said that it was a matter of urgency to discover their condition, and I determined to send a patrol there the same night. It would obviously be a hazardous and exhausting task calling for a tough and experienced officer. The choice seemed to me to lie between Gordon Pollard and Keith Ponsford. Both were troop commanders whom I could ill afford to lose, but it was vital to know what we were up against. Gordon Pollard had commanded the advanced guard during the morning and so I decided to send Ponsford.

After a short rest he set out accompanied only by Sergeant Gray, who after being wounded on D + 1 had recently returned. Each was armed with a sub-machine gun and wore plimsolls; they provided themselves with light sticks which they held just in front of them to give warning of trip-wires. The night was still and black as pitch, and though they moved at a brisk pace the way to the bridge seemed endless. Every hundred yards or so they stopped to listen. For a long time there was no sound, but at length halting once more to listen they heard low voices and metallic noises a little way ahead. Very slowly he and Gray approached to within fifteen yards and found that there were German posts on either side of the road. At this point the road began to slope upwards, showing that they had reached the first bridge. The night was so black that they could not make out whether it was still there. Hoping to find a way round to a flank, the two men now withdrew for about a hundred yards, searching for a gap in the hedge. After a while they succeeded and at the same time discovered two insulated wires; these they took to be German signal lines, and so they broke them—which was just as well as will appear later.

Beyond the hedge the fields were flooded. Realising that he could move more quickly and quietly without his clothes, Keith stripped. This time he went unarmed and alone, feeling that his tommy-gun would be an encumbrance in the water and that two would make more noise than one. Telling Gray that he would be gone about an hour, he lowered himself into the water. Except for a few ditches which he had to swim he found that the floods were only about two feet deep, and he advanced by paddling himself along, with his hands on the bottom. There was a good deal of water-weed floating about and this built up as he went along, so that he had to pause periodically and move it carefully out of the way.

The Germans were on the alert and it was slow work getting down to the river bank without attracting their attention. He started crawling towards the bridge, wondering whether the white parts of his body were visible, feeling horribly vulnerable and wishing he had not parted with his clothes. He could hear the Germans chatting to one another in undertones and assumed that so far nothing had aroused their suspicions. But he still could not see the bridge, except for a faint outline. Approaching as close as he dared, he lay on the bank, half-submerged, for about half an hour, his eyes straining into the darkness trying to make sure whether the bridge was still there. It seemed that it was. . . . By this time he was becoming very cold, though that did not account for stinging pains which now attacked various parts of his body. All the time he was hoping that the visibility would improve, but in vain. Eventually he withdrew stealthily by the way he had come; somewhat to his surprise he succeeded in reaching the hedge—long overdue—at the very place where he had left it. Gray had given him up for lost and had made his way back to our lines. As he pulled on his clothes Ponsford discovered the cause of the stinging—he was covered with leeches!

Nobody could have carried out his task more thoroughly, yet as ill-luck would have it we were still not absolutely certain of the state of the bridges owing to the uncommon blackness of the night. I decided, therefore, that despite the lack of cover the only way to solve the problem was to send out a fighting patrol in daylight.

On the Friday afternoon Lieutenant Thompson set out with twelve men of 3 Troop, while the rest of the troop stood by ready to go out and support them if necessary. Ponsford, exhausted by his adventures of the night before, was still sound asleep when they left. When he awoke, feeling that Thompson ought to have the benefit of the information he had gathered, he followed him with the other section of the troop.

Meanwhile Thompson had arrived at a building standing about four hundred yards from the bridges, at a place where the Germans had cratered the road. Here he was fired on from the bridge while an enemy standing patrol at the farm fell back. Almost at once a doodle-bug tank[1] moved into the road and started coming towards the patrol. This caused considerable consternation! We had never met one of these things before, although we had heard of them; moreover, the men had no anti-tank weapon with them. Nevertheless they engaged it with small-arms fire, and to their great surprise, not to say relief, it came to a halt and started spinning round in the middle of the road! The wire controlling it had been severed so that it refused to function. Two more were spotted not far away, but as they did not move it seems likely that Ponsford had cut the wires controlling them during his patrol the night before.

Ponsford now caught up the patrol and, leaving Thompson at the crater to give covering fire, took 5 Section across the fields to the right of the road near the bank of the Dives, hoping to get a better view of the Pont de Vacaville and the other bridge beyond. They crossed the open field under fire but reached the cover of a house before anybody got hit. They searched the building, before taking a look at the river bridge which, as we had concluded from the previous reconnaissance, was still in one piece. But was the other bridge still intact? The only hope was to take the first bridge and send a party over to have a look at the second—a desperate enough decision to take, for it meant crossing a flat field totally devoid of cover.

The Brens opened up and the 2-inch mortar laid a smokescreen which was very effective. Then Ponsford made his assault. As the troop charged in the near bridge went up! The air was filled with smoke and debris. In the confusion 3 Troop kept up a continuous fire, the Bren and rifle groups moved alternately and they dashed in and occupied the abandoned German weapon pits on either side of the road. Peering over the ruined balustrade Ponsford could see a group

[1] A form of remote-controlled tracked vehicle bearing a high-explosive charge.

of the enemy standing in the middle of the road. He called up a Bren-gunner, and while the latter fired, resting his weapon on the shoulder of his No. 2, Ponsford gave them a burst from a captured Schmeisser which he had adopted as his personal weapon. They then flung a Mills grenade into the group for good measure.

There was enough debris in the water to make stepping-stones, and Ponsford now called forward Sergeant Osborne, M.M.

"Take four men, get across and have a look at the bridge beyond. We'll give you covering fire."

Osborne and his men dashed down the bank unscathed, crossed the ruins in the water and scrambled up the opposite bank. A shot rang out and Melville, a Scots Guardsman, who had already been wounded on D + 4, was hit. To avoid further casualties Ponsford shouted to Osborne to bring his men back, which he managed to do. Melville, who was badly injured, died soon afterwards.

Next Ponsford ordered Thompson to move forward from his fire position. By this time the Germans had begun to mortar his position quite heavily and a 20-mm. Flak gun about two hundred yards farther up the road had opened fire, wounding Hawkesworth, the sniper, and another man.

Nevertheless Ponsford decided to have one more try. This time he sent Thompson and three men across, but they came under fire from a Spandau firing from the cover of a house and got separated. Thompson dashed back to report this development.

No. 3 Troop had quickly passed back the information they had gathered, and as soon as I heard that the first bridge had been blown I sent Colin Rae, the Intelligence Officer, to order them to withdraw. It was obvious that this might be difficult. I sent the Forward Observation Officer to help them with smoke, and Sergeant Agnew to thicken up the screen with our own 3-inch mortars. Barty went along to co-ordinate the proceedings.

The range was too great for our mortars and at first the 25-pounder smoke fell six hundred yards short. This was soon put right. Gradually the smoke blotted out the whole area of the bridges, but Ponsford sent word to Barty that he still had men across the river. The latter, however, quite rightly ordered him to withdraw immediately, and Ponsford, feeling that his men had a reasonable chance of getting back under cover of the smoke, reluctantly fell back. The men, Corporal Norris among them, made their way a little upstream, where one of them swam across. They then stripped their Bren into its five main parts and threw each across in turn. This done, the others followed; one, as it chanced, was a non-swimmer, but they dragged him across somehow and escaped unscathed. The rest of the troop also withdrew without further loss.

During the night that followed this brisk skirmish the German coast defence guns on the Heights between Houlgate and Angoville shelled us in Varaville. Ponsford was sleeping the sleep of the just in his bunker—German make—which sustained a direct hit. In the morning he was dug out by his batman, none the worse for wear. A hard man to kill.

The Heights of Angoville

Or in the night, imagining some fear,
How easy doth a bush become a bear.

I expected orders to move on Saturday morning, but nothing happened, and the pause gave us time to clean up and reorganise a bit; weapons were tested. It was evening before any orders arrived. We were to move by motor transport to Briqueville. I went ahead in my Jeep leaving Barty to bring up the unit. I found the Brigadier at his Headquarters and, rather to my surprise, was told that we were to advance that very night. This was awkward because I had not brought the troop commanders with me. It was dark before they arrived, and indeed it was not until half-past ten that the unit arrived at Le Plein Gruchet, having marched three miles from Briqueville.

During the afternoon Derek had received orders from General Gale to seize the Heights of Angoville, which were well behind the German lines and dominated the area west of the Dives. No. 4 Special Service Brigade was to attack the small town of Dozulé at the same time. It was essential that the Heights should be in our hands by dawn.

The enemy position seemed to be one of considerable strength. The country was open, absolutely flat and intersected by numerous ditches as well as the River Dives; the whole area was overlooked by a range of hills, the Heights. The Germans had been in position there for more than two months.

The Brigadier had little alternative but to attack by night. He determined to send 4 Commando to the south of the Dozulé road to a place called L'Epine and to advance with the rest of the Brigade against the Heights themselves. I was to lead with 3 Commando and was to take the village of Angoville itself. The route was left to me. Derek had provided a few hundred yards of white tape to mark any difficult places in case anyone should go astray in the dark.

A study of the map showed a railway line leading in the right direction which joined another running north towards Cabourg. The railway was far less likely to be watched by the enemy than the Troarn–Dozulé road which ran parallel with it. It would be hard going in the dark, but there was little likelihood of anyone getting lost. Nearer the Heights a footpath was marked going off in the direction of Angoville; it went to a place where a church was marked on the map and near that point we would have to cross a fairly wide tributary of the Dives. The map showed a bridge, but it was unlikely to be still standing and was in any case bound to be watched. After the bridge our route would take us across the fields, but we should be able to see the Heights looming up on our left hand.

It was obvious that the longer we argued the shorter time we would have to brief our unfortunate followers. Luckily the Brigadier and Nicol Gray, the commander of 45 (R.M.) Commando, agreed to the route I suggested, and after some argument Bill Coade of 6 Commando, who at first favoured some other approach, fell in with our views.

There was no chance of a proper look at the ground. I gave out my orders in a dimly lit room in a shack beside the railway and then the troop commanders had to brief their officers and N.C.O.s. The men did not receive the precise information that they could have had if there had been more time and better facilities.

Gordon Pollard wrote in his diary: *C.O.'s Order Group. Horrible scheme to advance to Angoville 250745. Crossing R. Dives and establishing salient into enemy lines. 4 Brigade are to take Dozulé. Not a pleasant prospect. Endeavoured to instil confidence and cheerfulness into the Section Commanders and through them into the Troop. They did extremely well.*

It certainly did not seem a particularly promising expedition, but the plan was a simple one. As long as the troops kept well closed up there was a good chance that we should at least find the objective, although it meant marching about five miles and crossing two small rivers. The order of march was to be 6 Troop, 5, 4, H.Q., 3, 1.

We moved off at 1 p.m. on 20th August. No. 4 Commando started twenty minutes earlier but soon branched off from the railway, leaving us in the van. No. 6 Troop, with Colin Rae acting as navigator, was leading. I went with them, escorted by Corporal Christopher, Trooper Turnock and a signaller with a wireless set, so that I could keep in touch with Barty who was leading the main body of my Headquarters. It was so dark that one could scarcely see the next man ahead, and certainly not the one in front of him. We crossed the River Dives on some sort of duckboard bridge, which had been put there, I think, by the Canadian Parachute Battalion. Once across we were in No-man's-land.

Crunching along on the cinders of the railway track we seemed to make an appalling noise, but the Germans were still far away. They were on the alert though. A gun somewhere up on the Heights was dropping shells on the road to our right. It was only harassing fire, but still I was thankful that we had chosen to use the railway.

After a time we came to a bend in the railway line; the path to the church should branch off soon after this. There was a pause while we checked up that we were really on the right track; Colin Rae was absolutely certain, and after a few minutes we pushed on. The men were still keeping well closed up. Now we had to advance with re-doubled care, not only because we were nearing the enemy, but for fear of missing the track to the church. After a while we came to a hedge leading off to the right; there was a footpath sure enough, but it was on the wrong side. Under the cover of a gas-cape we took another look at the map. This *must* be the place. Not without doubts we set off up the path laying a trail of white tape to show the route to the rest of the brigade. In the Stygian blackness it hardly showed.

The German guns had fallen quiet now and once we left the railway the sounds of the night were no longer drowned by our own footsteps. The brigade stumbling along the track behind us made enough noise to wake the dead. Surely if the Germans knew their stuff it would be only a matter of minutes before our leading section ran into their outposts. They could hardly fail to have a standing patrol on the footpath. No. 6 Troop kept steadily on, eyes straining into the dark, fingers on triggers, and when at last we reached the church—which turned out to be a farm—we were still undiscovered. Still it was nervous work and, as previously arranged, I now sent Alan Pollock forward to lead with 5 Troop, leaving 6 Troop to follow behind the rest of the Commando. For Colin Rae there was no relief.

The next thing was to find the bridge; this should be about one hundred yards north-west of the farm if it had not been blown up. It was still there. We began to cross; on the far side was a gateway leading into a field to the right of the road.

Surely the place must be guarded. One field away I could hear the tramp of many boots as the Commando came up the lane. Still no challenge came, no burst of tracer, no flares. No. 5 Troop crossed the bridge and pushed on across the field. We had run out of tape now and it was difficult keeping the men closed up. We could just make out the Heights not far to our left.

We were still pretty much in the open and it was beginning to get light. I was with 5 Troop when the column got broken. Somebody had failed to keep up. Luckily Gordon Pollard realised what had happened. He moved up to the head and managed to keep the brigade going in the right direction.

No. 5 Troop crossed an orchard, moving uphill now, crossed a fence and came to a rough country road. I had not gone far along it when a shot rang out, followed by a scream, and then another shot.

My first thought was that a German sentry had killed one of the men at the head of the column. It was a bad moment—too much for the nerves of some of those in front; they came galloping back down the road making a noise like a runaway cart-horse and nearly ran me over! I cursed them heartily and they had the grace to stop.

There were buildings ahead on both sides of the road and I directed 4 Troop, which had now come up, to search them. It was La Ferme du Manoir d'Angoville.

Alan Pollock, the commander of 5 Troop, had pushed on up the hill. When he reached the gate of the farm a sleepy German sentry had wandered out of the gate and Pollock had shot him. It was his scream that had for a moment so dismayed a few of the men. Alan himself had pushed on up the road with most of his troop and met a horsedrawn convoy of three 20-mm. guns coming down. In the dim morning light Troopers Saunders and Shillinglaw played havoc with their Brens and few of the crews escaped. The three guns were ours.

Meanwhile Gordon Pollard was clearing the buildings. Sergeant McDonald's squad entered a farm building and Pollard followed. Hearing someone moving about in the straw, and thinking it was the farm people, he ordered them out. Six frightened Germans emerged with their hands up. He handed them over to Leyland, now his Sergeant-Major, and went forward to reconnoitre the top of the orchard farther up the hill. Meanwhile there was much firing from near the road where Sergeant McDonald was clearing the farm buildings. They found half a dozen more Germans asleep in a house—by the simple expedient of striking matches over their faces. Coming out of the door they were fired on by the Marine Commando, who had just come on the scene, and did not realise that the Germans were prisoners. One of 4 Troop was killed, one wounded and in the confusion four of the captured men escaped.

By this time it was light enough to get the hang of the area. To our left was a feature, which we christened the Pimple (Point 72). If the enemy got it life would be very uncomfortable indeed, so I sent 6 Troop to hold it. Nos. 4 and 5 Troops, one either side of the road, were digging in just north of the farm.

Derek Mills-Roberts arrived and decided to send 6 Commando through us to get on to the high ground in front, although it was really beyond Angoville, the objective laid down by General Gale. It was obvious that if we let the Germans have it we would be in an impossible position. As a result of our night march we were now cut off from Division and it was up to the Brigadier as the man on the spot to decide how best to hold the position.

Derek discussed this point with me, and then, as the hill above us was a very long feature, he told me to detail a troop to hold the western end, La Ferme du Bassebourg. I was only too glad to do so, for it was vital to the security of our own position. Clive Collins moved up there with 1 Troop.

I established my Command Post in a deep ditch whose banks were covered with bushes. This I shared with the Brigadier and a good many German prisoners as well.

It had been an exhausting night, and after being awake for most of the previous twenty-four hours I felt pretty tired. It was still rather misty and I actually ordered Gordon Pollard to send a squad to occupy some houses that didn't exist. This may sound odd, but I saw them quite clearly at the time.

Not long after the Germans began mortaring and shelling the farm area; a self-propelled gun had appeared down in the valley to the east and had begun to bombard the Pimple. I sent Ponsford and his troop to deal with this menace, but they searched for it in vain.

Word came from 6 Troop that they were being shot up from two sides, and I walked over to see Donald Gurnsey and find out how things were. There was a fair amount of cover and I arrived without incident, to find that Trooper Warren had been killed and Sergeant Leech and another man wounded. While the self-propelled gun fired at them from the direction of Dozulé, riflemen were sniping them from the area of Le Quesnay. This did not alter the fact that the Pimple was vital to us. I impressed this on Gurnsey, who had his men in a reasonable position on the reverse slope. He told me that on arrival they had found a German section in position, but one of the soldiers had charged them, firing his Bren from the hip, and they had made off. This enemy position overlooked the bridge we had all crossed the night before at a range of 150 yards. Presumably the Germans had all been asleep—which was just as well for us. Taking Leech with me, I returned to my Command Post.

Meanwhile 1 Troop had moved up the hill to La Ferme du Basse-bourg, passing through 6 Commando, who had reached the summit and were in action. As they went by they heard a wireless operator reporting that the situation was obscure! Collins put one section into the farm buildings, while the other occupied the highest part of the hill, a splendid vantage point. Troop Headquarters was in the farm-house, lying between the two. They had not been in position long before they came under heavy artillery fire, but most of the shells went over the hill and burst beyond, in country still occupied by the enemy!

During a lull a Volkswagen drove into the position. It is an open question whether 1 Troop or the Germans were the more surprised. There was some pretty wild shooting, in which Trooper Furber—much to his indignation—was shot in the lobe of the ear by his own side and the three Germans escaped by diving down the steep wooded hillside, taking the ignition key with them! No. 1 Troop's sentries must have been badly posted or dozy, and I was extremely annoyed at their letting these people slip through their fingers. Later a German patrol came up the hillside, but when fired on took to flight, leaving a rifle behind them. Two Germans appeared to have been hit.

The rest of the day was reasonably quiet apart from occasional shelling. It was warm, but when night came I took up my quarters in a small outhouse of La Ferme du Manoir d'Angoville. We had no blankets and no rations; in fact, none of us had had a meal for at least twenty-four hours, and it looked as if we were in for a miserable night. Though it was possible to reach Le Plein Gruchet on foot, no vehicles had managed to get through as yet.

We had, moreover, a number of wounded to be evacuated. But there was no road open between us and the Bavent area, and it was obviously impossible for our transport to reach us that night.

Dusk was falling, and I was thinking of turning in when artillery fire broke out; this time it was our own guns. Shells were bursting in the valley between us and 4 Commando. There was some mortaring as well—probably enemy. Suddenly I heard the roar of engines. Jeeps were coming up the hill flat out. I could hear R.S.M. Allen directing vehicles into the farmyard; then Ned Moore and Slinger Martin talking as they came towards my outhouse.

"Slinger! Have you brought my rations?"

"I have, sir!"

"How the hell did you do it?"

He told me how the jeeps of the whole brigade had quietly concentrated in 4 Commando's lines and then in the gathering dusk had dashed across the valley, their movement covered by a smokescreen and the noise of it drowned by the clatter of 4 Commando's Vickers guns. It was a well-laid plot and our jeeps had all got through.

Corporal Christopher brought us mugs of tea and a tin of stew—undoubtedly the "best meal of all time"—and I told Slinger that I was concerned to get our casualties away. Each jeep had been fitted with stretcher-frames and there was room for all the wounded. By 2 a.m. they had been loaded into the jeeps, the cooking gear had been packed up and Slinger was on his way again.

I emerged next morning from my outhouse after a good night's rest to find a knot of soldiers gathered about a pair of German prisoners. I might not have slept so well had I known that these two, fully armed, were lying low in the loft across the yard, waiting for their chance to make a break!

There were still enemy outposts to the west of us, and at ten o'clock Barty took out 4 and 5 Troops to mop them up. Sergeant King, M.M., captured two Germans, and a little later five more surrendered to 5 Troop. I set them to work to clean up Le Quesnay farm and its outbuildings, and that afternoon, when they had made a tolerable job of it, moved my Headquarters there. The man who was set to dig the latrines was a bit dubious about it. He seemed to have the idea that he was digging his own grave.

A comfortable evening was spent there resting and drying out and a grateful government saw its way to allowing each of its servants a minute tot of rum to make up for the two wet and sleepless nights they had just passed.

Next day, the 22nd, we moved eastwards and spent most of the day waiting in an orchard. About 8 p.m. it looked as though we were going to spend the night there and so I put the whole Commando under cover in a farm some way from the road. It had been a fine day and the other units thought this was entirely unnecessary. We spent the night in comfort. About two o'clock in the morning it rained heavily, and when we next saw the rest of the brigade they were standing around in the sodden fields, blue with cold and green with envy.

That day we moved by transport to Drubes and occupied a big farm at Vasse. In the evening orders were issued for an operation which involved crossing a river of uncertain depth, advancing across a marsh on to some high ground, crossing the line of advance of the 4th Special Service Brigade and descending upon Pont L'Evêque from the rear. All this in the dark and at extremely short notice. Fortunately for all concerned this stunt was cancelled at the last moment and we had a night's sleep instead.

Next morning I inspected the turnout, weapons and boots of three troops. Soon after, the order came to advance. We went down through Pont L'Evêque, which was pretty much shattered, crossed the river on the surviving girders of the bridge and went into a new concentration area at Le Bas de Surville. Here we received orders for a further advance.

While we were waiting to move forward 1 Troop produced a German. He was an unpleasant-looking creature, who claimed that he was a non-Nazi and had therefore decided to desert. I was interrogating him through one of our German speakers. He was remarkably glib in his answers; watching his eyes, I realised that he was paying careful attention to everything I said to the interpreter.

"You speak English?"

"A little."

He was a well-educated man who had been to a university; as it turned out he understood English very well indeed.

We discovered that he belonged to a Regimental Headquarters which had fallen back beyond the line of the next river. It seemed likely, therefore, that our objectives for the night's march were short of the new German positions. We hurried this individual off to Brigade Headquarters, with the information extracted from him.

Occasionally before an operation one gets the feeling that all will be well; that nothing can go wrong; that the enemy for the time being has "had it". It is certainly a notion to be regarded with the gravest suspicion. I had it twice in Normandy. The first time was when 5 Troop patrolled Sallenelles on D + 4, the second was before the advance to Quetteville. I cannot account for this, I merely state the case, but in neither case did this sixth sense, or whatever it may have been, play me false.

On this occasion 6 and 45 Commandos went on ahead and passed through the 5th Parachute Brigade, who had been held up at a demolished railway bridge, to clear either side of the main road to Quetteville. No. 3 Commando, followed by Brigade Headquarters and 4 Commando, were to make a wide move round the left flank.

Our troops had suffered quite a lot of casualties from mortaring, and as we moved forward in the evening the road we were following came under fairly heavy mortar fire. As quickly as possible I got the men off the road and made them double forward through the fields and we got through without losing a man.

About 8.30 we moved off, with Colin Rae navigating as he had for our advance to Angoville. Our route lay across fields, up steep banks, through woods, up hill and down dale. In front marched a group of men armed with stens, who had orders to open up and charge if we met any opposition. Other men, like the pioneers of old, were detailed to hack down any fence we might come to so that the column should not be delayed. On either flank moved officers and sergeants, eternally hissing "Close up! Close up!" to their weary men. It was exhausting work, and at one brief halt I actually went to sleep on my feet.

"They've gone on, Colonel," said Christopher, who was next to me. For a moment I did not believe him, and then, shaking myself, ran on to catch up.

As dawn was breaking we began to near Quetteville. We fanned out and began to go forward in extended order, and still moving as quietly as possible. Glancing around, to my horror I saw someone fling a rifle through the next hedge behind me. I was so indignant that I bellowed, "Care of arms!" at the top of my voice.

Brigadier Mills-Roberts stepped through the gap.

"As you were."

He explained afterwards that it was only a German rifle that he had picked up.

Not long after we reached our objective. The birds had flown.

. . . . .

That day we rested, but about 10 p.m. there was a flap. It seemed that Division wished us to move round Beuzeville to Boulleville, cut the roads and capture a substantial proportion of the Wehrmacht. This plan was regarded unfavourably by the Commando Brigade, which was not so much weary as sceptical. As a compromise one troop from each Commando sallied forth—3 Troop represented us—and reached Boulleville at 6 a.m. on 26th August. The Germans had departed at 4 a.m. They were now back over the Seine and so that was the end of Operation Paddle. It had cost us four killed, one missing, and eleven wounded.

We moved into billets at Boulleville where we had our first real rest after eighty-five days in the line. Glorious weather, a lovely country-side of shady orchards and lanes, it was all one could wish. I slept soundly in a room that a week ago had been the quarters of a German officer.

John Durnford-Slater, Derek Mills-Roberts and Philip Dunne came over to supper on the 27th, and Barty, no mean forager, feasted us nobly. Next day we went down to watch the Maquis parading through the town, the former collaborators in their midst. In front came the resistance fighters, the first few ranks fairly well armed. In the rear, looking distinctly self-conscious, marched a couple of ranks of uniformed police. We were told afterwards that the women collabor-ators were forced to kneel down while they had their heads shorn.

"C'est moyenageux," as a French friend remarked to me, but having avoided invasion ourselves it is hard to judge.

A few days later the Commando returned to England.

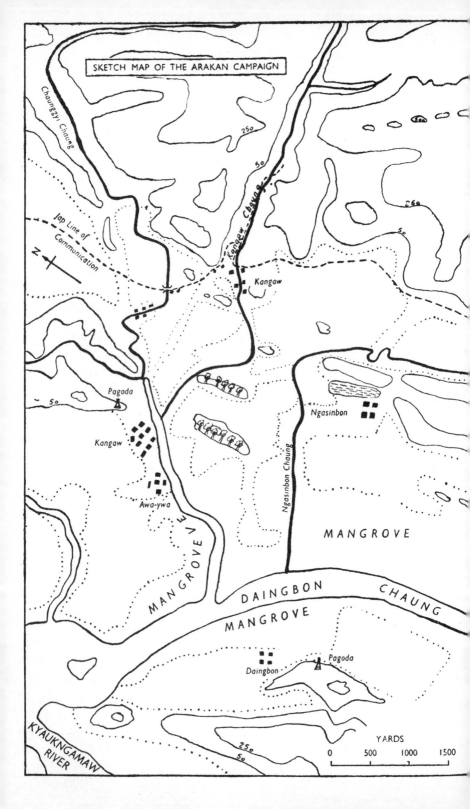

SKETCH MAP OF THE ARAKAN CAMPAIGN

Chaunggyi Chaung

Jap Line of
Communication

Kangaw Chaung

250

50

260

50

Kangaw

N

Pagoda

50

Kangaw

Awa-ywa

Ngasinbon

Ngasinbon Chaung

MANGROVE

MANGROVE

MANGROVE

DAINGBON   CHAUNG

MANGROVE

Daingbon

Pagoda

KYAUKNGAMAW
RIVER

250
50

YARDS

0   500   1000   1500

PART IV

BURMA

Chapter XIII

THE ARAKAN COAST AND KANGAW

WHEN we were still in the Bois de Bavent I was summoned
one day to Brigade Headquarters, where I found Major-
General Sturges, G.O.C. Commando Group. He wished me,
he said, to go out to Burma as Deputy Commander of the 3rd Special
Service Brigade with the rank of Colonel. Nobody has less objection
to promotion than I have, but since we were still in the middle of a
campaign I asked him to defer his decision. He said he would let me
stay with 3 Commando for another fortnight.

When we returned to England I had had plenty of time to think
things over and I had come to the conclusion that it would be better
to stay with 3 Commando. However, the General meant to be obeyed
and so on 2nd October 1944 I found myself in a York flying over the
scenes of past adventures in Sicily.

After a night in Malta we flew on to Cairo West, touched down at
Shaiba and so to Karachi and on to Colombo.

I had been told in England that I should find the brigade at Trin-
comalee, and 5 and 44 (R.M.) Commandos were indeed there. The
rest of the formation was, however, in the Arakan. It seemed strange
that such a major move should have taken place without Group knowing. When eventually I arrived at Teknaf it was to find that Brigadier
W. I. Nonweiler, R.M., had fallen ill and was in hospital. A week
later he was sent home to recover his health, leaving me temporarily
in command of the brigade.

The 3rd Commando Brigade was made up of two Army and two
Royal Marine Commandos. No. 1 Commando, under Lieutenant-
Colonel Ken Trevor, whom I had first met in 1942 when we had

both served for a few months on the staff at Combined Operations Headquarters, had seen a great deal of fighting in North Africa. No. 5 had been in action in Madagascar as long ago as 1942. The two Royal Marine Commandos had seen no active service before going out to Burma.

In March 1944 Nos. 5 and 44 Commandos had made a landing near Alethangyaw to support XV Indian Corps in an attack on the Maungdaw–Buthidaung road, but otherwise the brigade had scarcely been employed.

The beginning of November found the brigade concentrated at Teknaf. The men were eager for action, which had been long denied them, and it was only the acute shortage of landing-craft that prevented our embarking on a full raiding programme.

Eventually General Christison, the Commander of XV Indian Corps, was prevailed upon to lend us a Eureka,[1] which I believe was kept for him to use whenever he wished to travel up and down the Naf River. It was decided to raid Elizabeth Island in Hunter's Bay, forty miles south of Akyab, in order to collect information and if possible a prisoner. No. 42 Commando provided the landing party of thirty Marines.

I decided to accompany this expedition myself. Douglas Drysdale, the Brigade Major, insisted on coming as well, and I hadn't the heart —or the sense—to refuse him.

It was a lovely day and sailing down the Arakan coast was like a pleasure cruise. We reached Hunter's Bay without difficulty, the landing-craft towed behind a motor launch. Night fell long before we reached the lowering position, but we found it without any difficulty and transhipped to the landing-craft. On the run-in I saw what appeared to be a small craft lying at anchor offshore, but, running alongside to board it, found it to be a large rock.

Landing near the village of Ondaw, the Marines marched two and a half miles across country, harassed by wild boars as they went, and fell upon a Japanese section post guarding another beach. What casualties they inflicted I cannot say, but they returned without a prisoner. One man, Marine Chappell, missed his way in the dark and was trapped by Burmans in the pay of the Japanese about ten days later, though not before he had accounted for several of the enemy. Evidently they thought him dangerous, for they bound his hands behind his back when they took him to Myebon, rather an unnecessary

[1] A landing-craft of the type in which we went to Dieppe.

THE ARAKAN COAST AND KANGAW

precaution when the nearest British forces were forty miles away!. Happily Chappell survived to be repatriated at the end of the war.

The withdrawal was complicated. There was a good deal of surf; and, worse still, the craft broke down. Douglas Drysdale and I stood on the beach and watched it drift farther and farther away, and felt more and more idiotic. A gallant Indian seaman worked in the water for forty minutes and freed the propeller of the weeds which were clogging it; the craft came to life again. Even so we had to swim for it. It says much for the discipline of these Marines that not one of them lost his weapon.

Taking two civilians who had volunteered as prisoners we returned to Teknaf.

. . . . .

Since large-scale raiding was not to be had I asked XV Corps to lend us a sector of their front line so that we could give our people a little battle inoculation. In 1940 the battalions of the B.E.F. had gone to the Saar for similar experience, and it had paid them hand-somely. This was agreed to and later in the month 1 and 42 Com-mandos crossed the Naf River to Maungdaw and took over the positions of the 6th Battalion of the Oxfordshire and Buckinghamshire Light Infantry in the foothills of the Mayu Range.

The 25th Indian Division had been about eight months in the Arakan, and, such was the fanatical nature of the Japanese soldier, they had so far failed to take a single enemy prisoner. I was determined that the Commando Brigade should be the first to put a Jap in the bag. Easier said than done. A story from the first war suggested the solution. A colonel taking his battalion into the line in the First World War offered a fiver to the first man who got a German prisoner. This did the trick, so I decided to do the same thing.

No. 1 Commando won the prize. Captain Garner-Jones, an officer who had already distinguished himself in North Africa, took out a fighting patrol one day and overran the edge of a Japanese position. In the first exchange of fire the enemy commander was wounded, and a number of his men assisted him to the rear. In the confusion that followed a grenade stunned one of the enemy and before he could recover two of our men grabbed him, and trussed him up. Bound and gagged, he was hustled back to our lines. He was big for a Jap and well-made; when he came to he put up a struggle and is actually said to have swallowed his gag!

The men of 1 Commando soothed him, probably with the butts of their muskets, and by the time I saw him at my Headquarters he was as meek as a lamb. He was a fisherman from the north of Japan, and a simple soul. Like all Japanese prisoners he knew nothing of security and would answer any questions to the best of his ability. They just did not expect to be captured; it was against honour. He was offered some rice to eat but refused it.

"Aren't you hungry?" said the interpreter.

"Yes, I am."

"Don't you like rice?"

"Yes, very much."

"Why don't you eat, then?"

"Because you will then pour water down my throat and jump on my stomach."

He was persuaded that this was not in fact our plan. During the night he awoke and, plucking up his courage, made a noise to attract the military police who were guarding the prisoner-of-war cage. He made signs that he wanted food. To this the redcap wittily replied:

"You may be an honoured guest, but I'm buggered if I'm going to drum up for you at this time of the night."

. . . . .

For this successful patrol, in which several casualties were inflicted on the enemy, Garner-Jones was awarded the Military Cross and the two men who took the prisoner won the Military Medal. They also got a fiver each and a hundred rupees apiece from the Brigadier. Soon after we were allowed to send the first batch of men home on leave. No. 1 Commando selected these two to go with their batch. While they were at home their awards were announced and they returned to Burma too late to take part in any further fighting. Some people have all the luck!

. . . . .

I remained in command of the brigade until mid-December, when Brigadier C. R. Hardy, D.S.O.,[1] arrived from England and took over.

Campbell Hardy was already celebrated throughout the Commando Group for his exploits in Normandy, where he had twice won the

[1] Now General Sir Campbell Hardy, K.C.B., C.B.E., D.S.O. Commandant General of the Royal Marines.

D.S.O. in three months. Before the war he had been well known for his prowess at bayonet-fencing and he was a formidable-looking character. His iron-grey close-cropped hair and aquiline nose lent him a Prussian air when he chose, but since people seldom crossed him he was usually pleasant and light-hearted. He arrived somewhat the worse for wear as the result of a farewell Guest Night at Eastney, the famous Royal Marine Barracks. Some barrack-square brigadier, jealous no doubt at Campbell Hardy's rapid advancement, had made a speech in which he said: "We are very glad to have Captain Hardy with us tonight." It is said that they shelled this pompous individual with thunderflashes, fired from an antique cannon, while he was playing snooker after dinner and in the ensuing brawl the newly-promoted brigadier got a cracked rib.

The greatest gift a commander can have is the gift of making his men feel that if *he* takes them to a battle they can't possibly be beaten. I have several times served under commanders who gave me this feeling. Monty is obviously the supreme example from the last war of an officer who gave this feeling. Campbell Hardy soon had the 3rd Commando Brigade thinking the same way.

Christmas came and went and the time came for XV Corps to take its part in the final push for Rangoon. The monsoon was due to break in the middle of May and the Burmese capital lay almost a thousand miles from Maungdaw by sea.

The first move was to capture Akyab island.

On 2nd January the largest amphibious lift yet seen in Burma was assembled off Kyaukpyu. Cruisers, destroyers, sloops, Landing-Craft Infantry, old river-boats, rice barges, sampans—it was a strange flotilla indeed that had been assembled for the assault. But at dawn next day we heard that the Japs had already left; it was rumoured that they had departed as much as a week beforehand. A Royal Air Force officer flying over the place had thought it looked rather deserted and had landed to investigate. The bombardment was cancelled and 3 Commando Brigade and the 26th Indian Division landed unopposed. It was not an absolutely dry landing, but I was able to sit down on the beach, take off my boots and socks and dry my feet in peace. A gentlemanly operation.

In intense heat the heavily laden soldiers tramped across the island by dusty tracks made worse by the tanks that rumbled in the van. The Japanese had scarcely left one house in the place undamaged.

Captain "Chips" Heron, M.C., was selected to lead a patrol of 5 Commando to Pauktaw. He made his way up river in a landing-craft and surprised a party of ten Japs at close range, killing six of them, one an officer.

"The fellow had his back to us, sir! Thought I ought to shout 'Oi', or something."   .   .   .   .   .

It was now decided to launch a second amphibious assault. This time the objective was the Myebon Peninsula. Campbell Hardy and a small party set off in the R.I.N. Sloop *Narbada* to reconnoitre for a suitable landing-place. He patrolled along the shore in a motor launch, seeing nothing very remarkable except a derelict steamer. They fired a few shells at her, and at once Japs opened up with a concealed gun, a captured British 2-pounder. This the motor launch soon silenced, but not before she herself sustained slight damage and one or two casualties.

From the reports of agents and scouts the position appeared to be that the Myebon Peninsula was a concentration area for Japanese re-inforcements going north and for wounded travelling south along the Daingbon and Min Chaungs.[1] There were dumps of ammunition, food and clothing there, guarded by part of the Reconnaissance Regiment of the 54th Division, about three hundred strong.

Campbell Hardy's plan was a simple one. The beach defences at Agnu were to be obliterated by a bombardment both from the air and from the sea, and then, at high tide, the brigade was to land. There-after we would press forward to Kantha, and 50 Brigade of the 25th Indian Division, with a troop of 25-pounder guns, would follow up.

Douglas Drysdale and Tony Pigot, the D.A.Q.M.G., produced elaborate landing tables, so as to ensure that the troops fitted neatly into the various craft, but otherwise there were only brief written orders. Our information was too sketchy for a cut-and-dried plan. The first thing was to get the brigade ashore—the rest would follow.

At 8.30 a.m. on 12th January 1945, heralded by an armada of Mitchells, Thunderbolts, Lightnings, Spitfires and Hurricanes, 5 Com-mando made towards the shore. The sloops *Narbada* and *Jumna* added to the din with their gunfire. The strafe was a complete success. Agnu was a ruin and our assault wave was ashore with hardly a shot fired. Several light guns, including the one silenced during the Brigadier's reconnaissance, were captured in their bunkers. No. 42 Commando

[1] Chaung is Burmese for River.

lost a few men, some from mines and some when one of their craft was hit by a 75-millimetre gun.

It was just as well that the landing was a surprise. The tide began to recede rapidly and from the bridge of *Narbada* I could see the soldiers toiling ashore in mud up to their armpits. When it came to the turn of 44 Commando they had nearly four hundred yards to wade. Under fire it would have been murder.

There was a miniature peninsula to the left of the beach, joined to the land by a natural causeway of rocks. Seeing the misfortunes of the rest of the brigade, I went round the outside of this peninsula and landed on the rocky neck. I was about the only person to get ashore dryshod!

By nightfall the brigade had formed a bridgehead. "No. 1 Commando was on some hills to the west; 44 was in the area of Agnu village; 42 on Pagoda Hill to the north-west, with 5 slightly forward. A quantity of food, clothing and blankets was found in the bunkers and tunnels of Pagoda Hill. Only one wounded Jap was taken, but he died in the dressing-station.

It was a fairly quiet night, though medium machine-guns were heard firing from Myebon and a few shells fell in the area.

Dawn, to our surprise, brought no Japanese counter-attack and so during 13th January the brigade advanced. As yet we had no artillery ashore, and the only Sherman, which had attempted to wade to land, had become almost completely submerged in the mud. Finding the original beach entirely unsuitable, I suggested building up across the beach west of the little peninsula, where I had landed on the previous day. The great difficulty here was to make a road through the rocks which formed the neck of the peninsula. The Madras Sappers and Miners and a company of Gurkha porters attached to the brigade worked wonders here, and by that afternoon I had a road joining the two beaches. No mechanical equipment was available, the rocks were pushed aside by brute force or smashed with sledgehammers.

No. 5 Commando assaulted Point 140, eight hundred yards south-west of Myebon village, and by midday we had got three Shermans ashore belonging to the 19th Lancers (Indian Army). They managed to cross the neck without breaking their tracks and went straight into action, wreaking havoc among the Japanese, who had no long-range anti-tank weapons.

No. 1 Commando pushed on along the main ridge, while 42, passing Myebon itself, met severe resistance in the hills to the north and lost four officers including the Colonel, David Fellowes,[1] and a number of Marines.

The Lancers, who had refuelled and rearmed, were called up and climbed on to a pagoda-crowned hill. The next objective was Kantha, a village lying astride a swampy creek, whose bridge had been demolished.

By midday 1 Commando, opposed only by a few snipers, had taken Point 200 and the bunker on its summit. The Lancers supported the attack with their customary dash, and in this action one of their tanks turned right over on the steep slope and toppled down the incline. By some extraordinary chance none of the crew was any the worse for this mishap! The Japanese abandoned Kantha, leaving arms and documents behind them. No. 74 Brigade passed through.

The 3rd Commando Brigade had won its first battle, inflicting 150 casualties on the enemy for a loss of four men killed and eight officers and thirty other ranks wounded.

The brigade now had three days' rest, which was not unwelcome. It was a season of hot days, temperatures of 100 degrees and cold nights; drinking-water was hard to come by. Ammunition and weapons had to be manhandled forward, most of the work falling on the company of Gurkha porters, a hundred strong. Tough and inexhaustible, these men were quite unarmed except for the few who owned kukris, but they were always prepared to carry their heavy burdens right up to the forward posts. At night the Japanese would try and infiltrate snipers into the Commando "boxes", making a complete rest practically impossible.

We concentrated at Agnu for a day's rest, and on the evening of 20th January the brigade was briefed for its next battle—Kangaw.

While we were at Myebon I was joined by Corporal Christopher, who had so long followed my fortunes and had now come out from England with a draft of reinforcements. Lieutenant George Knowland, who as a Sergeant had distinguished himself with 3 Commando in Sicily, arrived to serve in 1 Commando.

Kangaw

This was now the situation in the Arakan—the West African divisions of XV Corps had been driving down the Kaladan Valley

---

[1] Now Major-General H. D. Fellowes, C.B., D.S.O.

towards Myohaung. The 26th Division had embarked at Akyab and was due to assault Ramree Island on 21st January. Simultaneously Marines from the Fleet were to occupy Cheduba. So much for XV Corps.

The main forces of the 14th Army were pushing towards Mandalay, determined to break the line of the Irrawaddy before the Monsoon.

No. 3 Commando Brigade's stock soared sharply after the capture of Myebon and the market remained steady thereafter. There had been room for improvement, for XV Corps were not used to employing Commandos and had failed to conceal their suspicion that they were utterly useless. As I stood on the beach at Akyab watching the soldiers embarking for Myebon, a general officer had come up to me and said:

"Do you think this will be all right?"

"Oh yes, I think so, sir!"

"Are the men for it?"

"Yes, they're quite keen really."

The conversation, all in this vein, lasted for some minutes, and when eventually he went his way, apparently somewhat reassured, I couldn't help thinking it a little odd that he, who after all was not going on the expedition, had to be reassured about it by someone who was. In the past it had usually been the other way about.

The Kangaw project was more ambitious and original than the attack on Myebon. The place was a junction on the Japanese lines of communications at the point where the motorable track from Myohaung turned from the plain into the hills to follow the Kangaw Chaung and then went south to Dalet. It was a minor naval base and supply point. The 54th Japanese Division opposing the West Africans was falling back along the road through Kangaw, and the aim of the operation was to cut off and exterminate as many Japs as possible before they could reach the An Pass.

The plan involved a five-mile approach in landing-craft up the Daingbon Chaung, a river about a hundred yards wide. If the Japanese happened to have posts along the banks it would be just too bad; concealed in the bushes, they would wreak havoc on the crowded boats.

No. 1 Commando was to land at noon and capture Hill 170, a long narrow wooded ridge, one and a half miles inland from the river. No. 42 Commando was to land on both sides of the Daingbon Chaung to protect the landing-place. No. 5 Commando was to reinforce the defenders of Hill 170, and 44 Royal Marine Commando was to form up in the beach area and lead the advance on Kangaw on the following day.

At 4 p.m. on 21st January I embarked with Campbell Hardy and his staff on H.M.S. *Narbada*, our Headquarters Ship. We had 1 Commando aboard and a hundred men of an Indian Field Ambulance, all crowded together in the most astonishing fashion. The last arrivals were hard put to it to find room to lie down on the deck of the sloop. Still, it was not for long and the crew were generous hosts. For the next fourteen hours they ladled out endless mugs of "char" to one and all. After a night at anchor in Hunter's Bay the convoy set sail next morning at 8.30, reaching the lowering position at ten o'clock. No. 1 Commando embarked in their landing-craft and in line ahead the craft wound their way up the river, a procession of boats stretching as far as the eye could see.

About 12.30 I transferred to a L.C.I. for the run-in. We were greeted by desultory shelling, but the wooded banks of the river concealed us from the Japanese observers and no harm was done. No. 1 Commando had landed just after 1 p.m.

Being the most experienced unit in the brigade they had been specially selected to seize Hill 170, which, we realised, would be vital to us as it was impossible to dig proper trenches in the mangrove swamps between it and the river. They pushed inland at great speed, while an air strike went in against their objective. Attacking from the south end, they cleared much of the hill, with a loss of three killed and nine wounded. By nightfall the whole of 1 Commando was more or less dug in on the centre of the ridge, with the Japs to the north of them and 5 Commando and Brigade Headquarters to the south. Nos. 42 and 44 were down on the flat ground, but during the night three troops of the latter unit attacked and carried the next ridge east of Hill 170, thus giving some depth to our position.

During the same night the Japanese were active also. They put in a determined attack on the two forward troops of 1 Commando, hurling grenades as they came. One rather keen Jap came running forward with a box of ammunition and planted it on the edge of a slit-trench, which happened to be occupied by a Commando soldier. This was a fatal mistake on the Jap's part. Some more of the enemy found their way to a hut which was occupied by one Lance-Corporal Littleton and some of his friends, who, according to one of the Sunday papers, promptly strangled the Japs with their bare hands. Be that as it may, they certainly had some bodies to show next morning.

In this fierce midnight clash the Japanese were beaten off, leaving behind nine dead, including an officer. No. 1 Commando lost one man killed, and an officer and ten others wounded.

At ten o'clock the next morning, after an artillery barrage, 4 Troop of 1 Commando advanced and occupied the north end of Hill 170 without opposition. The eminence they now held was divided from the rest of the ridge by a saddle. They were therefore cut off from the main body of the brigade.

Meanwhile, in the early hours 44 Commando had advanced and seized yet another hill to the east, not far short of Kangaw.

During the morning the Brigadier asked me to reconnoitre a landing-place for the Hyderabad Battalion under Lieutenant-Colonel Thimayya,[1] which was coming in to reinforce us. During this reconnaissance I discovered a sampan hidden under the bank of a chaung full of Japanese equipment, including many pairs of boots.

When the Hyderabads arrived I went in a landing-craft to show their second-in-command the beach I had found that morning. Moving up a narrow chaung north of Hill 170, we came under fire from a Japanese 75-millimetre gun on Pagoda Hill. We were returning the fire when our gun jammed. There was nothing for it but to turn round. The chaung was so narrow that this took a long time, and as the enemy gun was firing at us point-blank from about four hundred yards away he certainly ought to have hit us. We departed undamaged, but it was decided after this to bring the Hyderabads in behind Hill 170.

During the afternoon I visited 44 Commando's position. They were on a steep wooded hill known as Pinner and had dug shallow slit-trenches to a depth of about two feet. I urged them to go on digging, but they clearly thought I was unduly concerned about their safety. There were strong Japanese bunkers on the hill, and I asked them why they did not occupy these; I was told that this would be unsound since the enemy would know where they were. Still it's a great deal better to have a bunker the enemy knows about than no cover at all. I walked back across the paddy-field much disturbed by what I had seen and reported to Campbell Hardy.

About eleven o'clock that night we heard the sound of a severe bombardment. After a time a message came through on the wireless

[1] Now General.

from 44 Commando who reported that they had had eighty casualties. Although we had been unimpressed by the amount of digging done, neither the Brigadier nor I believed that things could be quite as bad as that. However, as it turned out there was little exaggeration.

At break of day the Brigadier took some stretcher-bearers and walked up to 44 Commando's position. He found that they had been shelled by 75-millimetre guns at a range of only a few hundred yards and had then been charged. Sixteen men were killed and forty-five wounded before the Japanese were beaten off, leaving twenty dead behind them.

The Brigadier sent up the Hyderabads to relieve 44, who fell back behind Hill 170.

During the morning Major-General G. N. Woods, the commander of the 25th Indian Division, came up to see us, a tall man armed rather incongruously with a minute American carbine.

With the aid of Corporal Christopher I dug an *abri*—not quite up to the Bois de Bavent standard—near the top of the hill.

Meanwhile the build-up was going on steadily in our swampy beach-head. Here Tony Pigot and his Staff Captains laboured to form dumps of food and ammunition. Water was a problem and had to be carefully rationed. A bomb-hole at the back of our hill served as our bathroom; the water in it left something to be desired. The dump areas were continually shelled, but the soggy ground minimised the damage done, and an encouraging proportion of the shells were duds. These were always greeted with derisive shouts of:

"Ya, you missed me!"

Nevertheless, as many as eight hundred shells landed in the beach-head during a single day.

One day, sitting on Hill 170, we were watching a line of Indian soldiers bringing up supplies; when some shells came down a man was hit and the rest scattered at top speed—all save one gallant soul, who knelt down beside the wounded man and there amidst the shells patched up his wounds. It was all done in a cool and matter-of-fact way, but in that flat exposed paddy-field it called for an iron nerve to behave as he did. The Brigadier sent a messenger to discover his name and he was decorated for his bravery.

It was on this day, 24th January, that 51 Brigade began to come ashore; after very severe fighting and many casualties they cut the road at Kangaw.

Despite the counter-attacks against 1 and 44 Commandos the Japanese reaction had been remarkably slow. The 25th passed without serious incident, and the 26th also—except that Campbell Hardy and Douglas Drysdale occupied my *abri*. I decided to build a bigger and better one, a tunnel leading out of a bomb-hole halfway up the hillside. I reckoned that the shell that got in there would have to go over the hill, stop in mid-air and then start going backwards! By this time 1 Commando were so well dug in that they only had five casualties in a week. This respite was invaluable to us.

On the morning of the 27th there was a heavy "stonk" when the Japs put over 164 shells in the half-hour between 6.30 and 7 a.m. Even so they caused few casualties, though one shell was a direct hit on a trench where three artillerymen were acting as flash-spotters. Hearing the shell land and the screams that followed, I ran up to see a ghastly scene. One man was practically unrecognisable as a human being, another was running about temporarily unhinged by the horrible sight of his dismembered friend.

.   .   .   .   .

The 28th passed with nothing more remarkable than heavy shelling throughout the evening. About this time the Brigade Ordnance Warrant Officer appeared and provided me with a fresh jungle-green battle-dress. What greater luxury could there be than a complete change of clothes after a week or two in the line!

The next three days were quiet enough, though on one of them a piece of a shell hit me on the thigh whilst I was walking along the ridge through 1 Commando's position. I heard this one coming but as it was obviously going over I did nothing about it and it burst in the paddy-field beyond. By some fluke a fragment came wandering back and drew a trickle of blood, but there was no harm done.

.   .   .   .   .

Then at long last the Japs struck. At 5.45 on the morning of 1st February they put down the heaviest barrage they had managed yet on to the positions held by 4 Troop of 1 Commando, the semi-detached hill at the north end of Hill 170.

Just before dawn I heard a loud explosion from the western end of the saddle. Three of the tanks, the only three we had ashore, had spent the night here protected by a platoon of the Bombay Grenadiers. I could see one of the Shermans blazing.

It was getting light now and from the paddy-field at the rear of our position we could hear the rattle of musketry. The Japs had slipped a party round behind us.

Meanwhile the forward section of 4 Troop, under George Knowland, was fighting an epic battle. Supported by heavy machine-gun fire from the Fingers, platoon after platoon of Japs came on in waves for two hours. Knowland and his twenty-four men, reinforced from time to time by the rear section of 4 Troop, beat off every attack while his ammunition lasted. He himself was everywhere, hurling grenades, manning a Bren, encouraging his hard-pressed soldiers. He was last seen engaging a horde of Japs with a 2-inch mortar, firing it right in their teeth with the base-plate against a tree. His first bomb slew six men. Then the Japs surged forward. By 8.30 his section position was partially overrun and he himself was dead, but this stand had saved the day. No. 1 Commando was never dislodged from the high ground north of the saddle.

.   .   .   .   .

I walked over to talk to the Brigadier. The first reports were coming in from 1 Commando. They were very modest in their claims, estimating that 4 Troop was being attacked by perhaps forty Japs, who had surrounded them. Even this did not seem particularly likely.

"As soon as this attack is over," Campbell Hardy said, "they'll put down another 'stonk'! You see! That's what they'll do." We waited, but the shelling had quite ceased. The small-arms fire grew louder and louder, but that was all.

I walked along to 1 Commando's lines to see Ken Trevor, the C.O. From his slit-trench we could see a few Japs in the paddy-field below. It was quite light now; all along the back of the hill men were taking pot shots at them. Presently one made a dash for it, but did not go far. There were only a few Japs, but they included an officer. Mike Cotton of 42 Commando ran out and got the officer's sword as a trophy and got hit for his pains. I took out a party to try and get a prisoner. As we approached, a badly wounded man killed himself with a grenade: the two others were already dead.

There was a lull in the fighting about 8.30, and I went with Christopher to see what had happened to the tanks. One had been utterly destroyed and another damaged. There was only one in operation. The Bombay Grenadiers had been dug in on the slope above the Lancer's tanks, but the Japs had rushed in from the other direction, across the open paddy. A party of twenty had charged in two groups. An officer with a pole-charge had actually climbed on to the destroyed tank. He lay beside it, his sword still at his side. Near him, with no turban, his long black hair flowing about his head, sprawled a tall slim Sikh, one of the crew. At least ten Japs lay dead round the tanks, perhaps more. One had his finger through the ring of a British Mills bomb. Examining the prostrate Japs I found one who still breathed and sent some men to carry him to the Regimental Aid Post.

The battle flared up again. First 3 and 6 Troops of 1 Commando went in to counter-attack; then W and X Troops of 42 were thrown in. These reinforcements prevented any further progress by the enemy and secured the flanks of 4 Troop. The one and only tank, supported by a swarm of Commandos, made several sorties against the right flank of the enemy. Massed mortars behind the saddle brought down fire just in front of our forward positions. All this time Ken Trevor directed the battle in person from a slit-trench in the heart of 4 Troop's position.

A never-ending stream of casualties was borne past to the casualty clearing station just south of Brigade Headquarters; fighting in the thick undergrowth at point-blank range, the casualties were sure to be heavy. The firing was so intense that the visibility gradually increased a few yards at a time as bushes were literally shot away.

Towards midday the heat was terrible. The sun beat down till you could hardly see straight. I went back to Brigade Headquarters to see what was going on.

Corporal Christopher produced a tin of pears, which served as a midday meal, and we then went off to find the Brigadier, who had gone forward to visit Ken Trevor. We reached the saddle and found a number of soldiers in extended order waiting to reinforce 1 Commando. There was a lot of shooting going on, but I could see no Japs anywhere. Suddenly the man next to me, a yard away to my right, gave a sort of choking noise and fell to the ground, dead. Then Charles Pollitt, who had come up with a troop of 5 Commando, was carried past on a stretcher. He had been up to see Ken Trevor, with whom he had served in North Africa, and had been shot in the knee. This was about 3.30. A little later I met the Brigadier. The line was intact. There was nothing much I could do to help for the time being.

Later Campbell Hardy sent two platoons of Indians into the paddy to keep the right flank of the Japs in check. I went with them to point out the situation—we had no common language but they were quick in the uptake and very well trained. There was no cover in the paddy-fields and so I thought it imprudent to put them nearer than three hundred yards from the Japs. The enemy were too busy to take much notice of us and caused us no casualties.

At 5 p.m. 5 Commando, now under Major Stuart, the Second-in-Command, moved up in rear of 1 Commando. The Brigadier was anxious to relieve the latter unit altogether, but thought it might not be possible with the enemy so near. Nevertheless, it worked. In fact by this time the Japanese attacks were beginning to slacken. Reports came in from the hill to the east that small parties of Japs could be seen retreating northward across the chaung. It began to look as if they had had enough.

As evening fell I hurried along the ridge trying to make sure that after this day of confusion all the key peaks, six of them, were securely garrisoned for the night. By the time I reached Brigade Headquarters it was dark. Some time before, the Brigadier, because of our heavy casualties during the day, had given orders that there should be no more counter-attacks by our own troops.

The night was quiet enough; the battle had died away. I rose in the early hours and went to see Robin Stuart.

"I think they're gone," he said. "If only we could make one more shove, we'd push them off the hill."

He seemed absolutely confident of this. There had been a little shooting or grenade-throwing some time before and then complete quiet.

"Well, you know the orders as well as I do. No more counter-attacks."

"Yes."

For a minute or two we discussed the situation in whispers, and I confess I told him that should he take it upon himself to give the enemy one more push, I would try to make his peace with the Brigadier. Indian troops of the 25th Division were supposed to be relieving us on Hill 170 that very day and we could not very well say to them: "This is the position, but unfortunately the north end is in the hands of the enemy."

No. 5 Commando thrust forward. The Japs had gone, leaving the hillside carpeted with their dead. When it was light enough I went forward to look at the ground where 4 Troop of 1 Commando had fought. I could hardly move a step without treading on a dead Jap. There were nearly three hundred of them and only one who still showed signs of life.

I was deeply impressed by the murderous onslaught of the Japanese and the almost incredible staunchness of the forty men who had held a battalion at bay. The Japanese had attacked with a fanatical, brutish courage which lacked subtlety and made little use of manœuvre. But the man who put them in to attack Hill 170 had put his finger unerringly on the key to the whole position. Any failure there and our whole bridgehead was in danger of collapse.

The danger had been very real, and troops less resolute than 1 Commando would have been swamped by this ferocious assault. The determination of the Japanese could be seen from the fact that most of them had two or three wounds, any one of them fatal. They had to be very thoroughly slain. They were mostly armed with long clumsy rifles, with long French-style bayonets like spears. Their dwarf-like figures under their medieval helmets, their mongol faces, many with glasses and gold teeth, made them look like creatures from another world.

Almost the first of our own dead I saw was Knowland. He lay on his back, one knee slightly raised, with a peaceful smiling look on his face, his head uncovered. Farther down the hill twenty paces from our forward trenches two of our men lay side by side as if they had together made a private counter-attack. I saw one soldier dead in his slit-trench with three Japs. They were dead too.

That evening we returned to Myebon.[1]

. . . . .

[1]Casualties at Kangaw.

Commando	Killed		Wounded		TOTALS	
	Offrs.	O.Rs.	Offrs.	O.Rs.	Offrs.	O.Rs.
1	2	20	1	43	3	63
5	2	17	3	21	5	38
42	1	3	2	20	3	23
TOTALS	5	40	6	84	11	124

In all, the Japanese lost about 450 men in their final attack on Hill 170.

For his victories at Myebon and Kangaw Brigadier Campbell Hardy won a second bar to his D.S.O.—an award which he had now won three times in six months!

For their gallantry in this battle 1 Commando won many awards. Ken Trevor, their Colonel, won the D.S.O., to the great delight of his followers. There were also three M.C.s and a bar to the M.C.; one D.C.M.; 12 M.M.s; Six Mentions in Despatches, and a Victoria Cross. The only man of 3 Commando to win the highest award of all won it after he had left our ranks—George Knowland.

.   .   .   .   .

The rest of the story is quickly told. A few months after the end of our brief but bloody Arakan campaign I returned to England, where, on 19th June, I took over the command of the 1st Commando Brigade from Derek Mills-Roberts.

The Brigade then consisted of 3, 6, 45 and 46 Commandos. Walter Skrine, somewhat recovered from his wounds, came to be my Brigade Major; Terry Donnelly was D.A.Q.M.G. and more than willing to do all our work.

We were quartered in Sussex and were busy training to go out to Malaya and fight the Japanese. Then they dropped those atom bombs and it all came to an end—but it was good while it lasted!